Wisconsin Sentencing
in the Tough-on-Crime Era

Wisconsin Sentencing in the Tough-on-Crime Era

How Judges Retained Power
and Why Mass Incarceration
Happened Anyway

Michael O'Hear

The University of Wisconsin Press

Publication of this book has been made possible, in part, through support
from the Anonymous Fund of the College of Letters and Science
at the University of Wisconsin–Madison.

The University of Wisconsin Press
1930 Monroe Street, 3rd Floor
Madison, Wisconsin 53711–2059
uwpress.wisc.edu

Gray's Inn House, 127 Clerkenwell Road
London EC1R 5DB, United Kingdom
eurospanbookstore.com

Printed in the United States of America
This book may be available in a digital edition.

Library of Congress Cataloging-in-Publication Data

Names: O'Hear, Michael, 1968- author.
Title: Wisconsin sentencing in the tough-on-crime era: how judges retained   power and
why mass incarceration happened anyway / Michael M. O'Hear.
Description: Madison, Wisconsin: The University of Wisconsin Press, [2017] |
Includes bibliographical references and index.
Identifiers: LCCN 2016013661 | ISBN 9780299310202 (cloth: alk. paper)
Subjects: LCSH: Imprisonment—Wisconsin—History. | Sentences (Criminal procedure)—
Wisconsin—History. | Imprisonment—Political aspects—Wisconsin.
| Sentences (Criminal procedure)—Political aspects—Wisconsin.
Classification: LCC HV9475.W58 O34 2017 | DDC 364.6/509775—dc23
LC record available at https://lccn.loc.gov/2016013661

ISBN 9780299310233 (pbk.: alk. paper)

With love and gratitude to my wife

Jennifer Madden O'Hear

Contents

Illustrations

Figures

Tables

Preface

This book tells the story of Wisconsin sentencing policy and politics since 1970. I first encountered the Wisconsin sentencing system in 2001 during my first year of teaching at Marquette Law School. Sentencing had been my primary academic interest ever since I was a law student, so I was quite pleased when I was given the opportunity to develop a new course on the topic at Marquette. Through my scholarly research and my time in law practice in Chicago, I had become quite familiar with the federal sentencing system, but I thought my new course should also cover the sentencing law of the state system in which most of my students would be working.

As I began to research sentencing law in Wisconsin, I was immediately struck by how little of it there was. Federal sentencing was governed by a voluminous and maddeningly intricate set of guidelines, which were quite justifiably compared to the federal income tax regulations. Federal judges had little discretion to consider a defendant holistically or otherwise to bring their own views of a case to bear in determining punishment. By contrast, Wisconsin judges had vast discretion at sentencing. The law gave them very little definite guidance about what factors should be considered and how they should be weighed. With so little Wisconsin law available to teach, my students ended up learning far more of the arcane federal sentencing law than they probably wanted to know.

I was left to puzzle over the question of why the two systems had developed so differently. The federal system was dominated by law, probably to an unhealthy extent. Meanwhile, the Wisconsin system was dominated by discretion—also probably to an unhealthy extent.

As I grew better acquainted with Wisconsin's on-the-ground realities, another question came to puzzle me. The law-dominated federal system was notoriously harsh. Among those of us who studied the system, it was conventional wisdom that giving the federal judges more discretion would result in more humane punishment. Yet, the high-discretion Wisconsin system could hardly be characterized as lenient. Indeed, Wisconsin had not proven the least bit immune to the national trend toward mass incarceration. Quite the contrary, Wisconsin's prison population had been growing more rapidly than the national average, and its rate of black male incarceration, in particular, had reached scandalous proportions. It seemed that the basic structure of the sentencing system—high discretion or low discretion—mattered less to outcomes than many people assumed.

These two questions—Why did Wisconsin give its judges so much discretion? And why did that discretion not provide greater protection from mass incarceration?—lurked in the back of my mind for many years and eventually led to this book.

Law professors customarily base their research on *law*—on statutes, regulations, and published judicial decisions. However, those sources would obviously not serve me well for this project. After all, my original motivation was to discover why there was so little sentencing law in Wisconsin. Law could not explain an absence of law. My research thus led me in a variety of different directions. I combed a multitude of dusty government reports, some decades old. I reviewed the minutes of dozens of meetings of long-defunct commissions and committees. I gathered copious data compiled by many different agencies. I reviewed the coverage of all of the key events in the state's leading newspapers. And I collected the official drafting files for most of the notable legislative proposals discussed here. Hardly any of this would have been possible without the very able and timely assistance of Elana Olson of the Marquette Law Library, to whom I am deeply indebted.

I was not, however, content to rely on even this expansive paper record. I also wanted to speak to many of the individuals who were involved in making the key policy decisions. Not all of them were as eager to speak with me, but many proved remarkably generous with their time and insight. In the end, I completed about fifty interviews for this book, most of them about an hour in length and some considerably longer. I spoke with governors, legislators, corrections officials, sentencing commission staffers, judges, prosecutors, and defense lawyers, most of whom have experience in the Legislature or the criminal justice system dating back to the 1970s or earlier. I spoke with leading Democrats and leading Republicans. I spoke with many representatives and officials from Milwaukee and Madison, the state's largest urban centers and the source of a disproportionate share of the state's criminal defendants, but I also spoke with a number of individuals from small towns and suburbs, who tended to have quite different views about the criminal justice system. Many of my interviewees are identified more specifically in the endnotes. All provided helpful information, and I am extremely grateful for the time they spent with me.

I am no less indebted to my dean, Joseph Kearney, who provided patient and unstinting support for this project through its many years of gestation. Dean Kearney has long promoted engagement by the Law School with state public policy, and I can only hope that this book lives up to the high standards he has set for such engagement. I hasten to add that the specific policy views I advance are mine alone, and do not reflect official positions of Marquette University or the University of Wisconsin.

Many others deserve thanks for their contributions to this book, but space precludes identifying all of them by name. The late Daniel Freed stimulated my interest in sentencing and encouraged my first writing efforts in the field more than twenty years ago. Michael Tonry provided helpful guidance in the plan of this book. Dean Strang, Lynn Adelman, and Kelli Thompson helped me make important connections for my research. Walter Dickey was especially generous with his time, patiently fielding several rounds of questions and follow-up questions. My colleagues Janine Geske, Daniel Blinka, Ryan Scoville, Jay Ranney, and Andrea Schneider provided helpful comments on earlier drafts, as did two anonymous reviewers for the University of Wisconsin Press. The participants at a conference on drug policy at Vanderbilt Law School offered constructive feedback on chapter 7. I am also grateful for the fine editorial input and other support provided by the staff of the University of Wisconsin Press, especially Gwen Walker, Sheila McMahon, and Sheila Leary, and for the timely and thorough work of Carol Roberts in preparing the index. Several research assistants helped with various parts of this project over the years, including David Behm, Joshua Bryant, Ben Hitchcock Cross, Laura Malugade, Katrina Seipel, Garret Soberalski, Robert Steele, and Elisabeth Thompson. Finally, my father, Michael F. O'Hear, not only read earlier drafts of this book but also more generally inspired my career as a teacher and scholar.

Abbreviations

ADA	assistant district attorney
AG	attorney general
ATR	alternative to revocation (of parole or probation)
CCJ	Council on Criminal Justice (Wisconsin)
CJC	Community Justice Council (Milwaukee County)
CPSC	Criminal Penalties Study Committee
DA	district attorney
DHSS	Department of Health and Social Services
DOC	Department of Corrections
DTC	drug treatment court
ERRC	Earned Release Review Commission
ISP	Intensive Sanctions Program
LEAA	Law Enforcement Assistance Administration
LWOP	life without the possibility of parole
MICAH	Milwaukee Inner-city Congregations Allied for Hope
MR	mandatory release
PO	probation officer
PSR	presentence report
SPD	state public defender
TAD	Treatment Alternatives Diversion
TIS	truth in sentencing
UCSA	Uniform Controlled Substances Act

Wisconsin Sentencing
in the Tough-on-Crime Era

Introduction

On June 30, 1973, Wisconsin's prisons held 2,046 inmates, amounting to 45 out of every 100,000 state residents.[1] The state's prison population had been remarkably consistent for two decades, ranging in size from a low of 2,036 to a high of 2,973.[2] Reviewing the year-end totals leading up to 1973, no particular trend stands out. Some years, the number went up by a few dozen or a few hundred; other years, the number went down by a comparable amount. A sort of gravitational pull seemed to prevent the population from straying far from 2,500 for long. So, when the population rose to 2,587 in 1974, observers might have thought this simply another instance of what statisticians call "reversion to the mean." Surely, no one in 1974 could have predicted that year's modest jump would prove to be the first in *three decades* of unbroken annual increases.[3] When the string of annual increases finally ended after 2004, the prison population had reached 22,966—more than ten times its 1973 size. Out of every 100,000 state residents, 417 bided their time in a prison cell. By comparison to historical norms, such numbers suggest a sort of indiscriminate use of imprisonment that might fairly be termed "mass incarceration."

The overall national numbers reflect a similar pattern. On June 30, 1973, America's state prisons held 178,835 inmates, or about 85 per 100,000 residents. Four decades later, on December 31, 2013, state prisons held nearly 1.36 million—more than a seven-fold increase—and the imprisonment rate had jumped to 437 per 100,000.[4] In 2013, Texas alone held nearly as many prisoners as all state prisons combined in 1973. Nor was the imprisonment boom limited to the big states with major urban centers. As indicated in table I.1, tiny North Dakota experienced an even faster rate of net growth in imprisonment than giant California.[5] Whether your state was big or small, or located in the North, South, East, or West, its prison population exploded in size between 1973 and 2013.

Table I.1. Imprisonment growth in selected states, 1973–2013

State	Prisoners, 1973	Rank (prison population), 1973	Prisoners, 2013	Rank (prison population), 2013	Change
California	18,534	1	135,981	2	+637%
Texas	16,289	2	168,280	1	+933%
New York	12,573	3	53,550	4	+326%
Wisconsin	2,046	24	22,471	19	+998%
Mississippi	1,985	25	21,969	22	+1,007%
Colorado	1,863	26	20,371	25	+993%
Maine	505	39	2,173	48	+330%
North Dakota	162	50	1,513	50	+834%

How We Got Here

There is no single right way to tell the story of mass incarceration in the United States. Researchers have used a wide variety of approaches to try to explain this unprecedented and profoundly important phenomenon. Each story has something to offer, but each also misses important dimensions of what happened. The complexity of mass incarceration defies reduction to a single cause or narrow set of causes.

One influential body of scholarship frames mass incarceration as a broad sociological phenomenon—a result of grand social forces unleashed by economic globalization, or the civil rights movement, or the sexual revolution, or some other epic social development at a national or even international level. This is the view of mass incarceration from thirty thousand feet. The perspective can be breathtaking. Sociologist David Garland's classic *Culture of Control* provides a fine example of this sort of study.[6] Garland's deeply insightful narrative focuses on the crisis of governance that faced the United States and other Western nations in the late twentieth century as global competition, deindustrialization, de-unionization, and other socioeconomic forces threatened standards of living and fueled feelings of anxiety and instability. Unable to address these challenges effectively, political leaders resorted to increasingly punitive crime-control policies, both because criminals were a convenient scapegoat for society's ills and because the decisive, tough treatment of criminals might reassure the public of government's efficacy.

Another fine study among many in the sociological tradition is *Harsh Justice* by legal historian James Q. Whitman.[7] Whitman contrasts mass incarceration in the United States with the dramatically lower incarceration rates found in western Europe, where most countries imprison at a rate that is only one-tenth to one-quarter of the American rate. Whitman attributes the divergence between American and European punishment to political and cultural patterns dating back to the eighteenth century, particularly relating to beliefs about equality and the role of government. Ironically, Whitman argues, Americans' stronger preference for formal legal equality and small government has resulted in the creation of a massive corrections bureaucracy that holds millions of Americans in a degraded legal status.

Yet another notable study is the best seller *The New Jim Crow* by law professor Michelle Alexander.[8] Alexander frames mass incarceration in racial terms, observing that people of color have been affected to a greatly disproportionate extent by the imprisonment boom. She argues that mass incarceration should be understood as a sort of backlash against the civil rights movement. By the 1970s, overt racism had become socially unacceptable in the United States. Expressing anger at criminals became an alternative way for whites to channel their resentment over black demands for more economic opportunity and political power. Increasingly punitive policies reflected these white attitudes and effectively reestablished social controls over blacks that were reminiscent of the old Jim Crow system.

I do not discount the value of these and other broadly framed sociological perspectives, which I draw on from time to time in this book.[9] In the end, though, my focus is quite different. Garland, Whitman, Alexander, and others help us understand the big-picture forces that drove up imprisonment everywhere in the United States in the late twentieth century. However, these forces expressed themselves to widely varying degrees in different states, as table I.1 makes clear. It seems that particular circumstances at the state level have served either to amplify or to dampen the general pressures for increased incarceration. These state-level particularities seem a crucial part of the overall mass-incarceration picture, and sorting them out is sure to offer some assistance to reformers seeking more effective strategies for undoing mass incarceration.

Another body of research on mass incarceration, statistical in nature, provides valuable insights regarding the state-level variations. This work employs the tools of econometrics: regression analyses that rigorously control for the overlapping effects of multiple variables. For instance, public policy professor William Spelman has found a statistically significant inverse relationship between a state's rate of imprisonment growth and its use of "presumptive" sentencing guidelines; that is, states with such guidelines in place tend to experience less dramatic imprisonment increases.[10] (Presumptive guidelines dictate a particular sentence, or a narrow range of sentencing options, for each case; the sentencing judge must follow the guidelines unless there is a good, legally accepted reason to deviate.) Likewise, sociologist Thomas Stucky and his colleagues have found a correlation between state prison admissions and Republican strength in the state's legislature, particularly when the state has many competitive legislative seats.[11] These and similar works offer a sense of what legal and political variables may drive mass incarceration, but they also have important limitations. Quantitative analysis requires that the rich complexity of the real world be reduced to a finite number of precisely defined variables. Many nuances of potential importance are lost. For instance, Spelman found that the adoption of presumptive sentencing guidelines in a state is correlated with lower rates of imprisonment growth, but there are many different ways that presumptive sentencing guidelines can be structured. A reformer reading Spelman's work might be intrigued by the potential value of presumptive guidelines in reducing imprisonment, but the multivariate regression analysis alone says nothing about the best way of designing a guidelines system. Nor does the regression analysis say anything about how to navigate the difficult politics surrounding guidelines adoption. Finally, the correlations found through regression analysis may not necessarily imply causation. For instance, it may be that guidelines do not *cause* lower rates of imprisonment growth; rather, there may be underlying, unmeasured features of the political or legal environment in a state that simultaneously predispose it both to adopt guidelines *and* to hold the line on imprisonment.

In these sorts of ways, *quantitative* analysis often raises more questions than it answers. In-depth *qualitative* analysis of particular states can help answer the questions. Law professors Richard Frase and Ronald Wright, for example, have authored wonderfully rich and insightful studies of the history of sentencing guidelines in Minnesota and North Carolina, respectively.[12] For the reformer interested in developing a guidelines proposal, the articles by Frase and Wright form an indispensable supplement to Spelman's.

Unfortunately, there are few additional states whose stories have been told in so thorough and nuanced a fashion.[13] This book adds Wisconsin to the short list. Indeed, as a book-length study covering the development of many aspects of sentencing policy—not just guidelines—over the course of several decades, this work joins an even shorter list. Social scientist Mona Lynch's exhaustive book on Arizona, *Sunbelt Justice*, may be the closest antecedent.[14] However, Arizona's experience with mass incarceration has been quite different than Wisconsin's—its imprisonment rate, for instance, is more than 50 percent higher—and different lessons may be drawn from the two states' stories.

Judicial Discretion and the "Lesson" of California

In recounting Wisconsin's experience, my focus is on the development and implementation of state-level sentencing policies. There are many aspects to this story, but a central theme throughout is judicial discretion—that is, the degree of freedom a judge has when selecting a sentence. Discretion can be wide or narrow. For a given crime, the law in one state might allow the judge to select a sentence anywhere from probation to twenty years in prison (wide discretion), while the law in another might dictate a sentence of two years to five years in prison (narrow). As we will see, an important lesson that emerges from the Wisconsin story is that wide judicial discretion provides no insurance against dramatic increases in a state's imprisonment rate.

In telling the Wisconsin story, I mean to challenge the common tendency to view California's experience with mass incarceration as archetypal. California has acted to restrict judicial discretion to a much greater extent than Wisconsin. Indeed, in the whole national history of mass incarceration, there is probably no story better known than that of California's infamous "three strikes and you are out" law, which has been the subject of several books and countless articles in both the scholarly and popular presses.[15] The three-strikes law, as adopted in 1994, imposed a mandatory life sentence for the commission of a third felony; judges had no explicit discretion to impose a lesser sentence, even if the third qualifying conviction seemed quite minor. Nationally publicized examples of the law's excessiveness included life sentences for stealing a slice of pizza and for shoplifting five videotapes. In all, more than 9,000 offenders have received life sentences under the law, more than 4,000 of them for nonviolent offenses.[16]

A lengthy 2013 article on the law in *Rolling Stone* neatly captures the common view that three-strikes legislation was archetypal—a distillation of what drove mass incarceration nationally.[17] The author, Matt Taibbi, reported that the "overwhelming support for the measure [in California] touched off a nationwide get-tough-on-crime movement. . . . A national craze was born. By the late Nineties, 24 states and the federal government had some kind of Three Strikes law." He opined, "This gets to the heart of what went wrong in America in the years following the mandatory-sentencing and three-strikes crazes. We removed the human element from the justice process and turned our courts into giant, unthinking machines for sweeping our problem citizens under a rug. And it isn't just in California, but all over the country, where there are countless instances of outrageous and brutal mandatory sentences for relatively minor crimes."

The lesson seems obvious, right? In order to get our national incarceration problems under control, we must overturn the mandatory sentencing laws and restore judicial discretion.

That lesson is far too simplistic. While discretion is clearly superior to the extreme excesses of California's three-strikes law, that law should not be viewed as at all typical. Although Taibbi conceded that "not all [of the three-strikes laws in other states] are as harsh as the California law," this was a gross under-statement. As we will see, no other three-strikes law was remotely as harsh as California's. Wisconsin's narrowly targeted law, for instance, applied to a grand total of only *three* defendants in its first four years. Nor have mandatory-sentencing laws proven more generally to be a prerequisite for mass incarcera-tion. Such laws had quite limited impact in Wisconsin. Indeed, if anything, judicial discretion actually *increased* in Wisconsin during the era of mass incar-ceration. Yet, as indicated in table I.1, Wisconsin's rate of imprisonment growth has been higher than California's.

The California story is a fascinating and important one, but it should never be assumed to be representative. Truly understanding the legal and political mechanisms of mass incarceration also requires the consideration of other states' experiences. These may suggest important qualifications to the lessons drawn from California. As we will see, the Wisconsin experience indicates that reformers should focus not only on judges' *power* to use alternatives to imprison-ment but also on their *incentives* to do so.

From Seventies Synthesis to Millennial Synthesis, and Beyond

The book's overall narrative arc is captured by Wisconsin's transition from what I call the "seventies synthesis" to the "millennial synthesis." By a synthesis, I mean the set of ideas, policies, and practices relating to sentencing that seem to predominate in a given period of time. Consider the seventies synthesis first. As discussed in chapter 2, Wisconsin sentencing in the 1970s was particularly marked by the following features:

- Wide judicial discretion, with the judge freely able to choose any outcome from probation to several years of incarceration in most felony cases;
- Wide parole discretion, with the Parole Board able to release most prisoners after as little as six months had been served; and
- Heavy reliance in practice on probation and short terms of incarceration, with few lengthy stays in prison.

These concrete aspects of the seventies synthesis reflected an underlying set of ideas about sentencing that might be called "managerialism."[18] Of central importance to the seventies synthesis, managerialism emphasized the use of professional expertise in order to address the varying public safety risks presented by different sorts of offenders, with imprisonment seen as an ineffective or overly expensive strategy for most. In the 1970s, managerial thinking typically included a great deal of faith in the ability of corrections professionals to promote offender rehabilitation—a faith that underwrote the era's heavy reliance on probation and parole.

The seventies synthesis slowly fell apart over the 1980s and 1990s. At an ideological level, managerialism faced the challenge of penal populism.[19] Populist views included harshly negative beliefs about criminals, who were seen as having little rehabilitative potential. Tough deterrence and incapacitation (imprisonment) thus appeared to be the only meaningful responses to crime. Populists had little patience for the fine-grained distinctions that managerial thinkers wanted to make between offenders, and tended to distrust the criminal justice experts and insiders, who were seen as overly lenient and insensitive to the public safety concerns of ordinary citizens.

In Wisconsin, populism's high point came in 1998 with the adoption of the state's truth-in-sentencing law. Passed by many states in the 1990s, such laws reduced or eliminated the ability of offenders to obtain early release from prison through parole. While many other states adopted truth in sentencing, Wisconsin's version stood out as the nation's toughest and most inflexible.

In the wake of the populist upheavals of the 1980s and 1990s, however, Wisconsin settled into a new equilibrium, the millennial synthesis, which differs in several important respects from the seventies synthesis. Judicial discretion, already wide in the 1970s, actually expanded by the 2010s, while parole discretion—a crucial check and balance in the 1970s—had been eliminated. The criminal code provided for much longer potential sentences, which attested to the continuing influence of populist views. At the same time, managerialism had staged something of a comeback, fueled by concerns over the state's burgeoning corrections budget and by a renewed interest in rehabilitation. For instance, diversion programs, which channel selected offenders from conventional prosecution into treatment, had become an entrenched part of Wisconsin's criminal justice landscape. Yet managerialism had plainly not regained the dominant position it held in the 1970s. Instead, the millennial synthesis seemed marked by a sort of long-term stalemate between populist and managerial impulses.

How did these various changes since the 1970s affect imprisonment rates? We may get a preliminary sense of this from figure I.1.[20] Between 1972 and 1989, Wisconsin's prison population rose in close correlation to the number of arrests in the state for major violent crimes. Over that period of time, the prison population grew by 234 percent, but violent arrests went up by nearly as much—213 percent. This provides an important reminder that the era of mass incarceration began in the midst of a long-term crime wave in Wisconsin and nationally. Starting in 1963, Wisconsin's rate of reported violent crime grew more or less

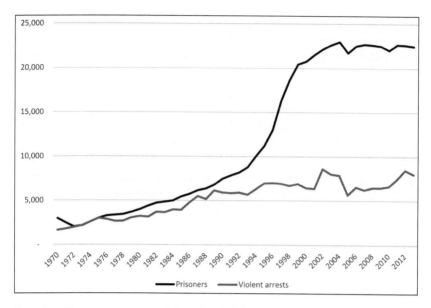

Figure I.1. Prisoners and arrests for violent crimes in Wisconsin, 1970–2012

steadily for three decades, increasing by 725 percent overall.[21] Quite apart from any changes in sentencing law and practice, it was probably inevitable that there would be large increases in imprisonment over a period of time when there were so many more offenders being arrested for serious violent crimes.

After 1989, however, there was a striking divergence between arrests and imprisonment. The prison population continued to grow without interruption for fifteen more years. By 2004, the number of prisoners was up 238 percent from the 1989 total. However, arrests for major violent crimes followed no such consistent pattern. The number went up in six of the fifteen years, but down in the other nine. Overall, the figure for 2004 stood only 28 percent higher than it had been in 1989. This contrast between skyrocketing imprisonment and relatively stable arrests points to a real increase in the severity of the criminal justice system. In the 1990s, more offenders were being sent to prison who would have gotten probation (or maybe even avoided prosecution altogether) in the 1980s. Additionally, those who would have been sent to prison anyway were serving significantly more time there.

Since 2004, we can see the emergence of a new equilibrium in the data. There have been small ups and downs in both imprisonment and arrests, with little overall net change. In 2013, imprisonment was down a paltry 2 percent from its 2004 peak, while violent arrests were up by a similarly small margin.

For decades, Wisconsin maintained a remarkably consistent relationship between its number of prisoners in any given year and the number of major violent arrests in the previous two years, a ratio that I refer to as the "parsimony index." Three arrests would produce two prisoners. However, under the millennial synthesis, the ratio had been reversed: since the late 1990s, Wisconsin has consistently held three prisoners for every two arrests. This is the mark of a much tougher system, and despite some increased interest in cost control and rehabilitation since 2000, there seems little indication of a real reduction in overall severity to anything like pre-1990 levels. Absent such a shift, the prison population is likely to remain near its historic highs for the foreseeable future.

What might cause the system to revert back to its historic severity norms? Not just in Wisconsin, but across all of the United States, reformers have been trying for many years to develop the political arguments and the specific legal changes that might bring the era of mass incarceration to a close. With very few exceptions, their efforts have proven a disappointment.[22] Consistent with the national pattern, the lessons from Wisconsin are less in the nature of "what works" than "what doesn't work": advisory sentencing guidelines, wide judicial sentencing discretion, and wide parole discretion, to name a few examples.

Still, there are a few positive lessons that emerge. For instance, while the imprisonment numbers for Wisconsin as a whole have been steady for more than a decade, the state's largest county, Milwaukee, has achieved remarkable decreases in incarceration over the same time period. The Milwaukee experience highlights the potential for productive innovation at the local—as opposed to the state—level of government. As we will see, state policies might be revised in various ways to provide even stronger incentives for local officials to take responsibility for addressing over-incarceration. Coupled with the implementation of presumptive sentencing guidelines, enhanced local ownership of the administration of punishment is a promising reform strategy.

Nonetheless, truly large-scale decarceration seems unlikely in the absence of fundamental changes in social attitudes toward criminal offenders. Years of populist political rhetoric and associated media coverage of crime have inculcated harsh "us-versus-them" attitudes in the area of sentencing policy. If voters and political leaders do not feel a sense of compassion for the incarcerated and recognize their potential for good, then it is hard to imagine the adoption of the sort of bold reforms that would be necessary to reverse the decades-long buildup of prison populations in Wisconsin and the nation as a whole.

1

Setting the Stage,
Meeting the Players

This book is concerned with Wisconsin's sentencing *law* and sentencing *outcomes*.
"Law" refers to the statewide rules governing punishment. For our purposes,
this means the sentencing-related statutes adopted by the Wisconsin Legislature.
"Outcomes" refers to the sentences actually imposed on the tens of thousands
of defendants convicted of crimes in Wisconsin each year. Law may tend to
push outcomes in a particular direction, but the one does not fully determine
the other. Indeed, whether as a matter of conscious design or unavoidable necessity, the officials charged with implementing sentencing laws have been given
considerable discretion to bring their own values and interests to bear in establishing outcomes.

Law and outcomes both result from the interaction of many different actors,
each operating under the influence of distinctive political pressures, resource
constraints, and relationships with other actors, among many other considerations. Legislative leaders do not simply dictate law any more than judges simply
dictate punishment. "Checks and balances" is not merely an abstract theory of
government but a central part of the day-to-day reality of the criminal justice
system, whether at the level of general lawmaking or the level of case-by-case
punishment determination.

The narrative that unfolds in the coming chapters assumes some familiarity
with the basic functioning of both levels. This chapter sets the stage, first introducing the key institutional players who determine punishment outcomes in
individual cases and then discussing the chief players involved in the lawmaking
process. To a considerable extent, the basic dynamics at both levels are much
the same in 2016 as they were in 1970, on the eve of the great imprisonment
boom. In other respects, profound changes have occurred; some such changes

are noted in this chapter, while others fit more naturally into the narrative of succeeding chapters. This chapter concludes with a consideration of the competing ideologies of punishment that have informed changes in law and practice over the past half century, and a brief note on the place of drug enforcement and race in my narrative.

Sentencing:
The Conventional Picture

When most people think of sentencing, they imagine a courtroom scene. A robed judge sits behind an ornate bench, gazing sternly—or perhaps simply glowering—upon the defendant. There are also lawyers in the courtroom, of course—a prosecutor and defense counsel. The lawyers wear suits, but they are probably a bit rumpled and baggy. This is a criminal courtroom, after all, not a corporation-litigation tableau with its $500-an-hour knights dueling in their tailored Armani and Brooks Brothers armor.

The case is called. The lawyers say a few words at the start of the proceeding. The prosecutor reminds the judge about the harm caused by the defendant and highlights whatever prior convictions he has—his "criminal history," as the lawyers put it. "No slap on the wrist will do, Your Honor; this defendant has been given second and third chances in the past and still continues to slip up." Defense counsel presents a more positive view of the defendant. "He has a supportive family, Your Honor, and he is working hard to overcome his addiction problem." Maybe a victim will appear and make a statement. Maybe a friend or family member of the defendant will make a pitch for leniency.

Then it is the defendant's turn to speak—a moment of undeniable drama. He has said nothing of any substance in the case so far. Most convictions are obtained by way of a plea bargain, not a trial. The presentencing proceedings in such cases are apt to be perfunctory—a formalistic ritual of question and answer to ensure that the defendant understands what he is doing when he surrenders his right to a trial. Even if there is a trial, the defendant will typically invoke his right to remain silent rather than testifying in his own behalf; this common strategic choice prevents the jury from learning about the defendant's prior convictions. Thus, at sentencing, the judge and anyone else who cares to show up will hear for the first time from the defendant's own mouth what he thinks about the crime. He may be sullen and say little. He may offer an artful excuse for his misdeeds or point the finger of blame at another. He may tearfully beg for forgiveness. He may promise to do better in the future. Perhaps we will even believe him.

After the defendant finishes his statement, all eyes turn to the judge. As she begins to speak, we immediately notice the stark contrasts between the sentenced and the sentencer. He was dark-skinned; she is fair. He was young; she is much older, with more than a few gray hairs and wrinkles to augment her natural gravitas. He was halting and awkward in his speech; she is confident and commanding, displaying the vocabulary and diction of a well-educated professional. Much more than just an orange jumpsuit and a black robe differentiates these two.

Will the defendant actually be spending any time behind bars? This is the question whose answer we most eagerly await. The judge will either order imprisonment or probation. If imprisonment, the judge will then have to decide the length of the term. If probation, the judge will decide what conditions the defendant must satisfy in order to stay out of prison. As the judge walks us through the technical details of the sentence, a certain amount of cold legalese is inevitable. Yet the judge's voice at sentencing is, above all, a voice of moral authority, channeling society's condemnation of the crime and beseeching the criminal to recognize his responsibilities to others. As the crack of a gavel concludes the sentencing, we may feel gratified by a sense of closure. The judge had the last words, and those words served to put the defendant in his place and to reassert the proper social order.

Such, anyway, is how we might imagine sentencing to work.

And, indeed, the courtroom ritual often does look a lot like my stylized description. The conventional image I have presented is not so much inaccurate as it is radically incomplete, missing the broader procedural, institutional, and political context in which the courtroom ritual occurs. Let's take a closer look at each of the key actors.[1]

Sentencing in Wisconsin: A More Complete Picture

The Prosecutor

Each of Wisconsin's seventy-two counties has an elected district attorney, who is responsible for criminal prosecution in his county. What this actually means in practice varies tremendously from county to county, based most fundamentally on population size. Many of Wisconsin's smallest counties, which are concentrated in the state's remote and heavily forested northern reaches and to a lesser extent along the state's hilly west-central border, contain fewer than twenty thousand residents. Two of these counties share a single DA, while in

Table 1.1. Arrests by county, 2012

County	Population (2010)	Homicide	Rape	Robbery
Menominee	4,232	0	2	0
Florence	4,423	0	0	0
Iron	5,916	0	0	0
Waukesha	389,891	1	29	20
Dane	488,073	11	51	90
Milwaukee	947,735	91	216	1,037

three others the DA's position is only a part-time job.[2] At the other end of the spectrum, Milwaukee County, situated on Lake Michigan and constituting the heart of Wisconsin's heavily populated southeastern quadrant, boasts nearly a million residents. Its DA is less lawyer than administrator, leading a staff of more than 120 prosecutors. This dwarfs even the state's second-largest DA's office. South-central Dane County, containing the state's capital city, Madison, and a population of half a million, maintains only about thirty prosecutors.

As might be expected, the number of cases sent to prosecutors varies tremendously from the small rural counties to the large urban counties. Table 1.1 compares arrests for three types of major violent crime in Wisconsin's three smallest and three largest counties.[3] The larger counties have many more arrests than the smaller, but even among the larger counties, there are stark differences in per capita rates, with gritty Milwaukee far ahead of suburban Waukesha.

Wherever based, Wisconsin's DAs operate with almost complete independence from one another. In contrast to Alaska and Connecticut, Wisconsin does not have an integrated, statewide prosecution bureaucracy. There is an elected state attorney general, but he has little authority over the DAs. Indeed, before 1990, the DAs and assistant DAs (ADAs) were not even state employees but were paid by their counties. Since then, the state has picked up the tab for prosecutor salaries and benefits, but the DA's electoral accountability remains local, with each DA facing the voters once every four years. Additionally, the DA must obtain funds for support staff and other administrative expenses from the county, which further enmeshes the DA in local-level politics.

The ranks of Wisconsin's prosecutors have been growing. In 1990, when prosecutors first became state employees, there were 332 positions spread across the seventy-two counties; by 2014, the number had reached nearly 430. Prosecutors nonetheless continue to complain about excessive caseloads. The

Wisconsin District Attorneys Association, for instance, estimates that an additional 260 or so ADAs would have to be hired for prosecutors to be able to handle their caseloads properly within a forty-hour workweek.[4]

Outside of the smaller counties, the bulk of the day-to-day prosecution work is done by the ADAs. Although the ADAs do not themselves face the voters, they are hardly likely to be oblivious to local sensibilities. For one thing, an ADA's prospects for advancement in his office may depend on the avoidance of missteps that make the boss look bad in the eyes of local voters. For another, many ADAs dream of running for DA or judge in the future, and for this purpose they will want to ensure that their record as a subordinate prosecutor is more of a political asset than a liability.

Whatever a prosecutor's interests and values, he will have no shortage of opportunities to bring them to bear. Like American prosecutors generally, Wisconsin's DAs and ADAs enjoy wide discretion in charging and plea bargaining. Police make arrests, but prosecutors are not required to charge every case police bring to them. As the Wisconsin Supreme Court has put it, "Full enforcement of the criminal laws is neither possible nor desirable."[5] Prosecutors may decline charges based on inadequate evidence, insufficient time or resources to devote to the case, the perception that no real harm was done, the prospective defendant's efforts to make amends, or any of a number of other considerations. Moreover, once the decision to charge is made, the prosecutor may still have additional choices to make about *which* charges to bring. American criminal codes are expansive, and a single act or series of acts may be charged many different ways. A given barroom fight might be charged as battery, substantial battery, or disorderly conduct. A given mugging might be charged as robbery, armed robbery, or theft. A drunk driver who speeds down the wrong way of an interstate might be charged with DUI, reckless endangerment, or both. In some cases, a prosecutor might have the option of piling on a dozen or more charges. All of these decisions can have an enormous impact on the defendant's sentencing exposure; each charge will carry its own maximum statutory penalty—one or seven or fifteen years behind bars, for instance—and the various maximums associated with each charge must be added together to determine the defendant's overall potential sentence.

Just as a prosecutor has discretion to decide which charges to bring, the prosecutor also has discretion to decide which charges to dismiss as a reward for a guilty plea. A prosecutor might initially charge the barroom fight as a battery, for instance, but agree to drop the charge to disorderly conduct as part of a plea deal. Or, to handle the case even more cleanly and efficiently, the prosecutor might never formally file the battery charge but merely threaten to do so in order to extract the desired guilty plea to disorderly conduct. However accomplished, such deals spare prosecutors the time, expense, and uncertainty of a trial. Recall the prosecutors' perennial demands for new ADA positions. Prosecutors cannot take to trial every case in which they would like to see the defendant punished. Plea bargaining helps the system establish accountability for a much larger number of defendants than would be possible if every case were tried, but at the cost of lesser punishment in some cases. When charges are dropped, the defendant's sentencing exposure is reduced, and the judge may ultimately be unable to impose as severe a sentence as she thinks best. Although the judge has the authority to reject a guilty plea if she thinks the underlying deal is unjust, busy judges have strong incentives not to do anything that might gum up the plea bargaining works, and in any event, the judge may not have enough information at the guilty-plea stage to see the problems with a deal. In the conventional image of sentencing, the judge appears to be in the driver's seat, but in some cases the most important decisions are actually made by the prosecutor before the judge even mounts the bench.[6]

Plea deals can also take other forms. In addition to or in lieu of reduced charges, a prosecutor might agree not to advocate in court for a stiff sentence or even to support the defendant's request for leniency. Such prosecutorial recommendations are not technically binding on the sentencing judge, but they tend to exert a strong influence in practice. Controlling for dozens of variables, one Wisconsin study from the 1970s found that the prosecutor's recommendation was the single most powerful predictor of whether a defendant would get probation or prison.[7] There seems no reason to think this has changed since then. Experienced practitioners recognize that judges only very rarely sentence above the prosecutor's recommendation. As long as the judge follows the prosecutor's recommendation, the judge has political cover if anything should later go wrong. For this reason, a savvy defendant might be quite interested in bargaining over the prosecutor's recommendation in his case.

Prosecutors thus exercise a great deal of subtle influence over the sentencing decision through their charging and plea bargaining discretion. We might imagine that prosecutors would attempt to use this discretion so as to maximize the aggregate amount of punishment across all of their cases, surrendering a little punishment in the plea-bargained cases so as to ensure more total convictions. However, prosecutors often exercise more restraint than one might expect if simple punishment maximization were the goal. Many other considerations might come into play. The prosecutor might sympathize with the defendant, for instance, or think that incarceration would be counterproductive and make the defendant more likely to reoffend over the long run, or fear a political backlash from excessive toughness, or wish to maintain friendly relations with a defense lawyer with whom the prosecutor deals regularly.

Many factors might push a prosecutor toward leniency, but lurking in the background in many cases is the fear that something might go terribly wrong. Prosecutors of a certain age will recall Willie Horton, the Massachusetts prisoner who was furloughed (temporarily released) on the watch of Governor Michael Dukakis and who then committed a brutal rape and assault. When Dukakis ran for president in 1988, a notorious television ad tying the governor to Horton turned the political tide and contributed to the election of George H. W. Bush.[8] While such catastrophic failures are not common in the criminal justice system, the possibility that they might occur tends to promote a certain conservative-ness among prosecutors and other officials. Moreover, prosecutors must appreciate that leniency can produce an unpleasant scandal even if the beneficiary does not pull a Willie Horton. For instance, in 2014, Jefferson County DA Susan Happ's campaign for Wisconsin attorney general was derailed by criticism over a case in which an ADA in her office reduced child sexual assault charges to disorderly conduct as part of a plea deal.[9]

Prosecutors thus confront a complex array of considerations that must be balanced in each case. However, at least in the busier counties, much of the balancing is largely subsumed into established habits and patterns of case resolution. Experienced lawyers and judges have a shared sense of "going rates" for the more common types of crime in the county. If we assume the lawyers understand the going rates and the defendant is reasonably compliant, little self-conscious effort need go into the charging or plea bargaining of routine cases.

The sense of bureaucratized justice in the larger offices may be enhanced by the DA's development of written internal policy documents to guide or control the exercise of discretion by line prosecutors in particular categories of cases. Those who have been involved in the system for many decades believe that line prosecutors had much more freedom back in the day. One former Milwaukee prosecutor who started in the 1970s recalls that the DA then "just told us to do the right thing."[10] A former Dane County prosecutor who started at about the same time bemoans the fact that the prosecutor has become "just another functionary in the system."[11]

A prosecutor in 2016 may feel hemmed in by bureaucratic controls from within his office, by the expectation of judges and defense counsel that established "going rates" will be respected, and by the pressure to resolve most of his cases quickly by guilty plea. The law, as it has been developed in the distant appellate courts, recognizes a vast field of prosecutorial charging and plea-bargaining discretion, but the in-the-trenches prosecutors may perceive themselves as much less autocratic than critics think. Still, it is important to recognize that the various practical and political constraints on prosecutorial discretion operate in a localized fashion. For the most part, Wisconsin's prosecutors work in a single county, subject to the cultural norms of a particular courthouse and to the guiding hand of a particular DA, who is himself accountable to a particular local electorate. Whatever coherence these forces may bring to the sentencing outcomes in a given county, we cannot expect similar coherence on a statewide basis.

Defense Counsel

The prosecutor's counterpart in all of this will be either a salaried public defender or a private defense lawyer. The United States Constitution guarantees a government-funded lawyer for most indigent criminal defendants but leaves states with considerable leeway to decide how to provide this counsel. For a time, Wisconsin put the responsibility on its counties. In the mid-1960s, though, a state public defender (SPD) position was created to handle criminal appeals, and a decade later the defender was also given responsibility for trial work.[12] Since then, the Office of the SPD has generally had responsibility for all legal representation of criminal defendants whose income falls below a certain level, which constitutes about half of the state's total criminal caseload. Other defendants must find their own lawyers, although counties may step in to help in some cases.

Most of the SPD's cases are assigned to its salaried staff attorneys, who are spread across thirty-five district offices. The remaining cases are mostly distributed to private attorneys for reimbursement at a rather low rate (for lawyers anyway) of $40 an hour; a smaller percentage of cases are handled through annual fixed-fee contracts. Unlike the prosecution function, the defense function in Wisconsin is not administered on a county basis by locally elected officials but by a state official who is accountable to a board of gubernatorial appointees. State law establishes a standard of about 185 felony cases per salaried public defender per year.

In theory, the motives of defense counsel should be much simpler and more straightforward than those of the prosecutor. While the prosecutor's duty is "to administer justice"[13]—whatever that means—defense counsel's duty is to aid a flesh-and-blood client according to that client's directives. In practice, though, there can be tensions between the lawyer's duty to the client and the lawyer's caseload and economic pressures. It is easy enough when the lawyer is able to charge a wealthy client market rates, confident that the bills will be paid no matter how hefty. But such cases are few and far between. Many defense lawyers, like their prosecution counterparts, feel pressure to plea-bargain away most of their cases as quickly as possible. The system of going rates helps to facilitate this process and may produce reasonably fair outcomes most of the time, even if defense counsel has not given the case the full Clarence Darrow treatment. Moreover, after the plea deal is reached, the going rates are not necessarily so firm and precise that counsel's performance at sentencing is inevitably just for show. Skilled advocacy can humanize the defendant and convince the judge there are grounds for a second (or a third or fourth) chance. Yet the business of pulling together all of the supporting information for this sort of advocacy can be constrained by the challenging economic realities of a criminal defense practice.

The Judge

The judge may be the star of the show in the courtroom sentencing ritual, but as our consideration of plea bargaining indicates, the courtroom ritual is only the tip of a much larger iceberg. The appellate courts describe judicial sentencing discretion just as expansively as they speak of prosecutorial charging discretion, but, in practice, sentencing discretion is importantly constrained or influenced by plea deals, lawyer recommendations and arguments, caseload pressures, the going rates established through earlier cases, and many other factors.

In Wisconsin, criminal cases are filed in the county-based circuit courts. A handful of the smaller counties share courts, but each of the remaining counties has its own.[14] Much as with DA offices, the state covers judicial salaries, but counties are responsible for support staff and operating expenses. The total number of circuit court judgeships rose from 190 in 1980 to 249 in 2014. Like the prosecutors, the judges periodically request even more new positions in order to address caseload pressures. Nearly half of Wisconsin's counties have just one judge. At the other extreme, Milwaukee has forty-seven judges and Dane County seventeen. Outside of Milwaukee County, judges are paid more than DAs; that, and the longer term of office—six years instead of four—helps to draw DAs and ADAs into judgeships.

Circuit court judges are elected locally to their six-year terms through nonpartisan spring elections. Normally, these elections are quiet affairs, with low turnouts and little serious competition. For instance, in 2012, Milwaukee County elected ten circuit court judges, eight of whom ran unopposed.[15] The highest vote total for any of the twelve candidates was less than 85,000. By contrast, later in 2012, President Barack Obama won more than 332,000 votes in Milwaukee County. Even Republican candidate Mitt Romney, who lost badly in Milwaukee County, received almost twice as many votes as the biggest judicial winner.

Although incumbent judges are normally reelected as a matter of course, judges recognize that the criminal side of their docket is an area of particular sensitivity; missteps here may encourage a credible opponent to enter the race—there is often a hungry prosecutor waiting in the wings—and bring an otherwise spotless judicial career to an early end. As longtime Milwaukee judge Lee Wells puts it, the "two most dangerous areas" for a judge wanting to hold onto his job are bail and sentencing decisions; these decisions can attract a great deal of public attention, and members of the public seem to think themselves particularly well qualified to second-guess them. Wells observes, "An error can be fatal in these two areas."[16]

This perception was surely reinforced by Wisconsin's 2008 Supreme Court election. Louis Butler became the first incumbent justice since 1967 to lose re-election after a campaign that featured attacks on his pre-judicial career as a criminal defense attorney. "Louis Butler worked to put criminals back on the street," intoned one television ad—an ad that also seemed to imply (incorrectly) that Butler had been responsible *as a judge* for the release of a repeat child molester.[17]

In the smaller counties, each judge is necessarily a generalist, shifting from civil to criminal cases regularly as needs demand. Milwaukee and other large counties, by contrast, rotate judges through different assignments, permitting specialization and greater efficiency in case resolution. On the criminal side of the docket, there might be separate courtrooms within a single circuit court for juvenile, felony, and misdemeanor cases.

In Wisconsin, there are special juvenile court procedures for most cases involving defendants sixteen and younger. Juvenile sentencing, handled quite differently than adult, lies beyond the scope of this book. As for the adult docket, the felony cases involve the more serious crimes. In general, a felony is punishable by at least one year in prison. To be sure, a probationary sentence *may* be imposed at the judge's discretion in most felony cases, but it is the *possibility* of a year or more in prison that most clearly distinguishes felonies from misdemeanors. Misdemeanor cases typically involve lesser penalties and employ somewhat more expedited procedures. Incarceration is a possibility for most misdemeanors, but this would generally be for less than a year, served in a county-administered jail or house of correction rather than one of the state-run prisons. This book focuses less on misdemeanor than felony sentencing, which has been the real driver of the state prison population.

Unlike the prosecutors, the circuit court judges work within a hierarchical state bureaucracy of sorts. Litigants can appeal unfavorable circuit court decisions to Wisconsin's intermediate court of appeals, which is divided into four geographically defined districts. A losing party at that level can then request the Wisconsin Supreme Court to take the case, although the state's high court only grants a small percentage of such requests. If the case involves a federal constitutional issue, then further appeal to the United States Supreme Court might also be a possibility; however, this level of the appellate process does not normally come into play in relation to state sentencing decisions.

Wisconsin's appellate judges (i.e., those on the court of appeals and supreme court) are elected, but the dynamics are a bit different than at the circuit court level. For one thing, elections occur at the district or state level, not the county level, resulting in larger, more diverse, and more geographically dispersed electorates.[18] For another, the state's seven supreme court justices only face the voters once a decade, in contrast to the six-year terms of judges at the circuit court and court of appeals levels.

Because electoral accountability is structured differently for appellate than for circuit court judges, the circuit court judge might feel herself in an awkward position. After all, she is answerable both to local voters and to higher-court judges who could have quite different values and beliefs than the local voters. However, for various reasons, this potential tension does not seem especially great in practice. For instance, despite profound political and social differences from county to county in other respects, criminal defendants, as a general matter, do not seem to elicit high levels of sympathy anywhere; thus judges at any level of the system will normally be on politically solid ground when they take a tough-on-crime stance. Further alleviating the pressure on circuit court judges, the appellate courts have developed various legal doctrines that mandate a high level of deference to lower-court decisions in many areas. This deference tends to be especially strong when it comes to sentencing.[19] That is why the appellate courts do not figure much in the narrative of the succeeding chapters. In any event, the reality is that sentencing judges have considerable freedom to play to the local voters if they wish to do so without fear of appellate reversal.

When selecting a sentence, the circuit court judge has a variety of sources of relevant information and guidance, only some of which will be apparent during the courtroom sentencing ritual. There is the statutory sentencing range, for instance—the minimum and maximum sentence that may be lawfully imposed in the case. The range is most commonly just a function of the offense of conviction. For instance, conviction of a Class D felony in Wisconsin may result in a fine up to $100,000 and a term of imprisonment not exceeding forty years. (Felonies are graded from Class A, the most serious, to Class I, the least.) In some cases, the basic sentencing range may be increased through the application of statutory sentence enhancers. For instance, distributing forty grams of cocaine is a Class D felony, but if the defendant has a prior drug conviction, then the maximum term of imprisonment the judge may impose increases from forty to forty-six years. Note that there is no *minimum* required term of imprisonment in this example; the judge could impose probation if she wanted. In comparison with some other jurisdictions, Wisconsin has few "mandatory minimum" prison sentences. The most important may be the mandatory life term for cases of first-degree intentional homicide, with potential release set by the judge at a date no sooner than twenty years into the life term.

In addition to the statutory range, the sentencing judge will also be able to draw on her recollection of earlier proceedings in the case. If there has been a trial, the judge will have a great deal of information about the circumstances of the crime and may also have a very definite impression of the defendant's character based on the defendant's demeanor during trial. More commonly, though, defendants are convicted by guilty plea, not trial. In such cases, the judge's interactions with the defendant may be perfunctory and formulaic. The judge will have access to the formal charging documents, but these may omit much information that seems necessary to assess the severity of the offense, such as the impact of the crime on its victims.

The judge may be able to obtain a fuller picture of the offense and the offender by ordering a written presentence report (PSR). These are prepared by probation officers (POs), who tend to be stretched quite thinly and may or may not be able to produce a reliable, comprehensive assessment of the case on a timely basis. Judges vary widely in the frequency with which they order PSRs and the weight they give to the PO's views. Traditionally, the POs have been less well regarded by the judges in the larger counties, especially Milwaukee, where there have been particular problems with high PO turnover rates. In smaller counties, judges are more likely to get to know their POs and develop trust in them.

At the sentencing proceeding itself, the judge hears additional information and opinion from the lawyers, and potentially also from the defendant, the victim, and other witnesses. There may also be written statements from such individuals submitted before the sentencing.

The judge is also likely to be influenced by her prior sentences in similar cases. The judge's natural desire to achieve some consistency in sentencing plays into the "going rates" phenomenon—the perception that outcomes normally cluster in various predictable ways for routine crimes. First-time unarmed residential burglars, for instance, may reliably get probation from a particular judge, while armed repeat offenders will get anywhere from five to seven years. A judge who is not predictable in this sort of way risks getting a reputation for unfairness. Such unpredictability may also disrupt the plea-bargaining process, which can cause case backlogs that reflect poorly on the judge.

These pressures for consistency do not imply any sort of statewide uniformity in sentencing. The practice of criminal law tends to be centered in just one county for judges, prosecutors, and, to a somewhat lesser extent, defense counsel.

In any given case, the practitioners may have little idea what is done in similar cases in other counties. Moreover, even if the practitioners know what is happening elsewhere, many believe that the needs and values of different regions of the state vary in significant ways. For instance, a burglary is hardly a shocking event in a large city but may have a much more profound impact in a rural community whose residents are accustomed to leaving their homes unlocked.[20] How, we might wonder, can the severity of a burglary be judged the same in these two different settings?

Nor do the pressures for consistency even imply there is much judge-to-judge uniformity within a single county. In baseball, it is said that each umpire has his own strike zone, which seems not to cause any particular consternation among the hitters and pitchers; the veterans know their umpires and can prepare for each game accordingly without any real unfairness. Similarly, the experienced lawyers know their judges and can adjust their plea-bargaining strategies and sentencing presentations accordingly. Additionally, Wisconsin makes it exceptionally easy for defendants to obtain a new judge if they fear the first one assigned will be excessively severe. Thus, although there have been occasional calls for greater sentencing uniformity, Wisconsin has seen little sustained effort to bring the judges into closer alignment with one another.

While judges may be inclined to stick to their own established patterns of sentencing, they can hardly be expected to act with mechanistic precision. A particularly delicate question is whether judges sometimes deviate from their norms based on electoral considerations. Some defense lawyers maintain that judges tend to sentence more harshly in cases that are receiving media attention, but judges contest this claim. It has also been suggested that judges sentence more harshly when they are facing imminent reelection. One study of the Wisconsin Supreme Court justices over a fifteen-year period did find that three changed their voting patterns in criminal cases in statistically significant ways in the two years prior to their reelection campaigns.[21] No similar study has been conducted of Wisconsin's circuit court judges, but research in other states has found that sentences do tend to grow longer as election day approaches.[22]

Any number of other dubious considerations may potentially come into play at sentencing, whether at a conscious or subconscious level—race, antipathy to the prosecutor or defense counsel, connections to the defendant or victim, and so forth. Suggestions that such factors play a role tend to generate heated denials. However, there are indications that race may play at least a subconscious role in some sorts of sentencing decisions, although much of the overall black-white imprisonment disparity in Wisconsin can probably be explained by reference to seemingly race-neutral factors, such as differences in criminal history.[23] We will consider racial disparity concerns in more detail in chapter 6.

Whatever subtle role hidden factors may play at the margins, most judges doubtlessly try in most cases to produce sentences that accomplish the officially sanctioned purposes of sentencing. The Wisconsin Supreme Court emphasized four such purposes in its leading case on sentencing, *State v. Gallion*: "the protection of the community, punishment of the defendant, rehabilitation of the defendant, and deterrence to others."[24] In practice, however, these "*Gallion* factors" are sufficiently indefinite that even the most thoughtful, well-informed judges might reach quite different conclusions about what sentence would be best in any given case. Consider just one of the factors, protection of the community. Objective risk assessment tools can give the judge a sense of the odds that a given defendant will recidivate (commit another crime) if released on probation rather than imprisoned. However, human beings are not machines—only very rarely will it be possible to say that the defendant is *practically certain* to succeed or fail on probation. Knowing that past defendants who are similar to the present one have recidivated, say, 20 percent of the time does not clearly dictate whether probation is the right or wrong sentence. Many additional considerations must be balanced, and various subjective value judgments must necessarily come into play.

There are no singular, objectively determinable right answers in sentencing, even though there may be some clearly *wrong* answers, at least at the extremes— life imprisonment for shoplifting, probation for murder, and so forth. The essential indeterminacy of the enterprise makes it easier to understand why judges might fall back on prosecutor recommendations, earlier sentences in similar cases, going rates, and the like—and also how electoral and other dubious considerations might creep into the process at a conscious or subconscious level.

Department of Corrections

Although not necessarily physically represented during the courtroom sentencing ritual, the Wisconsin Department of Corrections (DOC) nonetheless plays a pivotal role in punishment determination. Headed by the secretary of corrections, a gubernatorial appointee, the DOC handles both adult and juvenile corrections and also operates the Wisconsin Parole Commission.[25] Before 1990, all of these services were performed by divisions of the Wisconsin Department of Health and Social Services. The removal of these functions from the DHSS and the creation of the DOC in 1990 were seen by some as a symbolic repudiation of rehabilitation as a central mission of the state correctional system—the business of executing sentences seemed no longer a matter of "health and social services" but simply punishment. In any event, the administrative reorganization did nothing to slow down the long-term trend toward ever-greater corrections expenditures, which more than quintupled between 1984 and 2000.[26] By the 2014–15 biennium, the DOC's budget had reached $1.3 billion, including funding for more than ten thousand staff positions.[27] The DOC's sprawling size has contributed to the negative reputation it has among many observers. In particular, lawyers and judges have long tended to see the DOC as a clumsy, rigid, opaque bureaucracy—a reputation that, deserved or not, may color the sentencing process in important ways.

The DOC obviously determines in a very direct way the *conditions* in which a prisoner will serve his time behind bars, but this book is more concerned with the amount of *time* that is spent in prison. Here, the DOC's influence is less direct and, to some extent, even inadvertent, but still quite important. I have already noted one pathway of influence: the PSRs prepared in some cases by the DOC's probation officers, whose recommendations are sometimes given significant weight by sentencing judges. At least three other pathways merit consideration.

First, whether judges have confidence in the DOC's probation officers may influence the likelihood of a probationary sentence. This may not matter much with low-level offenders who present little risk of major recidivism incidents, but Willie Horton casts a long shadow over other cases. Indeed, Wisconsin judges do not even need to look to Massachusetts for an example of catastrophic failed supervision: in 1989, in the middle of his notorious killing spree, Jeffrey Dahmer was given probation by a Milwaukee judge on a sexual assault charge.[28] When Dahmer was finally arrested for his ongoing homicides two years later, it was not his probation officer who uncovered his grisly secrets.

Milwaukee's judges, in particular, have had all too many reasons to be skeptical of the reliability of probation supervision, including high-profile failures like the Dahmer case, high PO turnover rates in the city, and high client-to-agent ratios. Reflecting such concerns, it does appear that Milwaukee judges have tended to underutilize probation relative to their counterparts elsewhere in the state in some kinds of cases.[29] However, griping about the DOC's community supervision is by no means confined to Wisconsin's largest city. For instance, in 2000, the Governor's Task Force to Enhance Probation conducted a detailed survey of Wisconsin's judges regarding community supervision. When asked whether "corrections authorities sufficiently enforce court-ordered conditions of probation," only 48 percent of the non-Milwaukee judges—and only *6 percent* of the Milwaukee judges—answered in the affirmative.[30] Indeed, when asked what would need to be changed in order to divert more "marginal" offenders from prison to probation, the most common response from judges in and outside of Milwaukee was "increased supervision."[31]

Second, the DOC's determination of parole release dates may have both direct and indirect effects on the severity of prison sentences. Wisconsin's complicated parole story is discussed at length in chapter 5. In brief, those sentenced to Wisconsin's prisons for crimes committed on or after December 31, 1999, are not eligible for parole, but parole release was a routine aspect of prison sentences for most of the time period covered by this book. The Parole Commission, housed within the DOC, determined prisoners' actual release dates within certain bounds based on the sentence length. For instance, in the 1990s, most prisoners became eligible for parole at the one-quarter mark of the judge's sentence and were required to be released by the two-thirds mark. This left considerable room for the Parole Commission to exercise discretion, although the halfway mark of the sentence was an important benchmark in many types of cases. As the prison population exploded in the 1990s, however, parole became somewhat more generous in order to relieve the pressure on chronically overcrowded institutions.

The commission's exercises of discretion obviously had an important direct effect on the real severity of sentences. Indeed, over the early and mid-1990s, *nominal* sentences (that is, the prison term pronounced by the judge during the courtroom ritual) increased on average, but *real* sentences (that is, the actual amount of time offenders served) decreased. On the other hand, there can be offsetting, indirect effects on severity if judges give longer sentences to circumvent increased parole generosity. Judge Diane Sykes, formerly of the Milwaukee Circuit Court, refers to this phenomenon as "defensive sentencing."[32]

Third, and finally, the DOC controls revocations from probation and postprison supervision. Either type of community supervision—that is, whether imposed as an alternative to imprisonment or served after imprisonment—entails conditions; the offender must comply with these conditions or face revocation and imprisonment. In the event of a violation, it is the DOC that decides whether to initiate revocation proceedings. Then, if postprison supervision is revoked, it is also the DOC that determines the length of the return to prison. However, if *probation* is revoked, the case goes back to the judge for resentencing, unless the judge had already imposed a suspended prison term; in the latter situation, the suspended term is executed, and there is no need to go back to court. Either way, the DOC controls access to this secondary pathway to imprisonment.

In all of the DOC's complex interactions with the sentencing system, the agency may feel itself whipsawed between two competing imperatives. On the one hand, the DOC has a strong interest on multiple grounds in minimizing prison overcrowding. Overcrowded prisons strain the DOC's budget, create stressful institutional environments that are more difficult to manage, expose the DOC to the threat of litigation, and may require the building of expensive new facilities. On the other hand, the public expects the DOC to protect it from recidivism, and there can be few nightmares more terrifying for agents and managers than the commission of a highly publicized crime by an offender on community supervision. To note just one example discussed in more detail in chapter 4, when supervisee Patrick Neal Rucker was arrested for a double homicide in 1997, his probation agent was taken to task in a front-page story in Milwaukee's main newspaper.[33] Thus, at the same time that the DOC has strong incentives to recommend probation, expedite parole, and ignore violations of community supervision, the agency also has powerful, countervailing incentives to keep offenders in prison for as long as possible and to pull the revocation trigger quickly whenever there is any risk of re-offense.

In seeking to triangulate between the imperatives of imprisonment reduction and risk avoidance, the DOC's management faces challenges from above and below. Above the DOC stands the governor. The secretary of corrections is a member of the governor's cabinet and must necessarily be responsive to some extent to the governor's political needs and beliefs. In general, the secretaries have not been corrections professionals promoted from within the DOC but outsiders with backgrounds in law or law enforcement. Implicit in such leadership choices is the assumption that the secretary will not simply perpetuate existing practices but will move the DOC in new directions consistent with the governor's priorities, whether those emphasize greater imprisonment reduction, greater risk avoidance, or some particular balancing of the two.

From below, there is the classic challenge of bureaucratic inertia. The political appointees cycle in and out every handful of years, but the careerists in the trenches remain the same. New policies and priorities may come down from the secretary's office, but many layers of bureaucracy separate top from bottom, and office culture in the field may prove impervious to change.

Lawmaking in Wisconsin

Sentencing outcomes emerge from the complicated interactions between prosecutors, defense lawyers, judges, and corrections officials, all playing out against a backdrop of sentencing law. Wisconsin's sentencing statutes, in turn, have emerged from the complicated interactions between a different set of actors, playing out on a fractured and dynamic political landscape.

The Political Landscape

In the 2012 presidential election, Democrat Barack Obama carried Wisconsin by a respectable margin of 53 to 46 percent, but a closer look at his numbers

Table 1.2. County vote totals in 2012 presidential election

County	Obama votes	Romney votes	Obama percent	Oppose same-sex marriage (2006)
Milwaukee	332,438	154,924	68%	Y
Dane	216,071	83,644	71%	N
Waukesha	78,779	162,798	32%	Y
Brown	62,526	64,836	49%	Y
Racine	53,008	49,347	51%	Y
Outagamie	45,659	47,372	48%	Y
Winnebago	45,449	42,122	51%	Y
Kenosha	44,867	34,977	56%	Y
Rock	49,219	30,517	61%	Y
Rest of state	692,968	740,429	48%	Y

reveals much about the state's divided political geography. Table 1.2 provides the vote breakdown in Wisconsin's nine largest counties, which collectively represent about half of the state's total population.[34]

Obama rolled to huge wins in the state's two largest counties, both Democratic bastions. Milwaukee is the more sizeable of the two. For much of the twentieth century, the city of Milwaukee was not only an industrial powerhouse but also America's largest city with a Socialist mayor. After the 1950s, the Democrats elbowed the Socialists aside in city government, but organized labor and the economic liberalism of the blue-collar worker remained powerful political forces in the city. Later, a large influx of African Americans throughout the second half of the twentieth century helped to keep the city firmly in the Democratic camp even as the city's industrial base and unionized workforce melted away. Although Milwaukee *County* also encompasses an inner-ring of Republican-leaning suburbs, the city's numbers are normally large enough to ensure that Democratic candidates can carry the county as a whole.

Madison, Wisconsin's second-largest city and no less a Democratic stronghold, similarly tends to push Dane County into the Democratic column. However, Madison's liberalism has traditionally had a distinct flavor from Milwaukee's. Where Milwaukee's liberalism is rooted in its industrial past, Madison's liberalism is that of a college town—the city hosts the flagship campus of the University of Wisconsin system—and a seat of state government. Madison is more affluent, better educated, and less racially diverse than Milwaukee, and the capital city's liberalism more clearly extends beyond pocketbook issues. In 2006, when Wisconsin's voters considered a state constitutional amendment that would preclude same-sex marriage, Milwaukee County voted "yes," while Dane County voted "no."

Outside of Dane and Milwaukee Counties, Democrats face rougher sledding in Wisconsin, perhaps nowhere more so than in Waukesha, the state's third-largest county, where Barack Obama could not manage to win even one-third of the vote. The Milwaukee metro area—including the "collar counties" like Waukesha with their outer-ring suburbs—is thus among the nation's most politically polarized.[35] In the 2012 election, for instance, Milwaukee was second nationally only to New Orleans among large metro areas in the size of its urban-suburban voting divide.[36] Fueled in part by white flight, the collar counties have been growing rapidly. Between 1960 and 2010, Waukesha County's population increased by 146 percent, even as Milwaukee County's fell by nearly 9 percent. As white Milwaukeeans moved to the suburbs, and their places in the city were taken first by blacks and then by a more recent wave of Hispanics, the partisan divide has grown wider. In the 1968 presidential election, Milwaukee was only a little more Democratic, and Waukesha only a little more Republican, than the state average—in each case, about seven percentage points—but the gaps have grown steadily since then, doubling in Milwaukee and tripling in Waukesha.[37]

Democrats are competitive in the rest of the larger counties, but they are not nearly as dominant as they are in Milwaukee and Madison. These counties boast established urban cores with significant traditions of industrial production. Brown County, for instance, is centered on Green Bay (population 104,000), and Racine County on the city of Racine (population 78,000). The liberal economic agenda resonates in these counties, but the liberal social agenda less so. For instance, each voted against same-sex marriage in 2006. Such dynamics tend to make these counties important battlegrounds in state elections, especially the Fox River Valley counties of Brown, Outagamie, and Winnebago in Wisconsin's once-mighty paper-production corridor.

The rest of Wisconsin's population is dispersed among the sixty-three remaining, largely rural counties, located mostly in the northern and western halves of the state. Although these counties include some significant pockets of Democratic strength, they lean Republican as a whole, with Obama winning only about 48 percent of the vote.

Statewide elections, in sum, pit two large bastions of Democratic strength, Milwaukee and Madison, against the fast-growing, deeply Republican Milwaukee suburbs, with the rest of the state closely divided. As a practical matter, in recent years, this balance of power has meant that statewide elections depend on the turnout level of the Democratic-leaning voters of the cities. Blacks, Hispanics, and young people vote more reliably in presidential election years than otherwise, which means that Democrats tend to do quite well in Wisconsin every four years.[38] In off-year elections, however, Republicans have the edge because their suburban supporters do a better job of maintaining their turnout levels. This helps to explain why Democratic presidential candidates have won Wisconsin in each of the past seven elections, while Republican gubernatorial candidates (who run in presidential off years) have won six of their past eight campaigns. This also helps to explain why Wisconsin has both one of the nation's most liberal U.S. senators (Tammy Baldwin, voted in during the presidential election year of 2012) and one of the most conservative (Ron Johnson, voted in during the off year of 2010).

These contemporary political dynamics differ in a number of respects from the dynamics that existed in 1970, the historical starting point of this study. Over the past half century, the state's political landscape has been reshaped by at least three overarching, overlapping trends, in addition to the explosive growth of Milwaukee's suburbs.

First, Wisconsin has become much more racially and ethnically diverse. Initially little affected by the Great Migration of blacks from southern states, Wisconsin had a scant 12,158 African Americans in 1940 out of a total population of more than three million.[39] However, the explosion of industrial jobs in the state during and after World War II, especially in Milwaukee, proved a powerful magnet for poor blacks seeking economic opportunity. The state's black population topped 74,000 by 1960, 182,000 by 1980, and 304,000 by 2000. Reflecting continued but slowing growth, Wisconsin's black population surpassed 373,000 by 2013.[40] As a percent of the state population, African Americans increased from just 0.4 percent in 1940 to 6.5 percent in 2013. Wisconsin's non-Hispanic white population, by contrast, has been largely stagnant in size for decades.

It is possible that the black population growth might have been absorbed without much impact on the state's political system if it had been evenly distributed across the state. However, Wisconsin's burgeoning black population settled overwhelmingly in the city of Milwaukee, which saw its numbers increase from 13,000 in 1945 to nearly 230,000 in 2000, or about three-quarters of the state total.[41] Accounting for four out of every ten Milwaukeeans in the new millennium, African Americans have fundamentally reshaped both the city's and the state's political dynamics. The long-standing relationship of mutual distrust between Milwaukee and the rest of the state has become racialized, with Milwaukee becoming a majority-minority city—African Americans and Hispanic Americans together constitute a majority of the city's population—even as much of the rest of the state has remained racially homogenous.

Milwaukee's demographic transformation did not always go smoothly. The city had been a leading German and Eastern European outpost in the United States, and the earlier generations of immigrants and their descendants seemed to view the new arrivals from the southern United States with suspicion. In the ugly mayoral campaign of 1956, critics charged that Frank Zeidler, the incumbent Socialist, was placing billboards in southern states to draw more blacks to the city.[42] Zeidler's opponent supported time limits on public housing in an effort to keep the migrants away.

For their part, black Milwaukeeans also had their share of grievances, including discriminatory housing practices that helped keep them confined to blighted neighborhoods in the inner city and near north side. The bitter political fight for an open-housing law lasted for most of the 1960s. In 1967, Milwaukee's chief civil rights provocateur, the Roman Catholic Father James Groppi, led a group of protesters in a series of marches through the still-white ethnic neighborhoods of the near south side.[43] They were met with insults, bottles, and bricks.

At about the same time, tensions in the black inner city boiled over in a bloody riot that echoed the more infamous, and much larger, conflagration that struck Detroit during that "summer of love."[44] Mayor Henry Maier responded forcefully, effectively putting Milwaukee under martial law for twenty-six hours. His popularity soared to unprecedented heights, leading to a landslide reelection in 1968. The entire episode likely reinforced white perceptions of black dangerousness and of declining safety levels in the city, while also demonstrating the political dividends of tough responses to crime and disorder.

Although the protests and riots of the late 1960s largely died out, racial tensions have remained an important subtext of city, county, and state politics. These racial tensions have been inextricably intertwined not only with the city-suburbs divide, but also with issues of class and the fraught politics of welfare. The adoption of open-housing laws did not end black concentration in Milwaukee's northwest quadrant, and those black neighborhoods continue to be marked by the familiar indicators of urban poverty. Indeed, black Wisconsinites lag far behind the state's population as a whole when it comes to practically every major social measure: percent with a high school diploma, percent with a college degree, median family income, poverty rate, unemployment rate, incarceration rate, home ownership, percent of births to unmarried mothers, and infant death rate, to name a few.[45]

Although they do not figure as prominently in this story as African Americans, other minority groups have also grown in prominence in Wisconsin since 1970, including Hispanics, Asian Americans, and Native Americans. Hispanics, in particular, have come to rival African Americans in percent of the state population and, like the black migrants before them, are fast changing the cultural and political geography of Milwaukee in particular. Where blacks came to dominate the traditionally German neighborhoods of the north side, Hispanics settled in the traditionally Polish neighborhoods of the south side—taking over those urban spaces that had proved so hostile to Father Groppi in 1967. Census data from 2010 indicated that the city had become more than 17 percent Hispanic. Overall, the state's Hispanic population had quintupled from its 1980 level.[46]

In addition to such demographic changes, Wisconsin's political landscape has also been reshaped over the past half century by economic changes, perhaps most importantly the losses of manufacturing jobs and unionized jobs. Milwaukee was especially hard hit by deindustrialization, losing half of its manufacturing jobs between 1967 and 1987.[47] Other parts of the state were not as affected, or experienced a manufacturing rebound following the dark days of the early 1980s. Overall, in 2007, on the cusp of the Great Recession, Wisconsin had almost exactly the same number of manufacturing jobs it had thirty years earlier.[48] But, of course, this number of jobs was spread over a larger population. Moreover, the raw numbers fail to capture the long-term impact on families and communities resulting from the closure of iconic manufacturing facilities that long provided stable, well-paid blue-collar employment.

Along with the shuttering of many old-line, unionized factories came a sharp decline in the proportion of state workers who were union members. Between 1964 and 2015, the number dropped steadily from 34 percent to just over 8 percent.[49] Thus, while unionized industrial workers constituted a major political force in the state in 1970, these prototypical "Reagan Democrats"—more liberal on economic than social issues—have dwindled in number and influence. These changes made possible the adoption of an anti-union "right-to-work" law in Wisconsin in 2015, a development that would have been unthinkable a generation earlier and that will only further marginalize organized labor as a political force in the state.

The economic changes have also affected the political landscape in other ways. For instance, the concurrence of deindustrialization in Milwaukee with a dramatic increase in the size of the black population sharpened the economic competition between blacks and whites and thus likely exacerbated racial tensions. Deindustrialization also helped to ensure that Milwaukee's blacks would remain poor, and that the politics of race in Wisconsin would remain intertwined with the politics of welfare. More generally, there can be little doubt that the collapse of the economic arrangements that fueled postwar prosperity contributed to that particular late twentieth-century Middle American zeitgeist of anxiety and despair—a social setting in which the politics of law-and-order could take root and flourish.

Third, and finally, Wisconsin's political parties have grown far more ideologically polarized. In the 1970s, in Wisconsin and nationally, there were liberal Republicans, conservative Democrats, and plenty of moderates in both parties who could attract support from both the left and right. Along with this intra-party ideological diversity came a great deal of ticket splitting and crossover voting. As late as 1988, for instance, Democratic U.S. Senator Herb Kohl won a quarter of the Republican votes in Wisconsin, while his Republican opponent won one in five of the Democratic votes.[50] The long-term trend, though, has been for both parties to become more homogenous, and woe betide the politician who drifts too close to the center—both parties have seen prominent legislators successfully "primaried" (i.e., eliminated in a primary election, often by a more ideologically extreme candidate). Not surprisingly, the ideological polarization has been associated with a steady drop in ticket splitting. In 1994, with both a U.S. Senate and a gubernatorial race on the ballot, fully 36 percent of Wisconsin voters split their tickets.[51] In 2010, though, once again with U.S. Senate and gubernatorial positions at stake, ticket splitting fell to only 7 percent. Persuadable voters seem to have largely disappeared from the landscape, especially in the metro Milwaukee area, and politicians in statewide races focus mainly on maximizing turnout from their base.[52]

The critical features of Wisconsin's political landscape might be summed up this way: in a closely divided state with little crossover voting, the variable turnout of key Democratic voters often plays a decisive role in elections; these Democratic voters include blacks and Hispanics, who have increased dramatically in number over the past half century, especially in the city of Milwaukee; the explosive growth of Milwaukee's black population generated considerable racial tension, which continues to play a role in Wisconsin's sharp Democratic-Republican and city-suburbs divides; and, partly as a result of late twentieth-century deindustrialization, Milwaukee's black neighborhoods serve as Wisconsin's most visible zone of chronic, concentrated poverty, making these neighborhoods a perennial focal point of social policy debates.

This political context has helped to determine, among other things, which individuals have been in a position to influence the development of state sentencing law.

The Governor

Occupying the most prominent and powerful position in state government, Wisconsin's governor is uniquely well situated to shape state sentencing law. Through his bully pulpit, the governor can influence public perceptions of the crime problem and potential policy responses. He also has a variety of more direct mechanisms of influence over state lawmaking. For instance, the governor initiates the biennial budget-writing process with his own budget proposal. Since everyone recognizes that the budget simply *must* pass every two years, budget

Table 1.3. Gubernatorial elections, 1970–2014

Year	Winner	Party	Percent vote	Party control— senate	Party control— assembly
1970	Pat Lucey	Dem.	54%	N	Y
1974	Pat Lucey	Dem.	53%	Y	Y
1978	Lee Dreyfus	Rep.	54%	N	N
1982	Anthony Earl	Dem.	58%	Y	Y
1986	Tommy Thompson	Rep.	53%	N	N
1990	Tommy Thompson	Rep.	58%	N	N
1994	Tommy Thompson	Rep.	67%	Y	Y
1998	Tommy Thompson	Rep.	60%	N	Y
2002	Jim Doyle	Dem.	45%	N	N
2006	Jim Doyle	Dem.	53%	Y	N
2010	Scott Walker	Rep.	52%	Y	Y
2014	Scott Walker	Rep.	52%	Y	Y

bills are always a tempting vehicle for nonbudgetary policymaking, and Wisconsin's governors have indeed used this process on several occasions to accomplish important changes in sentencing law. The governor can also call a special session of the legislature to deal with a specific problem; although the governor cannot dictate how the legislature responds to the problem, the calling of a special session helps focus public attention on an issue and builds pressure on the legislature to do something about it. Moreover, at the back end of the legislative process, Wisconsin's governor wields an unusually strong veto power: the governor need not veto an entire bill in Wisconsin—as the president must in the federal system—but may simply strike out individual sections or even words with which he disagrees.

In recent years, as we have seen, Wisconsin's ideological polarization and related voting trends have tended to favor Republican gubernatorial candidates. This represents a marked departure from the 1970s, when Democrats dominated state government. As indicated in table 1.3, most gubernatorial elections since 1970 have been close, with the notable exception of Republican Tommy Thompson's landslide reelections in the 1990s.[53] Whatever their own vote total, though, Wisconsin's governors have typically faced the difficult reality of divided government. Between 1970 and 2006, seven out of ten gubernatorial terms began with the opposing party controlling at least one chamber of the legislature. Since 2010, though, Republicans have managed to replicate the Democratic dominance of the 1970s.

If the overall trend since the 1970s has been toward greater Republican power in state government, and if Wisconsin's Republicans have at the same time become more uniformly conservative, then one might suppose that the state's sentencing policies have become much tougher. In some respects—most notably, the 1998 truth-in-sentencing law—there clearly has been a movement toward greater severity in punishment. However, as later chapters detail, state sentencing policy has hardly followed a consistent path, and many tough-on-crime enactments have been more symbolically than practically significant. This has been due, in no small measure, to the restraining influence of Wisconsin's governors, including the Republicans. Carrying the ultimate administrative responsibility for the Department of Corrections and its budget, governors from both parties have been mindful of the potential impact of sentencing laws on the size of the prison population. Tommy Thompson, for instance, recalls that he was very concerned about the fiscal burdens of Wisconsin's continuous prison construction in the 1990s.[54] Among other things, this concern helped to ensure that Wisconsin's "three strikes and you are out" law was much more modest in its impact than similar laws adopted in other states at about the same time.

The Legislature

The Wisconsin Legislature consists of a senate, whose thirty-three members serve four-year terms, and an assembly, whose ninety-nine members serve two-year terms. In the early 1970s, as the legislature was entering the mass-incarceration era, it had just completed a transition from part-time to full-time. It also stood on the verge of a long period of Democratic control, as indicated in figure 1.1.[55] Democrats took the assembly in the 1970 election and the senate in the 1974 election. They would hold both without interruption until the mid-1990s. Since the 1994 election, party control of the closely divided senate has switched back and forth repeatedly, but Republicans have had nearly continuous control of the assembly. Since 2010, this Republican lock hold has been strengthened by gerrymandering that packed Democrats into a small number of districts, some of which are 90 percent "blue."[56] Thus, even in the good Democratic year of 2012, with Barack Obama winning a clear victory at the top of the ticket, Democrats could not manage to win 40 percent of assembly races.

Not surprisingly, Wisconsin's increasing political polarization has affected the legislature. Those who served in the legislature in the 1960s and 1970s recall a time when strong friendships formed across the aisle, and bipartisanship was a more common aspect of lawmaking. This changed over time, as moderates in both parties disappeared, sometimes after being "primaried" and sometimes

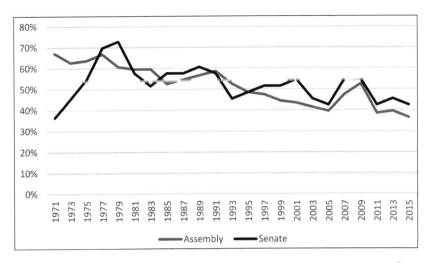

Figure 1.1. Democratic percentage in Wisconsin Legislature, 1971–2015

voluntarily—often with a feeling of frustration at how "nasty" the legislative process had become.[57]

The legislature also became much more preoccupied with crime in the mass-incarceration era. Bills were often proposed in response to the latest crime in the news—"government by headline," as one former senator disparagingly puts it[58]—and many legislators recall a steady drumbeat of constituent demands for longer sentences.

Along with the growth of partisanship and government by headline came a reduction in the influence of Wisconsin's nonpartisan legislative service agencies, the Legislative Council, the Legislative Fiscal Bureau, and the Legislative Audit Bureau. The Legislative Council, in particular, had a notable history in the development of state criminal justice policies. Overseen by a bipartisan committee of legislators, the council maintains a staff of attorneys who advise the legislature's various standing committees. The council also regularly forms "special committees" to deal with complex issues of particular concern. These special committees, comprised of a combination of legislators, other public officials, and interested private citizens, constitute what may be a nationally unique policy-development vehicle. The special committees typically hold a series of public hearings, consult with experts, issue staff reports, and systematically develop legislative proposals. Wisconsin's influential criminal-code reform of the 1950s emerged from just such a process. As described in chapters to come, Legislative Council special committees continued to grapple with criminal justice issues in the mass-incarceration era, but with much diminished relevance to policymaking.

External Influences

Only the governor and legislature have formally prescribed roles in the law-making process, but outside agencies and interest groups can nonetheless play a decisive role in determining which issues are prioritized and which solutions become embodied in law. In some policy areas, there are well-organized, well-financed interest groups that engage deeply and systematically with the law-making process. Medical malpractice, industrial pollution, highway construction, and school vouchers seem good examples. By contrast, in the criminal justice area, external influences seem more diffuse and ad hoc.

Consider the judiciary, for instance. Judges value their sentencing discretion, and we might imagine that judges would resist sentencing policy changes that curtail their discretion. And, indeed, at a few critical junctures, various individual judges have played an important role in preserving sentencing discretion in Wisconsin. However, the influence of judges in the sentencing area has not come so much from organized, collective self-assertion as from the fact that individual judges have been invited into the policymaking process. As elected officials in their own right, judges tend to be respected figures in their communities, and some have long-standing relationships with policymakers. Judges, moreover, are thought to have particular expertise in the sentencing field. These considerations naturally lead to their involvement in the making of sentencing policy, whether through informal conversations with legislators or through appointment to policy-development bodies.

Thomas Barland, a longtime circuit court judge from Eau Claire County, provides an illustration. Before becoming a judge, Barland served three terms as a Republican member of the assembly, leaving the year before Tommy Thompson began his pregubernatorial career in the assembly. Thompson got to know Barland's reputation as a dealmaker who could get difficult legislation passed.[59] Three decades later, Thompson then turned to Barland to head up the Wisconsin Criminal Penalties Study Committee, which was charged with developing a proposal to implement truth in sentencing. As detailed in chapter 5, the committee's proposal, enacted by the legislature in 2002, powerfully reaffirmed Wisconsin's commitment to judicial sentencing discretion.

As important as was the role of Barland and his fellow judges on the Criminal Penalties Study Committee, that role did not result from collective lobbying on the part of the judiciary but from a set of ad hoc decisions about whom to include on the committee. Although the judiciary maintains a legislative relations staff in Madison, this office has not traditionally focused much on sentencing policy.[60]

In addition to the judges, the prosecutors comprise a second group of officials with an obvious collective interest in sentencing policy. Tougher sentencing laws increase prosecutors' plea bargaining leverage and help ensure sufficiently long sentences in cases in which prosecutors believe they are necessary. However, like the judges, the prosecutors have not traditionally engaged in much systematic, collective lobbying on sentencing policy. To be sure, individual prosecutors may be consulted, or may proactively make their views known, on an ad hoc basis. Indeed, some legislators make a habit of seeking the opinion of their local district attorney on crime legislation.[61] At the same time, some prosecutors, like some judges, find the sausage making of the legislative process distasteful and try to keep their distance. One former prosecutor described to me a lobbying meeting that he attended with some colleagues many years ago; once safely out of earshot of the legislators, one of the prosecutors exclaimed that he felt the need to take a shower.[62] To the extent the prosecutors have engaged with the legislative process in a coordinated fashion, they have tended to emphasize other issues besides sentencing, such as their pay scale, number of authorized positions, and the length of district attorney terms.

An important obstacle to effective, coordinated lobbying by both trial judges and district attorneys is that, at the end of the day, each faces reelection locally and must maintain a strong local orientation. With a few obvious exceptions like increasing pay, efforts to establish a united policy front seem doomed to founder on the inevitably conflicting preferences and priorities of widely dispersed local officials who must deal with widely varying local circumstances. There are, however, two state-level criminal justice officials for whom engagement with state policy may seem easier and more natural. One is the state public defender. The SPD's office has become more engaged with policy issues in recent years,[63] but as with the prosecutors, budgetary matters have sometimes been a preoccupation. Then, too, the political clout of public defenders tends to be somewhat less imposing than that of prosecutors.

The attorney general is another independent state-level official who might have an ongoing interest in sentencing policy. The AG's office represents the state in criminal appeals, investigates and prosecutes some crimes, runs the state crime lab, and provides services to crime victims. Wisconsin's AG is elected in his own right and may or may not belong to the same party as the governor. Indeed, the AG is apt to have gubernatorial ambitions of his own and may be more rival than collaborator with the sitting governor. This rivalry became particularly important in the 1990s, when Republican Tommy Thompson was governor and Democrat Jim Doyle was AG. Doyle's outspoken support for truth in sentencing put pressure on Thompson to propose his own, even tougher "truth" bill. However, with a few exceptions, Wisconsin's AGs have not generally made tougher sentencing laws a high priority. This may reflect the fact that the state's AGs have mostly come out of DA offices; as longtime system insiders they are apt to feel comfortable with the highly discretionary, decentralized system in which they cut their prosecutorial teeth.

A variety of other interest groups might potentially wish to involve themselves in sentencing policy. Some groups, for instance, have an economic interest in mass incarceration, including the mostly rural, economically challenged communities in which prisons are located; the corrections officers employed by prisons; and the private firms that build, supply, and service prisons. Others who might feel a particular interest in sentencing policy include police agencies, crime victims, and county governments, which are financially responsible for the local jails holding shorter-term inmates. Civil rights organizations like the ACLU (American Civil Liberties Union) and NAACP (National Association for the Advancement of Colored People) might also see themselves as having a stake in sentencing policy. Suffice it to say, though, that I have found no evidence that any of these groups have served as a major driver of sentencing policy in Wisconsin, and none feature prominently in the chapters to follow.

Somewhat more influential have been a few researchers and idea entrepreneurs, mostly situated in academia and think tanks. For instance, one of Wisconsin's leading voices on sentencing policy has been Professor Walter Dickey of the University of Wisconsin Law School. Dickey headed state corrections in the 1980s under Democratic Governor Anthony Earle, but he was sufficiently well regarded across the aisle that Republican Tommy Thompson appointed him to chair a prominent gubernatorial task force on sentencing and corrections in the 1990s. On the other end of the ideological spectrum, the Wisconsin Policy Research Institute, a conservative think tank, gained attention in the 1990s with a series of reports that were supportive of mass incarceration—one was titled simply *Prison Works*. Still, if there is one thing that is clear from the recent history, it is that neither densely footnoted research reports nor gaudy academic credentials are sufficient to move state sentencing policy. Expertise has been forced to compete, often unsuccessfully, with populism, political opportunism and expedience, and emotional responses to crime.

The media also play a role as external influencers. Marc Mauer of the Sentencing Project has charged, "Most images of the crime problem [in the United States] communicate fear, anxiety, and a distorted sense of the actual extent of the problem. This serves to overwhelm any intelligent or informative discussion of the issues."[64] There seems no reason to think that the media's role in Wisconsin has been markedly different from this national story.

By contrast, almost entirely invisible in sentencing policymaking have been criminal offenders, their families, and the deeply disadvantaged communities that are home to a greatly disproportionate share of both offenders and victims. In some ways, their political marginalization seems obvious and inevitable. For instance, Wisconsin's felons cannot vote as long as they are under criminal justice supervision. Moreover, offenders and their families tend to be poor, and poor people cannot make campaign contributions. Cultural barriers and educational deficits may further impede the effectiveness of their advocacy. Still, there is an uncomfortable sense in which sentencing policy in Wisconsin is something that is done by one group of people to another group of people. A more inclusive policymaking process might be better informed and carry greater legitimacy. As a counterpoint to the more exclusionary general tendency in state policymaking, chapter 7 describes the efforts of WISDOM, a faith-based grassroots organization, to bring offenders and their families into the conversation about sentencing and corrections.

Four Competing Ideologies

The narrative of policy debate and legal change that follows is, in large part, a playing out of the tensions between three competing sets of ideas about crime and punishment: populism, managerialism, and judicialism. These constitute rival types of penal ideology, by which I mean a complementary set of beliefs and attitudes that tend to support a particular sentencing and corrections policy agenda. Various legal reforms we will consider can be characterized as distinctly managerial or populist or judicialist, based on the content of the reform and the public justifications given by its supporters.

Populism and managerialism contrast sharply with one another along two dimensions. First, populists see criminals—especially serious or repeat offenders—as essentially depraved and uncontrollable but through tough deterrent threats and simple physical incapacitation. Managerialists see more variation in the offender population and greater potential to manage the threat posed by criminals through individualized control strategies, which might often involve rehabilitative treatment in the community. Managerialists fear that a heavy reliance on incarceration may prove counterproductive to public safety, both because some offenders may be made more dangerous by time in prison and because the high costs of imprisonment may drain funding from the social services that could deliver greater crime control over the long run. Second, populists tend to be skeptical of criminal justice experts and insiders—elites who may appear insulated from the fear of crime that plagues ordinary citizens and out of touch with the common-sense intuition that bad conduct deserves severe punishment. Populists thus distrust official discretion, most especially the discretion exercised by unelected bureaucrats. The archetypal populist sentencing reform is the mandatory minimum prison term, which takes away discretion from judges to choose probation and from corrections officials to allow parole release. Managerialists, by contrast, have more confidence in the ability of criminal justice officials to exercise discretion appropriately, especially when the discretion is informed by research, data, and specialized expertise. Indeed, the sort of individualization of punishment favored by managerialists probably requires a considerable amount of freedom for front-line officials to take into account all of the particular circumstances of each case.

Judicialism combines aspects of populism and managerialism, with an overriding emphasis on preserving and legitimizing the judge's sentencing discretion. The legitimacy question—how, in a society founded on ideals of individual liberty, can it be legitimate for the state to exercise its coercive powers of punishment?—is the grand question that quietly hangs over all sentencing policy debates. For the populist, legitimacy comes from popular support—it is assumed that tough punishment reflects majority will. For the managerialist, legitimacy comes from the systematic application of expertise to advance the public good. For the judicialist, legitimacy comes from a particular model of public decision-making—the familiar model of court-based processes that has been used for centuries to resolve all manner of social conflicts in the Anglo-American legal system. The basic components include open, public proceedings; a fair opportunity for both sides to tell their side of the story; and a reasoned, individualized decision made by reference to general principles. The decision maker, too, is important. The judge is a curious figure in our cultural imagination who seems to combine expertise—she is normally a highly trained and experienced legal professional—with democratic legitimacy, especially in states that elect their judges. The judge, in other words, can present both a managerial and a populist face.

Judicialism thus offers a third path that allows policymakers to evade the basic push-pull of populism and managerialism—should we have more imprisonment, or less? Judicialism declines any global answer to this question, leaving it instead in the hands of hundreds of judges operating independently of one another in tens of thousands of cases. Judges can be populist or managerial according to their own personal proclivities, the preferences of their own constituents, and the particular circumstances of each case. At a policy level, judicialists share with managerialists a preference for judicial discretion over mandatory minimums, but at the same time share with populists a skepticism of corrections discretion, which is exercised by unelected bureaucrats in ways that typically lack the transparency and accountability of the courtroom.

Since the early 1970s, public debate over sentencing policy in Wisconsin has been dominated by these three basic perspectives—populism, managerialism, and judicialism. Yet a fourth has also been apparent on occasion, and presents a notable contrast with the others. To borrow a term from sociologist Vanessa Barker, we might refer to this alternative ideology as "penal egalitarianism."[65] If populism looks to majority will as the ultimate source of legitimacy for punishment, egalitarianism rests on a deeper sense of democracy. As Barker puts it, "[C]rime is perceived to be a common feature of modern social life, rather than the result of morally depraved criminals, and criminals are considered to be part of the political community rather than fully excluded from it."[66] Punishment emerges from and embodies a sense of mutual respect and concern running to all members of the community—offenders, victims, and others. Punishment should thus be restrained, particularly when it comes to incarceration, which is so inherently exclusionary. Egalitarianism shares with managerialism a preference for community corrections and rehabilitation but puts these matters in a different ethical frame. While the managerial perspective sharply distinguishes between the offender who is to be controlled by the criminal justice system and the "law-abiding" citizen whose interests are to be served by the system, the egalitarian frame downplays the distinction and aims to establish stronger communities that work for *all* of their members. Although this perspective has not been much heard in the sentencing policy debates, we will see it reemerge toward the end of our narrative in the work of WISDOM.

Two "Missing" Pieces

Before proceeding with the more-or-less chronological narrative that constitutes the heart of this book, I should note that this narrative gives less attention to two topics than some readers might expect. Mass incarceration is often attributed to the War on Drugs or to racism, but neither topic receives extensive treatment in the chapters that immediately follow. I have chosen instead to give Wisconsin's War on Drugs its own chapter at the end of the basic narrative. I have done so, in part, in order to demonstrate in a more cohesive way that drug enforcement has been a much less important driver of mass incarceration in Wisconsin than it has been elsewhere in the United States.

As for racism, there is indeed a yawning gap in the imprisonment rates of whites and blacks in Wisconsin, and this is true to an even greater extent than in most other states. This deeply troubling phenomenon is noted at several turns in the narrative and explored somewhat more systematically in chapter 6. However, racism does not play a central role in my account. This is not because I doubt the existence of racial bias in the criminal justice system but because its magnitude and practical importance are very hard to assess using the source materials on which this study is based. Thankfully, overt bias only rarely appears these days in legal and political rhetoric. Research on racial discrimination in punishment thus tends to focus on the statistical analysis of sentencing outcomes. Unfortunately, such research often raises more questions than it answers. By way of illustration, some research suggests that black defendants tend to come to sentencing with a worse criminal history than white defendants convicted of the same crime, which might arguably justify longer average sentences for black defendants.[67] Yet, on the other hand, black criminal history may not be a reliable indicator of elevated dangerousness relative to white offenders but instead merely reflects more intensive policing of black neighborhoods, which itself might conceivably result in part from racism. It is, in short, a daunting challenge to tease out the precise impact of racism on imprisonment disparities, and one that lies largely beyond the scope of this book.

2

The Seventies Synthesis

Wisconsin entered the 1970s with a stable, well-established sentencing system whose major features had been in place for many years. A decade later, the system's outward features remained basically unchanged. However, this superficial stability masked the emergence of widespread doubts about the system's fundamental premises. The push for reform culminated at the end of the 1970s in a comprehensive proposal for a fundamental restructuring of Wisconsin's sentencing system. Both the proposal and the process by which it was defeated demonstrate the extent to which political leaders had lost confidence in the status quo.

Institutions and Ideology

The sentencing system of the 1970s reflected a particular synthesis of institutional design, penal ideology, practice norms, and policymaking processes. More specifically, the "seventies synthesis" relied heavily on probation and parole; gave judges and corrections officials a great deal of discretion to decide what to do with offenders on a case-by-case basis; embodied a managerial view of punishment, with a particular emphasis on the goal of offender rehabilitation; and looked to systematic, deliberative policymaking for improvement of the system.

On a day-to-day basis, the two most visible institutional features of the seventies synthesis were probation and parole. Nationally, these two nineteenth-century innovations had become ubiquitous by the mid-twentieth century.[1] In Wisconsin, judges had broad discretion by the 1970s to order probation, and the Wisconsin Supreme Court even indicated that probation should serve as a sort of default sentence in most cases.[2] Mandatory minimum prison terms were established by statute only for three relatively rare offenses: first-degree murder, treason, and hostage taking.[3] For each of these offenses the mandatory term was life. For all other offenses, the judge could impose probation. Consistent with the supreme court's embrace of probation, at any given time in the 1970s, there were typically four or five times as many offenders on probation as in prison.[4]

There were similarly few constraints on the use of parole (that is, early release from prison on a decision by the Parole Board). Even in the life-sentenced cases, prisoners could be considered for parole release after serving twenty years, less time off for good behavior. A lifer who earned the maximum possible "good time" would be up for parole after just eleven years and three months.[5] All other prisoners could be considered for parole after just six months, regardless of the length of the imposed sentence. Of course, no prisoner could count on being released at the first possible opportunity. At the Parole Board's discretion, a prisoner might be required to serve the entire imposed term of imprisonment, less good time.

Probation and parole reflect the managerial ideology, permitting highly individualized punishment and encouraging restraint in the use of imprisonment. The probation decision was to be made on a case-by-case basis in light of "the nature and circumstances of the crime, the history and character of the offender, and the available institutional and community resources."[6] Likewise, parole decisions could take into account a wide variety of factors relating to the history and character of the offender.[7]

Wisconsin's highly discretionary, managerial system in the 1970s rested on a strong commitment to rehabilitation as a desired and realistic aim for most offenders. For instance, in 1972, Wisconsin's main institution for adult inmates identified its mission this way: "The Wisconsin State Prison, in accordance with the principles of modern penology, emphasizes the importance of vocational, physical, mental, moral, and social rehabilitation"[8]—strikingly omitting reference to deterrence, incapacitation, or retribution as central objectives. Similarly, the heavy use of probation and parole also reflected a focus on rehabilitation. For instance, Governor Pat Lucey's Council on Criminal Justice justified its preference for community supervision (probation or parole) over imprisonment this way: "It is only through maintenance in the community that work-release programs can be implemented, family ties maintained, and responsibility for individual actions meaningfully assumed. Here problems can be identified and treated, within context. Here an individual can develop a non-criminal lifestyle with the aid and support of the professionals in corrections. It is within their communities . . . that rehabilitation can occur."[9]

Importantly, this appealing vision of offender rehabilitation in the community reflected an easy confidence in the "professionals in corrections." More generally, the highly discretionary, managerial system of the 1970s necessarily implied considerable faith in professional expertise. The hundreds of judges and corrections officials who made the system work seemed to be experts in managing offenders, and it was their apparent knowledge and wisdom that justified the enormous discretionary power they were given over offenders' lives. A similar confidence in expertise may also be seen in the systematic, deliberative model of policymaking that seemed so prominent in the 1970s, an important component of the seventies synthesis that contrasts with the more reactive, ad hoc policymaking that grew increasingly common in the 1980s and 1990s.

The Wisconsin Council on Criminal Justice: Exemplar of the Deliberative Model

The seventies synthesis included an ongoing interest among policymakers in studying and improving institutional arrangements so as to help the criminal justice system better achieve its managerial-rehabilitative objectives. This interest was expressed through several ambitious policymaking initiatives. The basic process would look something like this: a commission comprising individuals with relevant expertise and diverse institutional roles would be assigned to study a policy problem; the commission would gather information and opinions in a transparent, systematic way from leading stakeholders and other members of the public; and the commission would then present detailed reform proposals in a public report. Although this model was hardly new to Wisconsin in the 1970s—the state had used this approach, for instance, to develop its nationally well-regarded criminal code reforms in the 1950s—the decade did witness an extraordinary flowering of deliberative initiatives. Many occurred under the umbrella of the Wisconsin Council on Criminal Justice (CCJ).

Council on Criminal Justice: The Early Years

In Wisconsin and across the United States, the federal government stimulated a great deal of criminal justice study and planning in the 1970s through its Law Enforcement Assistance Administration. The LEAA got its start in the Omnibus Crime Control and Safe Streets Act of 1968, adopted by Congress at a time of surging crime rates and bloody urban riots. President Lyndon Johnson was determined to increase the federal crime-fighting role, but conservatives and moderates in Congress wanted to retain the traditionally preeminent position of state and local governments in the criminal justice field.[10] The compromise solution was "block grants"—federal funds channeled through the states to enhance local crime-fighting capacity. As the dispenser of what would prove to be billions of dollars of federal aid over the years, the LEAA had a very attractive carrot to encourage state and local reforms. Central to the LEAA's work was the requirement that states engage in comprehensive criminal justice planning; if grants were not linked to a systematic plan, then there seemed considerable risk that much of the money would be squandered.

Wisconsin's Governor Warren Knowles, a moderate Republican, responded by establishing the Council on Criminal Justice in 1969 as the state's new planning agency. Formally housed in the Department of Justice and thus under the auspices of Republican attorney general Robert Warren, Wisconsin's CCJ ramped up quickly, disbursing more than half a million dollars in federal grants in 1969 and more than seven million dollars in 1970.[11] The CCJ's official state plans, which had to be submitted to the federal LEAA, reflected the late 1960s preoccupation with the threat of urban riots. Milwaukee had experienced a major disturbance in 1967, so the riot issue was no mere abstraction to state policymakers. Consistent with this preoccupation, Wisconsin's earliest plans emphasized the importance of new police hardware, especially communication devices. The CCJ's spending followed suit: police agencies received more than half of the total money in both 1969 and 1970, while courts, corrections, and crime prevention lagged far behind. All of this mirrored national trends. One LEAA official has recalled that his "top priority was to get hand-held radios into every cop's hands."[12] Police also acquired armored personnel carriers and other riot-suppression equipment.

As the 1960s gave way to the 1970s, priorities changed, and they did so even more markedly in Wisconsin than in the nation as a whole. Leading the way was Democratic governor Pat Lucey, who replaced Knowles following the 1970 election. Hailing from rural western Wisconsin, Lucey was a tenacious political organizer who had played a central role in the revival of the state's moribund Democratic Party in the 1950s.[13] He held a variety of political positions in the 1960s and became part of the inner circle of both John and Robert Kennedy. Introspective and owlish, Lucey lacked the Kennedy charisma, but he earned the admiration of many Wisconsinites—especially those on the left side of the political spectrum—for his principled stands on contentious issues and his willingness to fight tough political battles in the name of good-government reforms. He was an early and outspoken critic of the Vietnam War and one of the nation's first prominent political figures to call for the resignation of President Richard Nixon. Within Wisconsin, his legacies included consolidation of the University of Wisconsin system, tax reform, and greater equity in the funding of public schools.

This energetic reformer wasted little time after his election before turning his attention to the state's criminal justice system. Just two weeks after his inauguration, Lucey issued an executive order transferring control of the Council on Criminal Justice from Attorney General Warren to himself. The new governor had big ambitions for criminal justice improvement, and he saw the CCJ as the vehicle for change.[14] No longer would the agency's mission center on distributing radios to cops. Indeed, not long after Lucey reconstituted the CCJ, the agency specifically voted against any further funding of riot-control equipment.[15]

Lucey established a board to oversee the work of the CCJ's staff of twenty-four employees.[16] This large, diverse board nicely illustrates the 1970s ideal of inclusive, expert-driven policymaking. Chaired by Lucey and vice-chaired by Frank Remington, a much-admired criminal law professor from the University of Wisconsin who had played a lead role in the 1950s code-reform effort, the CCJ board also included several other state and local government officials, the director of a private social service agency, a prison chaplain, a tribal official, a university professor, and a private lawyer. Notably, the prison chaplain, Father Quintin Helline, was specifically designated as a representative of the interests of the state's incarcerated population. Such an inclusive gesture, which implicitly recognizes the legitimacy of prisoner interests, has not often been repeated in more recent decades.

The CCJ's first major task was the development of a revised criminal justice improvement plan for 1972–76. The plan demonstrated the CCJ's reorientation away from police hardware and toward systemic reform of courts and corrections. The plan also embodied all of the key features of the seventies synthesis. The CCJ warmly embraced probation and parole and simply took for granted the wide discretion given to judges and corrections officials in their administration. Community-based, as opposed to prison-based, programs dominated the specific priorities in the corrections area, which reflected the CCJ's belief that offenders were more easily rehabilitated if kept in the community.

All of this was perfectly consistent with a managerial ideology, but in a few places the plan seemed even more in the spirit of penal egalitarianism. Most notably, the CCJ emphasized that offenders "must be treated as community members with respect to decision-making and participation in their fates," and that the challenges posed by offender reintegration were essentially a *community*, not just a governmental, responsibility. "We must promote increased volunteer participation, encourage existing social service agencies to become more responsive to offenders and prod local business to increase offender employment," the CCJ said. "Our remote, state run penal institutions have had the effect of allowing the community to shirk its problems. These problems will never be solved until the community assumes them and tackles them accordingly."[17] Here, the

CCJ seemed to embrace a vision of deep democracy that contrasted with managerialism no less than with populism.

The CCJ Committee on Offender Rehabilitation: The Egalitarian High-Water Mark

Marking its first major commitment in support of the new priorities, the Council on Criminal Justice formed a Citizens Study Committee on Offender Rehabilitation in 1971. The committee would ultimately demonstrate both the visionary potential and the political pitfalls of an egalitarian reform agenda. Its forty-two members reflected an even more inclusive approach to policymaking than the CCJ itself. As Governor Lucey observed in his charge to the committee, "Amongst you are inmates, parolees, lawyers, doctors, and academicians. Several of you are presently professionally involved in our corrections system and different aspects of offender rehabilitation. Others among you have served time in Wisconsin Institutions, and we hope to benefit from the suggestions drawn from your own experience."[18] Serving as chair was Raymond Malmquist, a business executive from Madison.

A year in the making, the committee's *Final Report* contained dozens of policy recommendations, but all were overshadowed by what the committee itself characterized as its "most fundamental priority": the shuttering of all of Wisconsin's existing prisons by June 30, 1975.[19] The prisons were to be replaced by locally controlled, community-based treatment programs, supplemented by a few new places of confinement for the small number of offenders who "pose an imminent threat to the safety of the public-at-large."[20] The committee explained, "[N]o amount of resources, however great, can enhance a convicted citizen's chances for productive re-entry to a democratic society when that citizen has been confined in an institution too large to provide individual services, too geographically remote to provide vital life-contacts, and too regimented to [foster] self-esteem. In short, current Wisconsin institutions cannot rehabilitate."[21]

Although managerialism might similarly emphasize rehabilitation, the committee's references to citizenship and democracy point to the committee's essentially egalitarian orientation. Elsewhere, in a striking phrase, the committee referred to "rehabilitation for democracy."[22] The committee's hope was for imprisoned offenders to "assume the burden of citizenship" upon their release[23]— a seemingly more encompassing and egalitarian vision for the offender's future than simply staying out of trouble.

The committee similarly articulated a strikingly egalitarian vision for prison administration, termed the "collaborative model." The committee called for institutional self-determination based on staff and offender participation "on all levels of decision making regarding organizational decisions and individual self management decisions."[24] "Each institution would identify its own problems; their solutions should be left to those whose lives are significantly affected by what is done."[25] Similarly, the proposed community-based treatment programs would also be controlled by "the community," which was expressly defined to include offenders and their families.[26]

Other notable aspects of the committee's proposal included

- Curtailing the use of solitary confinement in prisons;
- Eliminating all minimum waiting periods before parole eligibility;
- Adopting a strong presumption in favor of probationary sentences;
- Limiting statutory maximum sentences to five years, except in cases in which there is a finding that the offender is "especially dangerous"; and
- Decriminalizing a host of vice offenses, including prostitution, marijuana distribution and possession, noncommercial gambling, and adultery.

Although much of the committee's proposal may sound hopelessly naïve to readers in the early twenty-first century, the committee was not out of line with other criminal justice reform proposals emerging at the national level in the late 1960s and early 1970s. For instance, the committee borrowed the concept of a collaborative prison from the report of President Lyndon Johnson's crime commission in 1967, while the committee's sentencing proposals echoed the American Bar Association's *Sentencing Standards*. As discussed in chapter 7, the committee's proposed decriminalization of marijuana also reflected a contemporaneous national trend. Most strikingly, in 1973, a National Advisory Commission on Criminal Justice Standards and Goals—sponsored by the staunchly law-and-order Nixon administration, no less—called for a ten-year moratorium on prison construction, a ban on private possession of handguns, reduced use of solitary confinement, earlier release of prisoners, and a maximum prison term of five years in most cases.[27] The prison, according to the National Advisory Commission, "is obsolete, cannot be reformed, should not be perpetuated through the false hope of forced 'treatment,' and should be repudiated as useless for any purpose other than locking away persons who are too dangerous to be allowed at large in free society." Back in Wisconsin, the members of the Committee on Offender Rehabilitation must have felt vindicated.

Any sense of vindication, however, would have been short-lived. The recommendations of the Committee on Offender Rehabilitation got no further in Madison than those of the National Advisory Commission did in Washington, DC. The prison guards union and other law enforcement groups were quick to denounce the goal of closing prisons at a time of rising crime rates, and

Governor Lucey promptly distanced himself from the committee's three-year timeline for implementing reforms.[28] Lucey had supported the idea of reduced reliance on imprisonment, but he had no appetite for closing down the prisons *en masse*. The closest he would come would be a proposal to shut down the Victorian-era Green Bay Reformatory, a badly outdated institution that housed younger offenders, but even that goal was surrendered as the state's prison population began to grow in 1973.[29] Meanwhile, overshadowed by the controversy over prison closures, the other recommendations made by the Committee on Offender Rehabilitation were largely forgotten. An unfortunate legacy of the whole episode may have been the disenchantment of the corrections bureaucracy with deliberative policymaking in general. Sanger Powers, a careerist who headed the Division of Corrections for nearly twenty years, said that the committee "left a bad taste in my mouth"; he felt that some members of the committee staff had manipulated the process to reach predetermined outcomes.[30] After his retirement in 1974, Powers dismissed all of Lucey's task forces as having little value.[31]

Despite the failure of the Committee on Offender Rehabilitation, the Council on Criminal Justice continued to issue its annual plans and to dole out federal money pursuant to the plans. A few representative expenditures from 1974 included

- $381,771 for an "urban prosecutor program" in Milwaukee;
- $142,096 for the evaluation of inmates in the Milwaukee County Jail;
- $25,369 for a bomb disposal program in Milwaukee;
- $90,972 for police training through the University of Wisconsin;
- $258,000 for the state Department of Justice's organized crime unit;
- $212,740 for an expansion of public defender services; and
- More than $500,000 for alcohol and drug abuse programs.[32]

As such quotidian grant-processing continued, the CCJ prepared to launch what would prove to be its most ambitious policy development initiative yet.

The CCJ Standards and Goals Committee: New Challenges to Rehabilitation and Parole

In 1975, the Council on Criminal Justice began a comprehensive, two-year review of Wisconsin's criminal justice system with an eye to developing long-term goals for improvement. Again, the federal Law Enforcement Assistance Administration in Washington, DC, provided a key stimulus. With the LEAA's grant budget reaching close to $1 billion, the agency continued to demand that states submit annual plans as the price of federal funding, but the LEAA was growing impatient with the low quality of many state plans.[33] The result was a 1973 mandate for states to develop comprehensive standards and goals for incorporation into the annual plans by 1976.[34] Supported by federal funding, Wisconsin's CCJ began its standards and goals project in 1975, with separate committees appointed by Governor Lucey to review the state's juvenile and adult criminal justice systems.

Handling the adult system, the forty-eight-member Special Committee on Criminal Justice Standards and Goals included no prison inmates, or even prison chaplains.[35] System "insiders" and other government officials predominated. Whereas the Committee on Offender Rehabilitation was chaired by a business executive, the Standards and Goals Committee was led by Middleton police chief Donald Steingraber—one of ten police chiefs and sheriffs on the committee. They were joined by three DAs and four judges. Most of the remaining members held some elected or appointed office in state or local government. Burned by the Committee on Offender Rehabilitation, Governor Lucey evidently decided to take a more cautious approach to his appointments this time around.

The committee was divided into various subcommittees, including one for courts and one for corrections. The subcommittees met regularly through most of 1976. Meanwhile, ten public hearings were held at locations around the state to gather input from interested citizens—about 425 attended—and staffers developed numerous research papers for members to digest. Draft subcommittee reports were circulated to regional planning bodies for comment. By December, the full committee had approved a *Final Report* that incorporated the contributions of all of the subcommittees.[36] At 375 pages, the voluminous report embodied the deliberative ideal of nuanced, informed, systematic policymaking.

From the Courts Subcommittee came two especially noteworthy recommendations that were endorsed by the full committee and the CCJ as a whole. First, the subcommittee advocated the creation of a new intermediate Court of Appeals, which would handle all of the routine cases coming up from the circuit courts and thereby free the Wisconsin Supreme Court to focus on the much smaller number of cases presenting the most significant legal questions. Second, the subcommittee also called for the creation of a centralized public defender office to oversee the trial-court representation of indigent criminal defendants statewide. Both recommendations were adopted by the legislature in 1977.

Sentencing proved to be a far more contentious issue. Most notably, the Courts Subcommittee pressed for the elimination of discretionary parole release. This startling proposal reflected the subcommittee's skepticism of rehabilitation-oriented approaches to punishment. Chaired by Judge Thomas Barland of Eau

Claire, who would reemerge as an important figure in sentencing policy in the late 1990s, the subcommittee was plainly influenced by an emerging national shift in expert opinion against rehabilitation in the mid-1970s. Among other scholarly works in this vein, the subcommittee cited a still-well-known 1974 article by sociologist Robert Martinson, "What Works: Questions and Answers about Prison Reform." After reviewing hundreds of prior studies, Martinson offered this much-quoted conclusion: "[W]ith few and isolated exceptions, the rehabilitative efforts that have been reported so far have had no appreciable effect on recidivism."[37] Others boiled down this conclusion to the even more pithy slogan "nothing works."

The elimination of parole seemed to follow logically from the "nothing works" mentality. If rehabilitation in prison had proven infeasible, it was hard to see what the Parole Board was supposed to do. Other than performance in prison, the sentencing judge seemed to possess all of the information that was relevant to how much time should be served, and performance in prison only seemed to matter to the extent that one wanted to assess rehabilitative progress. Take away any interest in such an assessment, and you also take away the Parole Board's reason for being. In a post-rehabilitation world, the Parole Board seems a redundancy, simply reweighing the same factors that have already been evaluated by the sentencing judge.

What would the guiding ideology be of the new, post-rehabilitation system envisioned by the Courts Subcommittee? In a word, judicialist. The subcommittee repeatedly emphasized the judiciary's preeminence in determining punishment. In the subcommittee's elliptical phrasing, "Clear lines of authority and responsibility emanating from the judge and ultimately returning to the judge are the foundation upon which [our proposed] sentencing structure is based."[38] Eliminating parole, of course, removed an important traditional check on the judge's sentencing power. The subcommittee also took aim at another check on the judge: plea bargaining. Although the subcommittee concluded—with seeming reluctance—that a ban on plea bargaining would be unenforceable and ineffective, it recommended numerous reforms that were intended "to increase visibility and fairness, and *to return the sentencing decision to the judge*."[39] Thus, the subcommittee would have prohibited prosecutorial recommendations on sentence length; this was "in keeping with the conclusion that the sentencing function must rest solely with the trial judge."[40] Other proposed reforms included a requirement that DAs maintain written, public policies on plea bargaining, with an equal opportunity for all "similarly situated defendants" to enter into negotiations.[41]

Through its discussion of plea bargaining and sentencing, the Courts Subcommittee brought to the fore a concern that had not figured prominently in earlier reports: disparity in the treatment of similarly situated defendants. This concern naturally becomes more important in a postparole, post-rehabilitation sentencing system. The centralized parole process had a natural tendency to even out disparities. The unlucky defendant with the unusually tough judge would likely end up serving a lower percentage of his long sentence than would his more fortunate peer with a lenient judge and a short prison term. Without parole, however, each judge's idiosyncrasies would become truly determinative of how long each defendant would spend in prison. Additionally, in a penal system centered on rehabilitation, it is hard to say for certain what disparity is and why it matters. Return from prison should be based primarily on rehabilitative progress and the likelihood of a successful reentry to free society—standards that cry out for deeply individualized assessments and that defy easy comparison across cases. On the other hand, if the system no longer emphasizes rehabilitation, then the basic facts of the offense—what was the nature and degree of the harm caused?—seem to stand out as the dominant considerations for punishment, and these facts more readily lend themselves to cross-case comparisons. Remove all of the imponderables of rehabilitation, and it becomes much more troubling that one armed robber gets probation, another gets two years in prison, and a third gets ten.

Thus, it should not be surprising that the desire for uniformity—that is, the elimination of unwarranted disparities—runs as a leading theme throughout the report of the Courts Subcommittee. Indeed, the subcommittee proclaimed as its overarching goal that "[r]ationally-based sentencing shall be promoted, and *disparity in sentencing shall be reduced.*"[42] To that end, the subcommittee proposed numerous changes in sentencing policy, including the identification of twelve considerations that should be taken into account by the sentencing judge; the preparation of a presentence investigation report in all felony cases; a prohibition on the use of consecutive sentences in most cases; the collection and dissemination of statewide data on sentencing practices; and mandatory appellate review of sentences of imprisonment.[43]

The Subcommittee's effort to promote greater uniformity in sentencing highlighted an important tension within the judicialist position. Judicial sentencing discretion seemed desirable, but it could be carried too far. If judges were all over the map in their sentencing decisions, then the whole system might appear arbitrary and illegitimate. There should be enough guidance for judges so that their sentencing decisions would have that crucial law-bound character on which the legitimacy of judicial decision-making generally depends. Finding the right balance between discretion and guidance, however, would prove a contentious matter for many years.

In the end, the full Standards and Goals Committee endorsed the sentencing guidance proposals of the Courts Subcommittee, as well as its plea-bargaining reforms, but not the recommended elimination of parole. The Corrections

Subcommittee fought to retain parole and ultimately prevailed. That controversy resolved, the full committee issued its final report, but few of its recommendations were enacted. The proposals were doubly orphaned. First, just six
months after the report's publication, Governor Pat Lucey stepped down to
become President Jimmy Carter's ambassador to Mexico. Lieutenant Governor
Martin Schreiber filled the remainder of Lucey's term. A Democrat and career
politician from Milwaukee, Schreiber had not been significantly involved in
criminal justice policy during his long run as Lucey's understudy, and it was
not initially clear whether he would continue the Council on Criminal Justice
after Lucey's departure. Schreiber requested a report from CCJ executive director Charles Hill on the agency's past accomplishments and possible future path.[44]
Hill's report, which touted the CCJ's role in the creation of the statewide public
defender system, did not appear until the very end of 1977. Moreover, while
Schreiber was evidently swayed by Hill's work, it took an additional six months
before the CCJ's continued existence was formally approved by the governor
and legislature. By that time, Schreiber's own days in office were numbered; he
was defeated by Republican Lee Dreyfus in the November 1978 gubernatorial
election. Although Dreyfus preserved the CCJ through his one term in office,
the momentum behind the standards and goals reforms had been irretrievably
lost.

Second, quite apart from the political turmoil in Wisconsin, the CCJ was
undermined by events in Washington, DC. The federal Law Enforcement
Assistance Administration had always played a key role in encouraging and
supporting the CCJ's efforts to serve as a comprehensive planning agency. The
CCJ's control of millions of dollars in annual LEAA grants, for instance, gave
the agency considerable leverage over the state's criminal justice leaders. Moreover, the LEAA directly funded the state's ambitious deliberative policymaking
initiatives, such as the work of the Standards and Goals Committee. However,
by the time of Governor Lee Dreyfus's inauguration in 1979, the LEAA was
nearing the end of its tumultuous run. Over the years, tales of wasteful spending
accumulated—one rumor even had it that an LEAA grant had been used to
purchase a submarine[45]—yet the agency's efforts to impose discipline on the
use of grants produced tremendous resentment on the part of local officials.[46]
By the late 1970s, the LEAA had few friends on Capitol Hill. Nor were there
many fans in the Carter Administration. Carter himself had clashed with the
agency when he was governor of Georgia.[47] Finally, under pressure to cut the
federal budget deficit during the election year of 1980, the administration announced its intent to eliminate the LEAA altogether.[48]

The CCJ's funding from the LEAA declined from a peak of $13.4 million in
1976 to only $5 million in 1980, and then nothing at all after 1983.[49] The CCJ

stumbled forward as the administrator of a much smaller federal grant program for juvenile justice. Additionally, the CCJ retained a role as the official collector of Wisconsin's criminal justice data. Gone, however, were the council's days as an agenda setter for the adult criminal justice system. The end of the LEAA thus marked the end of a golden age for deliberative policymaking in Wisconsin. The era had witnessed a number of important criminal justice reforms, including the creation of the current state public defender system and the Court of Appeals, but nothing happened that fundamentally altered the structure of the *sentencing* system.

Emerging Pressures on the Seventies Synthesis

The seventies synthesis—encompassing most visibly the almost unlimited discretion of sentencing judges to grant probation, and the almost equally unlimited discretion of corrections officials to grant parole—survived the decade intact, but not without enduring significant challenges along the way. Our review of the CCJ's history highlighted three. First, the Committee on Offender Rehabilitation represented a sort of radical egalitarianism—a last gasp, it seems in retrospect, of the postwar social energies that fueled the civil rights movement. The committee's agenda, including the decriminalization of most vice offenses and the capping of most prison terms at five years, would have substantially undercut the discretionary power of judges and corrections officials. By the mid-1970s, however, Governor Lucey's quiet burial of the proposals of the Committee on Offender Rehabilitation marked the end of the egalitarian moment.

By contrast, the Courts Subcommittee highlighted two additional challenges that would prove more enduring: the loss of confidence in rehabilitation and a related increase in concerns over the disparate treatment of similarly situated offenders. These two developments posed a threat to the wide discretion enjoyed by sentencing judges and the Parole Board. Neither development led to any major reforms in the 1970s, but both would continue to be part of sentencing policy debates in Wisconsin throughout the 1980s and beyond.

Perhaps the most fundamental challenge to the 1970s status quo came not from these theoretical critiques, however, but from the on-the-ground reality of ever-swelling crime rates. Wisconsin's rate of violent crime increased every single year between 1962 and 1975, save for one tiny dip in 1969.[50] By the end of those thirteen years, the rate had more than quintupled. Once up, violence remained high. A short, shallow downturn after 1975 gave way to a new record high in 1979, and then an even bigger number in 1980. As the new decade began, violence was more than six times greater than what it had been in the early 1960s.

Wisconsin's experience mirrored trends in other states and likely resulted from much the same causes as the broader national crime wave. Demographics surely played a role, as baby boomers hit their peak crime-committing years.[51] More speculatively and controversially, a wide variety of other explanations have also been offered, including, to name just a few, the expansion of the constitutional rights of criminal defendants in the 1960s, inadequate funding of social services for the poor, brutality or incompetence on the part of the police, and suburbanization and the resulting breakdown of "community-maintenance functions" in the cities.[52]

Whatever the causes, the dramatic increase in crime tended to discredit everything about the status quo. Probation and parole, it seemed, were not working. Judges and corrections officials, entrusted with vast discretion, seemed incapable of stemming the tide. Rehabilitation, the system's official ideal, seemed a pipe dream.

The great crime wave not only engendered mounting public frustration and anger but also imposed enormous strains on the correctional system and likely diminished whatever ability it actually had to accomplish its rehabilitative objectives. In 1974, Wisconsin had more prison space than it needed, but by 1984 the prison population had grown to 123 percent of capacity.[53] Moreover, even in the mid-1970s, probation caseloads in Milwaukee stood at a 70:1 ratio.[54] Such numbers help to explain why recidivism rates were high—more than 50 percent, for instance, for male juveniles[55]—and repeat offenses only further reinforced perceptions that the system did not work.

These perceptions, in Wisconsin and nationally, helped to fuel the rise of penal populism, with its emphasis on greater use of imprisonment and its skepticism of official discretion. Populism found its paradigmatic expression in mandatory minimum sentencing statutes. Beginning in the 1975 legislative session in Wisconsin, and then accelerating in the 1977 session, legislators began to introduce a series of mandatory minimum bills, mostly relating to violent crime.[56] Although none was adopted, their appearance signaled that populism was gaining some traction—bad news indeed for the seventies synthesis, with its emphasis on official discretion, rehabilitation, and community supervision.

High crime rates and routine recidivism undoubtedly contributed a great deal to the rise of penal populism, but the dispiriting crime trends did not, strictly speaking, *require* acceptance of the populist narrative of elite failure and inherently depraved criminals. An egalitarian might argue, for instance, that the real problem was a brutalizing prison system—this was essentially the position of the Committee on Offender Rehabilitation. Or a managerialist might argue that the real problem was insufficient funding for community supervision.

Explaining the growing prominence of penal populism in the 1970s thus requires more than just crime data.

Sociologists, historians, and other commentators have offered a variety of intriguing theories to fill the gap, and some certainly resonate with the Wisconsin experience. For instance, there can be no doubt that mandatory minimums and other populist legislation in the late twentieth century had a disproportionate impact on people of color. Perhaps this indicates there was a conscious or sub-conscious agenda of racial control fueling the populist wave. Thus, for instance, Michelle Alexander, in *The New Jim Crow*, characterizes mass incarceration as a "backlash against the Civil Rights Movement."[57] Escalating black demands for political, social, and economic equality posed a threat to whites, especially the working-class whites who were clinging to a tenuous middle-class status that had been made possible by the New Deal and the postwar economic boom.[58] Changing legal and social norms made it difficult for whites to express their resentment through overt racism. Anger at "criminals" became the more socially acceptable alternative. On this view, "tough on crime" should be understood as essentially a hostile white response to the perceived threats posed by people of color—threats that had as much to do with economics, political power, and cultural values as with public safety.[59] Although this "white backlash" phenome-non may not fully account for penal populism, it likely did play some sort of role in Wisconsin. As described in chapter 1, the Wisconsin of the 1970s was in the midst of a dramatic, long-term increase in its black population, and this increase had generated considerable social tension, especially in the Milwaukee area.

Another line of commentary emphasizes the role of certain political leaders in promoting penal populism for partisan advantage. On the national level, for instance, a common narrative attributes the politicization of crime to Richard Nixon and other Republican strategists, who used crime, along with welfare and affirmative action, as wedge issues to break apart the New Deal political coalition and peel away white working-class voters from the Democratic Party.[60] Similarly, in Wisconsin, some Republican leaders—most notably Representative and then Governor Tommy Thompson—embraced penal-populist rhetoric as the Republican Party steadily grew in power between the mid-1970s and mid-1990s. This is not to say that Democrats consistently or uniformly presented a different vision—it would be far too reductive to say that the Republicans were the party of populism and Democrats the party of managerialism—but it is to note that penal populism interacted in significant ways with partisan politics in Wisconsin in the late twentieth century. Certain political leaders benefited from the rise of penal populism, but they also contributed to that rise by fanning the flames of public fear and anger regarding crime and by enhancing the legitimacy of populist responses. Indeed, research at the national level suggests that public concern over crime may be more influenced by political rhetoric and media coverage than the reverse; politicians do not simply follow public opinion but play an important role in shaping it.[61]

Another line of theorizing connects the rise of penal populism to "post-modernist angst," which resulted from the swift pace of deeply unsettling economic, technological, and social changes in the second half of the twentieth century.[62] As David Garland puts it,

> With a sudden and unexpected jolt, the oil crisis of the early 1970s ushered in a period of economic recession and political instability throughout the Western industrialized nations. The re-appearance of "negative growth," now complicated by a built-in inflation and the politically underwritten expectations of unionized workers, exposed underlying problems of the UK and US economies and opened them up to harsh competition from newly developing economies abroad. . . . Within a decade, mass unemployment re-appeared, industrial production collapsed, trade union membership massively declined, and the labour market restructured itself in ways that were to have dramatic social significance in the years to come.[63]

As detailed in chapter 1, these economic disruptions hit Wisconsin with particular force. Combined with a bewildering array of contemporaneous social changes, such as the breakdown of traditional norms relating to family structure, deindustrialization and de-unionization fueled a generalized sense of social disorder. However, as Michael Tonry observes, "Because most of the forces and developments that destabilize our lives are distant and impersonal, but criminals are near at hand and identifiable, broad-based anxieties are displaced onto blamable criminals."[64] In the words of Julian Roberts and his colleagues, there is a "mood of receptivity to policies that exclude and punish any group that might reasonably be implicated as a source of public insecurity."[65] Politicians are strongly tempted to take advantage of this "receptivity"; doing so, after all, offers them "a respite from the complexity of diffuse global threats over which they have limited control."[66]

There are doubtlessly many other overlapping factors that contributed to the rise of penal populism, which might include diminished public trust of government in the wake of the Watergate scandal, the war in Vietnam, and other prominent failures of government competence or integrity;[67] the ascendance of neoliberal political ideologies premised on the belief that "each individual's fate is their own responsibility";[68] pervasive television coverage of crime, which broke down middle-class insulation from violence and disorder and made crime a more vivid, everyday reality for everyone;[69] the "moral panics" caused by especially tragic or horrific crimes;[70] and a shift in the pendulum-like movement of American social sensibilities from tolerance of deviance to intolerance.[71]

In short, the penal populism that became more evident in Wisconsin across the 1970s drew its strength from numerous social, political, technological, and economic forces, many of which seemed deeply rooted and unlikely to dissipate any time soon. With penal populism standing in stark opposition to all of the major components of the seventies synthesis—managerialism, confidence in rehabilitation, trust in judges and corrections officials, preference for community supervision over imprisonment, and reliance on deliberative policymaking— big changes to the status quo were only a matter of time.

The McClain Committee: Reimagining Managerialism in a "Nothing Works" World

The last gasp of deliberative policymaking in the 1970s came not from the Council on Criminal Justice but from the Legislative Council, a research agency overseen by the Wisconsin Legislature. Among other activities, the Legislative Council regularly sponsored "special committees" to study issues of public concern and propose legislation. These committees were normally composed of legislators, state and local officials, and other citizens with relevant interests or expertise.

The Legislative Council did achieve one notable reform of sentencing law in the 1970s: the creation of a uniform system for crime classification.[72] To this end, the council appointed a Special Committee on Criminal Penalties. Serving as chair was Madison's lanky liberal senator Fred Risser. A lawyer by training, Risser was first elected to the legislature in 1956 and would still be in office six decades later, earning recognition as the longest-serving state legislator in American history.[73] As Risser's committee began its work in 1972, Wisconsin's criminal code lacked classifications; each enacted crime contained its own maximum (and, in a very few instances, minimum) sentence. To bring order to this messy system, the committee established five classes of felonies (A being the most serious, and F the least) and three classes of misdemeanors. Each class had its own sentencing range, such as zero to twenty years for Class B felonies. The committee then divided more than two hundred crimes among the new categories, thereby replacing the crazy quilt of existing sentencing ranges with a small number of new ranges. Consistent with the seventies synthesis, the wide felony ranges provided considerable discretion to sentencing judges.

The legislature adopted the Risser committee's proposal in 1977—the same pivotal year that also saw the release of the CCJ's standards and goals report, Governor Pat Lucey's departure for Mexico, the adoption of the statewide public defender program, and the creation of the new Court of Appeals. It was also the year of a rising tide of mandatory minimum bills introduced in the legislature, indicating the growing influence of penal populism. None became law, but the general ferment surrounding sentencing policy did lead in 1978 to a directive for the Legislative Council to study "determinate sentencing," that is, the elimination of parole. (In the next decade, supporters would rebrand determinate sentencing as "truth in sentencing.") Among the sponsors of the determinate sentencing initiative was Tommy Thompson, then a fast-rising young Republican representative from rural Elroy, Wisconsin, who felt that the state had become "too tolerant" of crime.[74] Thompson was also the principal author of a pending mandatory minimum bill.[75]

The directive touched off a two-year deliberative policymaking process that makes for an intriguing "what if" question. For decades, Wisconsinites have been puzzling over why their state's imprisonment rate is so much higher than that of their western neighbor, Minnesota. Although the two states are very similar demographically and politically, and although Wisconsin has generally had a slightly *lower* rate of reported violent crime, Minnesota's imprisonment rate has remained consistently about half of Wisconsin's since the mid-1980s.[76] A number of different factors likely contribute to the disparity, but one obvious candidate is Minnesota's well-regarded system of presumptive sentencing guidelines, which went into effect in 1980 and which are thought to have promoted greater restraint in the use of prison sentences in that state.[77] Indeed, national studies have found that states with presumptive sentencing guidelines have tended to experience lower rates of imprisonment growth, holding other factors constant.[78] In any event, the Legislative Council's determinate sentencing project marked the closest Wisconsin ever got to adopting the Minnesota model. Had Wisconsin done so, the state's prison population might not have diverged so dramatically from Minnesota's in the ensuing decades.

The Legislative Council established its Special Committee on Determinate Sentencing in June 1978. The membership included legislators from both parties and a variety of criminal justice officials. Leading the effort was Representative Ed McClain, whose background as a college philosophy professor seemed reflected in the committee's ambitious efforts to craft a theoretically coherent sentencing system. Although a Democrat, McClain was not regarded as anything like a soft-on-crime liberal and, in fact, was well respected by many Republicans. With McClain at the helm of a diverse and well-credentialed committee, prospects must have seemed good for a thoughtful, well-informed proposal capable of gaining broad support.

McClain's committee put considerable effort into the initiative, meeting thirteen times between August 1978 and January 1980. With the help of the Legislative Council's professional staff, sentencing and corrections data were analyzed, more than a dozen working papers and staff briefs were prepared, and testimony was received from numerous corrections officials, prosecutors, judges, defense lawyers, and even former prison inmates. The committee also consulted with the ubiquitous Frank Remington and his protégé Walter Dickey of the University of Wisconsin Law School—part of the coterie of "usual suspects" who regularly engaged with the Legislative Council and CCJ deliberative policymaking efforts of the 1970s.[79]

As McClain and his colleagues were aware, many other states were also considering fundamental sentencing reforms in the 1970s. California and Minnesota offered leading, and somewhat different, models of reform. Both states established determinate sentencing by eliminating discretionary parole and also sought to guide and limit judicial sentencing discretion. For its part, California expressly rejected rehabilitation as a legitimate purpose at sentencing in favor of punishment pure and simple, and limited the judge's discretion to the selection of just one of three possible sentence lengths for any given crime.[80] By contrast, Minnesota chose to establish an expert commission that was authorized to draft sentencing guidelines; although judges were not required to adhere to the guidelines in all cases, they did have to justify any departures from the guidelines, subject to appellate review. Such guidelines are referred to as "presumptive"— they have real legal weight, but are not strictly binding. In drafting its sentencing guidelines, Minnesota's commission, like the California Legislature, chose to emphasize retribution over other purposes of punishment but also prioritized keeping the prison population size within the state's prison capacity.[81] California's approach thus leaned toward populism, while Minnesota's reflected more of a managerial orientation.

McClain's Committee initially inclined toward the California model but ultimately submitted to the legislature a comprehensive reform proposal that was closer in spirit to what Minnesota was doing.[82] The committee's proposal embodied three key policy decisions: (1) "the recognition of just [deserts] rather than rehabilitation or individual predictions of dangerousness as the major factor in sentencing and release decisions," (2) the abolition of parole, and (3) the adoption of presumptive sentencing guidelines.[83] The committee's criticisms of parole reflected both its philosophical commitment to desert-oriented sentencing, in which punishment is based on the severity of the offense rather than the offender's rehabilitative progress or potential, and its skepticism of the accuracy of individual dangerousness determinations. Also of concern was the "disrespect for the system" that was bred by sentencing disparities and the unpredictability of parole.[84]

The committee seemed to acknowledge only one plausible justification for retaining parole, which was that the prison population would surely grow after the implementation of determinate sentencing if judges failed to take account of the change and adjust their sentences downward. It was for this reason that the committee favored presumptive sentencing guidelines, which were to be designed by a sentencing commission based in part on prison capacity constraints.[85]

In essence, the McClain Committee was confronting the same fundamental problem as the CCJ's Courts Subcommittee had three years earlier—what should replace the seventies synthesis in a world that no longer had much confidence in rehabilitation?—but McClain and his colleagues arrived at a quite different solution. The Courts Subcommittee rejected managerialism in favor of judicialism, preferring to leave it to the judges to sort out what purposes of punishment should be emphasized on a case-by-case basis, subject only to some light constraints intended to reduce disparity. By contrast, the McClain Committee tried to adapt managerialism to the emerging "nothing works" conventional wisdom. Although rehabilitation was jettisoned in favor of desert, the committee's sentencing guidelines retained the managerial ideal of careful selectivity in the use of imprisonment. They also amounted to a much more significant limitation on judicial sentencing discretion than anything contemplated by the Courts Subcommittee.

In the end, the committee's work—embodied in a technically complex, sixty-four-page bill—failed to connect with the tough-on-crime sensibilities that had caused the committee to be created in the first place. Although McClain succeeded in shepherding his bill through the Wisconsin Assembly's Criminal Justice and Public Safety Committee, which he himself chaired, the proposal was gutted on the assembly floor. Tommy Thompson and tough-on-crime Milwaukee Democrats like Tom Hauke and Louise Tesmer had been among the original sponsors of the determinate sentencing initiative, but they were evidently unhappy with the end result of the process. They wanted tough but got technocratic—including a mandate for restraint in the growth of the state's prison population. Thompson was particularly disappointed by the extent to which the judges retained discretion under the McClain bill. His concerns regarding judicial sentencing discretion had been sharpened during his unsuccessful bid for Congress in a 1979 special election; a notorious child-murderer in the district in which Thompson ran received a sentence that was widely perceived as too lenient. That sentence was among a handful of similarly unpopular outcomes in high-profile cases in the 1970s that, he says, "precipitated my opinions" on sentencing policy; by 1980, he decided—in good populist fashion—that he wanted to "take it out of the hands of the judge."[86] Apparently, presumptive guidelines, although considerably more restrictive of judicial discretion than the existing system, did not go far enough.

Thompson thus voted against the McClain bill in the Criminal Justice and Public Safety Committee. Then, when the proposal reached the floor, he, Tesmer, and Hauke sponsored a substitute amendment that fundamentally altered McClain's bill. Once adopted, what remained was a much simpler ten-page bill whose centerpiece was a requirement that, in cases of felonies committed while an offender was on probation or parole, a determinate (i.e., no parole) sentence be imposed that was at least equal to 50 percent of the maximum possible sentence for the felony. The bill also established new restrictions on the use of probationary sentences in other felony cases.[87] Thus amended, the sentencing reform bill passed by an overwhelming 75–23 margin. For the moment, populism triumphed over managerialism.

Whatever populism's appeal in the assembly in 1980, however, the senate proved much less hospitable, and the amended bill died quietly in committee in the upper house. Nor did McClain's original version of the bill find any champion in the senate. Never again would Wisconsin come as close to adopting presumptive sentencing guidelines on the Minnesota model. Indeed, it would take a long time before another such sweeping sentencing reform proposal would emerge from a truly deliberative policymaking process. Much of the story of the next thirty-five years would be of more narrowly focused reforms, often adopted with little research as ad hoc responses to immediate political needs.

Conclusion

The key institutional features of the seventies synthesis survived the 1970s, but their durability may have owed less to enthusiastic or widespread support than to the inability of critics to achieve consensus around any alternative approach. In particular, the failure of the Legislative Council's sentencing reform initiative of 1978–80 demonstrated the fundamental tension between supporters of populism and managerialism. Reformers on both sides shared concerns about parole and judicial sentencing discretion, but populists wanted to replace the old system with something much tougher, while managerialists wanted to navigate the transition to a post-rehabilitation world without a large increase in the size of the state prison population. With populist sensibilities strong in the assembly, but much less influential in the senate, a political impasse blocked structural reform. But even as both populist and managerial reform stalled in the Wisconsin Legislature, a different sort of reform initiative was quietly gathering steam in the judiciary.

3

The Equivocal Assault on Discretion, 1980–1995

A central component of the seventies synthesis was official discretion—the judge's broad discretion in selecting a sentence and the Parole Board's equally unfettered discretion to grant release from prison. Legislators were already challenging discretion at both levels by the late 1970s. Continued efforts to restrict or guide discretion would dominate the sentencing policy story in Wisconsin throughout the 1980s and 1990s.

These efforts came from two distinct sources, both of which were foreshadowed in the 1970s. First, there were ongoing concerns about disparity in punishment, that is, dissimilar treatment of similarly situated offenders. High levels of discretion seemed to make disparities inevitable, so it was natural for concerns over disparity to lead to calls for closer regulation of discretion. Second, populist sensibilities remained a prominent part of the public conversation regarding crime and punishment, especially after the mid-1980s. Such sensibilities included a reflexive distrust of experts and insiders, as well as an impatience for tougher sentences, and thus ran counter to Wisconsin's high-discretion tradition.

Although disparity concerns and the populist critique were conceptually distinct from one another, they were related in at least this sense: the efforts to address disparity were motivated, in large part, by a perceived need to shore up the criminal justice system's standing with the public at a time when populist rhetoric was casting the system in a very harsh light. Thus, system insiders might support modest disparity-reducing reforms in order to head off more radical populist reforms, such as mandatory minimums or the elimination of parole.

Despite two decades of pressure, though, sentencing and parole discretion were still only loosely constrained in Wisconsin in the mid-1990s. This reflected the equivocal nature of the challenges to discretion. On the one hand, many of those who supported disparity-focused reforms were really doing so in order to *preserve* discretion; as a result, the reforms they sought tended to be rather superficial. On the other hand, populist sensibilities were consistently held in check by managerial concerns, especially those relating to the costs of the state's burgeoning prison population. This was in part a matter of partisan politics: Democrats retained control of at least one chamber of the legislature until 1995, and several leading Democrats, most notably in the senate, regarded the populist agenda with disdain. But some Republicans also played a role in preserving discretion. Indeed, support for populism often seemed more rhetorical than substantive. Perhaps most importantly, once installed as governor in 1987, Republican Tommy Thompson proved sensitive to managerial considerations and declined to pursue an aggressively populist sentencing agenda.

This chapter recounts efforts to regulate discretion in Wisconsin through 1995. I first discuss a failed experiment with sentencing guidelines, which emerged chiefly from disparity concerns, and then turn to reforms with a more populist flavor, focusing particularly on Wisconsin's "three strikes and you are out" law.

Disparity-Focused Reform: Wisconsin's First Sentencing Guidelines

Wisconsin may have rejected Minnesota-style presumptive sentencing guidelines in 1980, but that did not mean the state would forever go without guidelines. Indeed, Wisconsin has had *two* failed guidelines experiments, both involving advisory guidelines. While sentencing judges are obligated to follow *presumptive* guidelines unless they have a good reason to do otherwise, judges are entirely free to disregard *advisory* guidelines. To a great extent, "disregard" is precisely what Wisconsin's judges did when confronted with such guidelines, and both experiments ended amid widespread perceptions that the guidelines were irrelevant in practice.

The first of the two guidelines experiments lasted from 1980 to 1995. Although the guidelines had no lasting impact on sentencing practice in Wisconsin, the story of their rise and fall neatly illustrates, among other things, how strongly committed judges were to maintaining unfettered sentencing discretion, and how weakly committed lawmakers were to addressing the disparity issue.

The Path to Legislative Adoption of the Guidelines, 1980–1984

In 1980, Jon Wilcox, a novice judge in rural Waushara County, gave a stiff sentence to a robbery defendant, while a fellow judge handed down a much lighter sentence to another defendant who had been involved in the same robbery. Perturbed by the disparity, the parents of Wilcox's defendant lodged a complaint with Republican governor Lee Dreyfus. Wilcox soon received a phone call from one of the governor's aides. Although Wilcox felt comfortable with the sentence he imposed, he was left troubled by the potential for unwarranted disparities in Wisconsin's highly discretionary sentencing system. His subsequent conversations with fellow judges about this issue helped to launch the guidelines initiative.[1]

In time, the state's Office of Court Operations provided funding for research on sentencing guidelines and formed a steering committee, the Wisconsin Felony Sentencing Guidelines Advisory Committee, whose members included Wilcox and seven other judges, as well as a smaller number of other lawyers and public officials. The committee hired the Wisconsin Center on Public Policy (WCPP) to gather and analyze data on existing sentencing practices. Headed by Sandra Shane-DuBow, an energetic researcher with expertise in legal decision-making, the WCPP team undertook an ambitious empirical study of thousands of rape, robbery, and burglary cases, ultimately analyzing 3,634 charges by reference to 142 offense and offender variables.[2] Based on the results, Shane-DuBow and her colleagues developed sentencing guidelines for four offenses. Similar to the Minnesota guidelines, the proposed guidelines were structured around a two-dimensional matrix, with a criminal-history score on one axis and an offense-severity score on the other.

Figure 3.1 presents the key components of a representative guideline, that for armed robbery.[3] Based on about a dozen questions, the sentencing judge would assign the criminal-history and offense-severity scores. Putting the two scores together would take the judge to a specific box in the matrix, which contained a range of potential prison terms expressed in months, for example 60–72 months for a moderately serious armed robbery perpetrated by a first-time offender, or 78–102 months for a less serious armed robbery committed by an offender with a lot of criminal history. The ranges reflected the average sentences imposed in past cases involving the same level of criminal history and offense severity. Each box in the matrix also indicated the percentage of past cases in that category resulting in sentences of incarceration. Where that number was less than half, the guideline recommended probation. In other cases, the guideline recommended a prison term within the indicated range.

Offender criminal history (A scale)

<table>
<tr><th rowspan="2" colspan="2"></th><th>0</th><th>1–6</th><th>7–12</th><th>13+</th></tr>
<tr></tr>
<tr><td rowspan="8">Offense
severity
(B scale)</td><td>0</td><td>36–48 Mos.
45% Incar.</td><td>48–60 Mos.
74% Incar.</td><td>60–78 Mos.
100% Incar.</td><td>78–102 Mos.
88% Incar.</td></tr>
<tr><td>1–2</td><td>48–60 Mos.
62% Incar.</td><td>60–72 Mos.
95% Incar.</td><td>78–90 Mos.
100% Incar.</td><td>102–108 Mos.
95% Incar.</td></tr>
<tr><td>3–7</td><td>60–72 Mos.
74% Incar.</td><td>72–90 Mos.
95% Incar.</td><td>90–108 Mos.
98% Incar.</td><td>108–120 Mos.
100% Incar.</td></tr>
<tr><td>8+</td><td>72–84 Mos.
91% Incar.</td><td>90–102 Mos.
93% Incar.</td><td>108–120 Mos.
91% Incar.</td><td>138–156 Mos.
93% Incar.</td></tr>
</table>

Criminal History Scoring

Did offender have legal status associated with an adult felony at time of current offense?

      Yes = 1 point

      No = 0 points

If yes, type of legal status?

      ____ Probation

      ____ Bail

      ____ Parole/Supervised release

      ____ Other (e.g. escapee)

Does offender have more than three felony-type juvenile adjudications?

      Yes = 4 points

      No = 0 points

Number of offender's prior adult felony convictions?

____ Multiply by 2 = ____ points

Does offender have any prior adult convictions for violent felonies?

      Yes = 8 points

      No = 0 points

Total criminal history score (A scale) ____

Severity of Offense Scoring

Did offender have a gun while committing offense?

      Yes = 1 point

      No = 0 points

Was offender convicted of concealing identity during offense?

      Yes = 2 points

      No = 0 points

Did the victim suffer bodily harm?

      Yes = 3 points

      No = 0 points

List all instant convictions below.

_____   _____

_____   _____

Circle all instant convictions listed above as serious or more serious (by statutory designation) than this offense. Number of circled instant convictions: ____ Multiply by 4 = _____ points

Total severity of offense score (B scale) ____

Figure 3.1. Armed robbery sentencing guidelines, 1983

The proposed guidelines were thus *descriptive* in nature. As a general matter, sentencing guidelines may be classified as either descriptive or prescriptive. Descriptive guidelines attempt to codify, not challenge, existing norms. The recommended sentencing range for a category of cases will reflect the prevailing average sentence length for that category. Assuming that most judges cluster around the average in most cases, there should be only a few outlier judges who routinely find themselves at odds with the guidelines. By contrast, prescriptive guidelines are designed to achieve some other objective, or set of objectives, besides just bringing outlier judges closer to the overall average. The McClain Committee, for instance, called for prescriptive guidelines that were intended to achieve retributive (just deserts) objectives and discourage judges from basing sentences on rehabilitation or dangerousness. Such guidelines would pressure more judges to change their established ways of doing business.

Descriptive guidelines are thus a quintessentially judicialist response to the disparity issue. They validate, rather than challenge, what most judges are doing, and even to the extent they pressure outliers to change course, the governing norms come from established *judicial* practice, not the policy preferences of some external authority.

The Wisconsin Center on Public Policy's proposed guidelines were also judicialist in another sense: they were advisory, not presumptive. The guidelines contemplated that a sentencing judge could freely disregard a recommendation if there were aggravating or mitigating circumstances present that were not taken into account in arriving at the guidelines range. Such freedom does not *necessarily* mean that advisory guidelines are doomed to irrelevance, as judges may sometimes still feel subtle pressures to conform to the guidelines. A more lenient judge, for instance, might fear that a pattern of below-guidelines sentences could become grist for public criticism in an election year. Nonetheless, advisory guidelines are plainly more in the judicialist spirit of wide judicial discretion than are presumptive guidelines.

In May 1981, the advisory committee approved the WCPP's proposal and decided to launch a pilot program.[4] Judges in four counties initially agreed to give the four guidelines a test drive. Over time, the guidelines experiment—still administered by the Wisconsin Center on Public Policy—expanded to include eight counties and eight guidelines. By 1983, the results seemed sufficiently encouraging that the advisory committee petitioned the Wisconsin Supreme Court for a statewide rollout.

In making its request, the committee emphasized two overarching (and somewhat contradictory) aims: reducing sentencing disparities and preserving judicial sentencing discretion, especially from legislative action. The committee described the guidelines' mission this way: "The Wisconsin Felony Sentencing

Guidelines System is designed to allow the exercise of judicial discretion while reducing variance by providing guidelines sentences for similar offenders who commit similar offenses. . . . The ultimate responsibility in imposing sentence must and should remain with the sentencing judge. The judge must weigh, consider and apply competing values in circumstances as diverse and complex as each individual defendant. To dispel any perception of unequal treatment in sentencing, these guidelines have been developed to assist the sentencing judge charged with that difficult duty."[5]

In the end, the committee was remarkably candid that the "best argument" for guidelines in Wisconsin was that, in the absence of this reform, the legislature might well adopt something truly pernicious: "There is a perceived need to do something about judicial sentencing in Wisconsin. . . . For the judiciary to do nothing in the face of that perceived need is to invite others to solve what they perceive as our problem."[6]

In an appendix, the petition included twenty letters from judges who had been using the guidelines during the pilot phase. Although generally positive in tone, a careful reading of the letters reveals decidedly mixed feelings. The letter of Judge Thomas Barland—the chair of the CCJ's Courts Subcommittee back in 1976—was typical. Barland characterized the guidelines as "helpful" but also identified "some weaknesses," the "most important" of which was that "steps must be taken continuously to see to it that the Bar does not treat the guidelines as absolute rules." Despite such challenges, Barland concluded, "[T]here is no question but that the use of guidelines such as these is a far superior method of sentencing than the mandatory or fixed sentencing concept proposed by some in the legislature."

Aside from the preemption of more draconian reforms, judges saw little value in the guidelines beyond simply informing new judges of existing practice norms. Out of the twenty judges who contributed letters for the petition, not one indicated that unjustified sentencing disparities were an important problem in the state, and only a few specifically suggested that greater consistency in sentencing might result from the guidelines. Throughout, a distinct lack of enthusiasm for the project was apparent. As one judge put it, "Judging by the number of times I've had to list reasons for not sentencing within the guidelines, I believe the system has not really affected my dispositions. My participation has been motivated primarily by a worry about discretion being legislatively removed, but such an ulterior motivation combined with the [negative] attitude of the bar makes enthusiasm unrealistic."

Given such judicial ambivalence, it should not be surprising that the Wisconsin Supreme Court rejected the petition. The court concluded that even the proposed system of *advisory* sentencing guidelines "constitute[d] an unwarranted intrusion into the sentencing discretion and authority of the trial judge." Why "unwarranted"? The court saw no good reason for guidelines that were descriptive in character. "We believe that if we are to promulgate felony sentencing guidelines, they should reflect a reasonable sentencing policy, one based on rational policy decisions, rather than a mere compilation of sentencing averages." The advisory committee might have responded, of course, that a rational policy decision did undergird the guidelines, namely, the decision to promote sentencing uniformity—treating like cases alike. However, as with the first judicial users of the guidelines, the supreme court apparently did not find the reduction of disparity to be a compelling policy objective in and of itself. Indeed, the court even expressed doubts that there were significant disparities in Wisconsin.[7]

Despite their disappointment with the supreme court's decision, the guidelines' proponents did not give up hope for a statewide rollout but instead shifted their attention to the legislature. Representative David Travis, an influential Madison Democrat, provided the key support. Travis introduced a bill calling for the statewide use of descriptive guidelines to be administered by the supreme court, or, if the court declined, a new Wisconsin Sentencing Commission. The bill's single stated purpose was to address disparities: "sentencing of criminal defendants," the legislation declared, "should be even-handed and consistent."[8] Travis's bill reached the assembly floor in March 1984.

As they had done almost exactly four years earlier with the McClain proposal, Representatives Tommy Thompson and Louise Tesmer, the tough-on-crime Milwaukee Democrat, once again sought to derail a guidelines proposal through the amendment process. As Thompson recalls, his opposition to advisory guidelines in 1984 followed the same logic as his opposition to presumptive guidelines in 1980; in both instances, he felt the proposals were too "flexible" with judicial discretion.[9] This time, though, Thompson and Tesmer failed, as moderates and liberals in both parties voted in favor of the Travis bill. In the senate, support was even stronger. The upper chamber unanimously consented to the Travis bill just two weeks after it passed the assembly, and Democratic governor Anthony Earl promptly signed it into law.

The Commission and Guidelines in Operation, 1984–1995

The Travis bill offered administration of the guidelines to the Wisconsin Supreme Court. Although the court had turned down the opportunity to run a guidelines system a year earlier, there may have been some hope that the court would prove more responsive now that the guidelines were definitely going to be rolled out statewide; the only question was what body would superintend them. However, the court did not bite but offered a full-throated defense of unguided judicial sentencing discretion: "Neither the interests of the individual being sentenced nor those of the community in which that individual lives are susceptible of accurate assessment in terms of statistical data gathered from other sentencing courts in the state. While each convicted felon is an individual deserving of individual treatment at sentencing, the interests of the public, too, will vary according to the particular community in which the crime was committed, the capacity of the community to rehabilitate the criminal, and the needs of that community for protection from that type of criminal activity."[10]

The outcome could not have been a surprise, but it hardly amounted to a promising start for the new guidelines regime. Indeed, some observers felt that the supreme court's rejection undercut the guidelines' legitimacy and contributed to the subsequent resistance of sentencing judges to the new system.[11]

After the supreme court's rebuff, responsibility for the guidelines fell to the seventeen members of the new Sentencing Commission, most of whom were appointed by Governor Earl, subject to various statutory requirements intended to ensure representation from key stakeholder groups (judges, lawyers, corrections officials, crime victims, and legislators). Representative Travis served as the commission's first chair but was replaced in that role by Judge Jon Wilcox after fellow Republican Tommy Thompson became governor in 1987. Suitably enough for an instigator of the guidelines project, Wilcox would be the commission's longest-serving chair.

In 1985, the Sentencing Commission formally extended the guidelines pilot statewide. As mandated by the Travis bill, the new guidelines were advisory. While judges were theoretically required to take the guidelines into consideration and to provide reasons for deviating from the guidelines' recommendations, there was no enforcement mechanism—neither prosecution nor defense could appeal a judge's disregard of the guidelines. Judges were nonetheless asked to set forth their guidelines analysis in worksheets and then return the forms to the commission, which might thereby continuously revise the guidelines based on the evolution of sentencing practice.

For most of its decade-long history, the greatest challenge facing the new commission was gaining judicial buy-in. Even at the most basic level of filling out and submitting the guidelines worksheets, judges hardly provided strong support for the new system. Over the first five years of the statewide guidelines regime, worksheet submission rates consistently remained at about 60 percent.[12] Although the submission rate climbed after that, it still stood at only 83 percent in 1994, the commission's last full year of life.[13] Moreover, based on the worksheets that were returned, departures from the guidelines recommendations seemed common. In 1990, for instance, judges imposed sentences within the recommended range only 29 percent of the time in armed robbery cases. Even as to the forgery guideline, which had the highest compliance rate, judges deviated from the recommended sentences in more than one-third of the cases.[14]

Anecdotal evidence suggests that in some counties, the guidelines may have had even less of an impact than the statewide numbers suggest. Wisconsin's two largest counties, Milwaukee and Dane (Madison), were known to be particularly resistant.[15] For instance, one senior prosecutor in Milwaukee recalls the guidelines as an "embarrassment" that no one took seriously.[16] Even though the guidelines were perceived to be more lenient than the prevailing sentencing norms in Milwaukee, defense lawyers rarely even mentioned them at sentencing hearings; doing so would only be taken as a sign of desperation. Privately and publicly, the Milwaukee judges excoriated the guidelines for their supposed softness. One made headlines by announcing that not even Attila the Hun would get the statutory maximum under the rape guideline.[17] Meanwhile, at judicial education programs, judges would sometimes display overt hostility to the guidelines. One commissioner recalls simply, "The judges hated us."[18] The armed robbery guideline was a particular irritant; the Milwaukee judges regarded it as "laughable" that this guideline recommended probationary sentences in some cases.

Observers have suggested numerous reasons for the commission's difficulty with the judiciary. As already noted, the supreme court's sharply worded rejection of the guidelines likely diminished their standing in the minds of lower-court judges at a critical juncture. Additionally, Sandra Shane-DuBow's position as executive director of the commission may have been an issue. In some ways, it must have seemed a natural choice to hire her as the day-to-day leader and public face of the commission, given her prior work for the Wisconsin Center on Public Policy in designing the guidelines. Yet the judges and practitioners tended to be wary of the way that social scientists like Shane-DuBow approached sentencing issues.[19] In part, this reflected a belief that social scientists did not understand courtroom realities, including the extent to which each case was unique and incapable of neat categorization into a grid. There were concerns about the seeming preoccupation of social scientists with ferreting out evidence of racial bias in sentencing decisions. The fact that Shane-DuBow was a woman may have been a difficulty at a time when the judiciary was still overwhelmingly male.[20]

Quite apart from any skepticism of Shane-DuBow, though, the paperwork burdens of the guidelines were also a significant irritant for judges.[21] Partisan considerations may also have come into play. Although many moderate Republicans had supported the Travis bill, the guidelines were nonetheless always perceived as a "Democratic thing."[22]

The guidelines may also have suffered from the commission's painstakingly slow, data-driven approach to change. Rigorously adhering to the guidelines' descriptive mandate, the commission continuously reevaluated the guidelines in light of the constant inflow of new sentencing worksheets, which proved an extremely labor-intensive activity for the commission's five professional staffers. "To perform its revision of the sexual assault guideline, for instance, the Commission collected data on each of the over 1,700 sexual assault charges that had occurred in the previous twelve years, continuing to gather information on all of the dozens of variables that had been used in original development of the guidelines. By the Commission's own estimates, it spent approximately 3.75 hours per case analyzed to develop a guideline."[23] Such an approach precluded rapid amendment of the guidelines even when the legislature made important changes to the criminal code.

All of these issues doubtlessly contributed to negative judicial views of the guidelines, but these explanations miss what was almost certainly the commission's most fundamental challenge in dealing with the judiciary: Wisconsin judges resented bureaucratic oversight of their sentencing decisions and, by and large, did not recognize disparity as an important concern. Wisconsin judges were powerfully attached to the ideal of judicial independence.[24] Sentencing decisions, moreover, were an area of almost unique sensitivity to an elected judiciary, especially in an era of growing politicization of crime and punishment. The intrusion of purely advisory guidelines may seem small enough, but there were concerns about the proverbial "slippery slope." For instance, some feared that the commission's data might eventually be used in ways that would embarrass or put pressure on outlier judges.[25] Beyond such political concerns, moreover, there were significant, principled arguments against pushing judges toward greater statewide uniformity, based either on the view that each case was so unique that uniformity was a meaningless objective or the belief that important county-to-county variations warranted different sentencing norms. These fundamental objections to sentencing guidelines—*any* guidelines—were apparent in the supreme court's two decisions rejecting the Wisconsin guidelines, and it should not be surprising that the state's preeminent judicial body held views that were also widespread among rank-and-file sentencing judges.

In light of the deep judicial commitment to preserving sentencing discretion, some observers have concluded that the advisory guidelines project was "doomed from the start,"[26] and there does seem considerable merit to that view. To be sure, after 1990, the worksheet submission numbers did start to improve, and it seemed that judicial resistance was slowly diminishing. Wilcox thinks that only about 10 percent of the judges were strongly opposed to the guidelines. If the commission had been given a few more years to operate, it is possible that overt hostility would have continued to dissipate. Still, it seems significant that even supporters of the guidelines tended to emphasize their value to new judges and judges in rural counties who had limited experience with felony sentencing.[27] As judges acquired sentencing experience, they tended to develop their own sense of what was appropriate. To the extent a judge's sensibilities were out of sync with the guidelines, there seemed little reason to defer to guidelines that merely represented statewide averages— especially when those guidelines were unenforced. The judges faced local electorates and responded to local imperatives; the call for statewide uniformity did not resonate much with them. Against that backdrop, it seems unlikely that the guidelines would have ever had a big impact on sentencing practices.

The Demise of the Commission and Guidelines, 1995

Just eleven years after authorizing the Sentencing Commission and guidelines, the legislature reversed course and abolished both. The most immediate cause was a state fiscal crisis in the mid-1990s brought about by massive property tax relief; this provided Governor Tommy Thompson with a reason (or an excuse) to propose the elimination of *all* state commissions that were not revenue producing.[28] Thus, it does not seem that the Sentencing Commission was particularly targeted for elimination in 1995 but rather went down as part of a broader effort to shrink state government that also resulted in the elimination of other, unrelated agencies.[29] However, even if there were an absence of malice in the legislature's decision to kill the commission, that would still beg the question of why the commission lacked a champion to save it from the tidal wave of budget cuts.

The story of the commission's demise was, at least in part, connected to two larger shifts in state politics that were reaching a climax in the mid-1990s. First, under the leadership of Governor Thompson, who was first elected in 1986, the Republican Party slowly achieved a position of dominance in state government. In the late 1970s, Democrats had boasted two-to-one advantages over Republicans in both chambers of the legislature, but Republicans steadily whittled away at these margins, finally gaining a majority in the senate in 1993 and the assembly in 1995.[30] This mattered to the commission's future because Republicans had all along tended to be more skeptical of the commission's value than Democrats.[31] Second, at the same time that they were gaining power, Republican legislators were also growing more strongly and uniformly conservative.[32]

The significance of these shifts can be seen through a telling comparison between events of 1993 and 1995. In both years, Governor Thompson proposed the elimination of the commission. In 1993, a moderate Republican, Representative David Deininger, then serving as commission chair, took the lead in staving off Thompson's challenge.[33] With the support of other moderates in his party and Democrats, who still controlled the assembly, Deininger managed to save the commission. Two years later, however, Deininger was gone from the assembly, Democrats had been reduced to a minority, and the governor finally ridded himself of the commission.

But it may be too simplistic to say that the commission's demise was made inevitable by personnel changes in the legislature in 1995. After all, the new assembly Speaker, Republican David Prosser (a former prosecutor), was a supporter of the commission.[34] Why did Prosser not think it worthwhile to expend any of his political capital to save the agency? Why, for that matter, had legislative support for the commission been so persistently lukewarm even in better days? The commission had, for instance, been underfunded from the very start of its existence.[35] This suggests that the commission faced deeper problems than simply Deininger's departure from the assembly.

At the most basic level, the commission failed because it did not serve any function that was a high priority of any politically important constituency. The commission's fundamental purpose was to develop, continuously update, and promote the use of sentencing guidelines. The guidelines' stated purpose, in turn, was to achieve greater statewide uniformity in sentencing—in the words of the advisory committee that drafted the original guidelines, to "dispel any perception of unequal treatment in sentencing," ultimately with the hope of maintaining "public trust in the integrity of judicial process."[36] The Sentencing Commission itself later endorsed this statement of purpose and reprinted it prominently in the official sentencing guidelines manual.[37] Only the judiciary itself, however, had a clear, direct stake in maintaining "public trust in the integrity of the judicial process." This judicial interest was inadequate to protect the commission from fiscal pressures and changing political winds because the judiciary itself was basically ambivalent over the extent to which sentencing disparities were a genuine problem and descriptive guidelines an appropriate solution. Things might have been different if the guidelines had been designed to keep imprisonment growth within capacity constraints, as the guidelines envisioned by the McClain Committee would have done. Wisconsin's prison population quintupled between 1972 and 1995,[38] and, as we shall see, the resulting fiscal burdens had become a chronic concern for policymakers. If the guidelines were seen as an effective tool for containing and managing these burdens, then they might have found more support when Governor Thompson put them on the chopping block in 1995. Indeed, they might not even have been targeted for elimination in the first place; as we shall also see, Thompson quietly supported other initiatives in the parole and corrections area in the 1990s that ran counter to his tough-on-crime persona in order to ease imprisonment pressures.

In that time period, it might have been even more helpful for the guidelines if they had a reputation for toughness. In 1995, Wisconsin's violent crime rate was 50 percent higher than it had been in 1984, when the legislature adopted the guidelines system.[39] In the 1990s, lawmakers adopted a plethora of get-tough measures that were framed as responses to historically high crime rates. Yet the guidelines were not seen in the same light as these self-consciously punitive reforms; if anything, they were perceived to be quite lenient. Indeed, if you were inclined to view soft-hearted judges as a central part of the crime problem, as many politicians and voters were, then descriptive guidelines that merely codified existing sentencing practices would necessarily fall short; Shane-DuBow herself characterizes this as the "fundamental problem" with the Wisconsin guidelines. Moreover, even observers who were not cognizant of the subtle distinctions between descriptive and prescriptive guidelines, or advisory and presumptive guidelines, likely had a general sense that whatever the system was doing did not work and should be replaced by something tougher.

Although the guidelines lacked much of a constituency, the commission might possibly have survived anyway if it were perceived to be performing some important function beyond merely developing, updating, and promoting use of the guidelines. Sentencing commissions in other states have sometimes taken on an integral role in the policymaking process, especially through their ability to use sentencing data to predict the impact of proposed legal changes on prison populations.[40] The Wisconsin Sentencing Commission had the high-quality dataset and the technical know-how to serve such a consultant function, but it never really established itself as a neutral, widely trusted resource for policymakers.[41] As Representative and commission chair David Deininger puts it, the commission was simply "not engaged in an important way" in the work of the legislature.[42]

To some extent, the commission's failure to establish itself in the consultant role resulted from its labor-intensive approach to guidelines development and the challenges of dealing with judicial resistance, which left little time for other initiatives. Additionally, Shane-DuBow may have been personally ill suited to handle the political side of inserting the commission into the policymaking process. "My bread and butter is numbers," she points out, "not politics."[43] Others recall her tendency to rub politicians the wrong way.[44] On the other hand, even had all of these circumstances been different, there remained this problem: the commission could not contribute meaningfully to the policymaking process unless the legislature were committed to the deliberative ideal of data- and expertise-driven policymaking; to the extent the legislature had a populist orientation, the commission's database and technical expertise simply offered nothing of value. Wisconsin's tradition of deliberative policymaking in the sentencing area withered away in the 1990s. Given that broad shift in the state's political culture, the commission surely would have faced a steep uphill battle had it sought a more robust role in the policymaking process.

Thus, few tears were shed when the commission and its guidelines were eliminated. Indeed, contemporary press accounts noted the dismissive attitudes of the bench and bar. "Many judges and prosecutors say that crimes and criminals vary so widely that judges end up using their own judgment anyway," one reporter observed.[45] The judicial ambivalence apparent in the 1983 Wisconsin Supreme Court petition remained in 1995, but with perhaps one notable difference. As we have seen, some judges were willing to accept guidelines in 1983 as an alternative to more draconian sentencing reforms. By 1995, however, it was clear that the commission and guidelines were not an effective bulwark against new get-tough measures, which were adopted with some regularity beginning in the late 1980s. Moreover, as judges became increasingly accustomed to the new political environment, they may have realized that they had less to fear from penal populism than they once thought, for the punitive laws of the late 1980s and early 1990s did little to restrict judicial discretion but were largely symbolic in nature. There can be little surprise, then, that judges failed to rise *en masse* to the defense of the guidelines system when it was targeted for elimination.

Populist Reform and the Three-Strikes Law

Wisconsin's "three strikes and you are out" law, my focus for the remainder of this chapter, provides the paradigmatic example of an essentially symbolic tough-on-crime reform. It was, however, only one of a number of populist measures in the 1980s and 1990s that nominally took aim at official discretion. In the mid and late 1980s, for instance, the legislature was especially keen to adopt minimum sentences for drug-trafficking offenses. This story is more fully told in chapter 7. For now, suffice it to say that the legislature quietly moderated its populist gestures in 1990 by converting all of the new drug minimums from mandatory to presumptive, which restored the discretion of judges to sentence below the minimum.

Another notable populist enactment was the 1988 life-means-life law.[46] At the time, defendants sentenced to life in prison might be considered for parole after serving a little more than thirteen years. Introduced at the behest of Governor Tommy Thompson, "life means life" authorized sentencing judges to delay the parole eligibility of these defendants beyond the normal time. In a sense, the law shifted discretion from the Parole Board to the sentencing judge. Yet the law was clearly populist inasmuch as the judge's new power could only be exercised to *delay* release; judges were given no corresponding power to *hasten* parole. In any event, given that it affected only the very small number of defendants convicted of Class A felonies each year, the law had limited practical significance. Indeed, the Department of Health and Social Services estimated that only about five defendants per year would be affected.[47]

Six years after "life means life," Wisconsin adopted its three-strikes law amid a national wave of such enactments. The state of Washington launched the fad when it adopted the nation's first three-strikes law through a ballot initiative in November 1993. Although many states already had habitual-felon laws on the books at that time, these laws "were not widely used, nor were they an important issue in the modern politics of law and order."[48] Washington's was the first to employ the baseball metaphor and to demonstrate the concept's extraordinary popular appeal; the initiative passed by a three-to-one margin.[49] This success unleashed a torrent of copycat laws, including four enacted in the next five months alone.[50] Wisconsin was among these earliest adopters.

Senator Peggy Rosenzweig introduced Wisconsin's three-strikes legislation in December 1993, barely a month after passage of the Washington law. A moderate Republican, Rosenzweig was new to the senate, having won office in a special election in April 1993 following a decade of service in the assembly. Her special-election victory, in fact, accomplished the long-sought Republican goal of retaking the senate after two decades of Democratic control. Rosenzweig ran in a previously Democratic, blue-collar district in Milwaukee County, and her victory had been by no means assured. The hard-fought, expensive election campaign centered on crime, with both candidates seeking to stake out tougher positions than the other.[51] Rosenzweig distinguished herself in this regard through her support for mandatory sentencing laws.[52] She ultimately prevailed, but with only 52 percent of the vote.[53] It was clear that she would be targeted by Democrats when she ran for her first full term in 1994.

Once in the senate, Rosenzweig largely hewed to her independent, moderate reputation, even helping in October 1993 to defeat a Republican effort to reinstate the death penalty.[54] However, capital punishment was a high-profile issue in her district—Rosenzweig recalls that her "phone was ringing off the hook" as the senate considered the death penalty—and her vote created some political peril.[55] Although her views on the death penalty were shared by many in her old assembly district (suburban Wauwatosa), her new constituents tended to have higher levels of fear of crime and to take a tougher stance on punishment. Indeed, Rosenzweig felt that public safety was the number one public concern in her new district. She had not focused particularly on sentencing policy in her legislative career—her primary interests lay in the fields of health care and mental illness—but she felt it was important, as a general matter, to follow the wishes of her constituents.

It was against that backdrop that Representative John Gard, an ambitious young conservative from the rural northeast, approached Rosenzweig with a suggestion that she sponsor a three-strikes bill he was developing. "It will be good for you," Rosenzweig recalls him saying. Not surprisingly, under the circumstances, she took him up on his offer. (Gard would eventually rise to be Speaker of the assembly in the early 2000s.)

Like Rosenzweig, Gard had little expertise or experience in the field of sentencing policy. Neither was a lawyer or had worked in the criminal justice system. With a young family at home, though, Gard had been moved by the recent tragic slaying of Polly Klaas, a twelve-year-old Californian killed by a repeat offender who was out of prison on parole.[56] The case reminded him of another murder of a young girl that had occurred in his own district a few years earlier when he was first running for office. "These cases were so random, so vicious," he recalls. "You could see it being your own kid." To Gard, it seemed there were increasing numbers of violent and sexual crimes targeting children, and he wanted to do something to reverse this disturbing trend. He also recognized that being tough on crime was good politics, and that repeat offenders were a particular focus of public concern. Thus, with an eye to the success of the three-strikes legislation in Washington, Gard collaborated with a few fellow legislators in putting together a Wisconsin version.

Rosenzweig did not play a significant role in drafting the three-strikes bill and may have seemed an odd choice to serve as the chief senate-side sponsor of Gard's proposal. After all, the two legislators sat on opposite ends of the Republican ideological spectrum, and they did not have much of a track record of working together. Yet, Gard observes, "It was a big help to have Peggy be the lead on this."[57] "She created a level of credibility that I couldn't achieve myself." Among other things, as a woman and a mother, Rosenzweig brought an "additional perspective" on the sorts of crimes against children that were so troubling to Gard and that the three-strikes legislation was meant to address.

As introduced, the Gard-Rosenzweig bill closely resembled the Washington law, identifying a set of serious (mostly violent) felonies that would count as strikes; three convictions of any such felonies would result in a sentence of life without the possibility of parole (LWOP). Perhaps the most significant difference from the Washington model made the Wisconsin bill even tougher: juvenile offenses could supply the first two strikes.[58]

In advocating for the proposal, Rosenzweig highlighted the Polly Klaas case and played on fears of similar offenses closer to home.[59] Noting that "hundreds of . . . violent, persistent felons live among our citizens here in Wisconsin," she argued that further expansion of the state's prison population would be worth it "if that's what it takes to get three-, four-, or 10-time felons off the streets and away from our kids." A three-strikes law, she asserted, "will begin to seal the cracks in our legal system to make sure these criminals are locked up for life no excuses, no deals."[60]

Within three weeks of its introduction, and before any hearings had been held, the three-strikes bill had won the support of a majority of Wisconsin's legislators.[61] This was a startling, if implicit, repudiation of the deliberative policymaking norms of the 1970s. Although Governor Thompson did not immediately give his endorsement, he noted the bill's momentum[62] and eventually included the proposal in a larger anticrime package in his January 1994 State of the State address. "To those who break our laws, we have a very simple message," Thompson declared in his address, "Crime doesn't pay but you will."[63]

Whatever the political appeal of sending this populist message, it should have been clear to anyone paying attention that a three-strikes law would contribute very little to public safety. Even before Thompson's address, an official estimate from the Department of Corrections had projected that the three-strikes legislation would apply to only about nine defendants per year.[64] Moreover, since all of these defendants would, by definition, have serious current offenses and aggravated criminal histories, they would likely have faced long prison terms anyway. The three-strikes law might not have any effect for many years, until the first crop of three-strikers reached the time when they would have been paroled. For many, this would be well beyond their peak crime-committing years. The greatest practical effect of three-strikes legislation might thus be to prolong the imprisonment of dozens of offenders past the time when there was any appreciable public safety benefit to doing so, with the potential long-term costs including the construction of a new prison or the establishment of new geriatric facilities in existing institutions. Other tough-on-crime measures advocated by Thompson in his annual State of the State speech would even further diminish the practical value of the three-strikes legislation; these included the elimination of mandatory parole release for certain categories of offenders and a doubling of maximum sentences for many of the most serious felonies.

Critics were quick to note the flaws of the three-strikes proposal. "We ought to get tough and smart," said University of Wisconsin law professor Walter Dickey. "Right now we are getting tough and stupid."[65] In light of the long-run cost concerns—"Three-Strikes Law May Carry a Big Price Tag," blared one newspaper headline[66]—Rosenzweig's bill was referred to the legislature's evenly divided Joint Finance Committee, where it seemed likely to remain indefinitely. Senate Democrats successfully resisted efforts to have the bill withdrawn from the committee for floor consideration.[67]

Meanwhile, though, the assembly version of the three-strikes bill had progressed. Still controlled by Democrats, the Assembly Criminal Justice and Public Safety Committee amended Representative Gard's original proposal so that three-strikers might be eligible for parole after serving twenty years, subject to the discretion of the sentencing judge.[68] However, the committee also added a "two-strikes" feature that would have imposed new presumptive minimums following a second conviction for a serious felony. Based on DOC projections, this change would have resulted in a sixfold increase in the number of defendants affected by the bill. Thus modified, passage of a three-strikes bill seemed inevitable. A public opinion survey at the time found 75 percent support for three-strikes legislation among Wisconsin residents.[69] Rosenzweig also touted a new study showing that one-third of the violent offenders released from Wisconsin's prisons were eventually returned to prison for committing a new crime.[70] In that environment, even liberals like assembly majority leader David Travis—the sentencing guidelines sponsor—saw the three-strikes bill as a "political necessity."

But would the committee compromise on parole eligibility at twenty years hold? No, it turned out. On March 16, in a chaotic, politically charged floor session, Republicans pressed amendment after amendment in order to toughen the bill. Speaker Walter Kunicki "acknowledged that the crime issue would play well with voters in November and derisively waved a white flag in surrender."[71] "Vote how you want to vote," he told his fellow Democrats. "Let [the Republicans] live with this. They like building prisons." Back into the bill came LWOP (no parole eligibility) for the third strike. Also added were a host of new crimes that would count as strikes. Yet in the end, Democratic skeptics of three-strikes legislation somehow managed to have the last laugh; one of *their* floor amendments delayed implementation of the three-strikes bill pending a more thorough study of the costs. A red-faced minority leader conceded afterward that he had not fully read the amendment before the vote.

Rosenzweig decided to start over again from scratch, introducing a fresh, modestly scaled-back three-strikes bill. She now proposed that only one strike could be a juvenile offense, and reduced the number of qualifying felonies from thirty-three to twenty-eight.[72] In truth, although she doubted that Gard was happy about the new version, Rosenzweig herself preferred the more narrowly focused bill, which was more in keeping with her own moderate views.[73] In any event, the new version successfully avoided a potentially fatal referral to the Joint Finance Committee (where, coincidentally, a sexual predator bill also based on a recent Washington model was just then losing a decisive vote).[74] Said the Republican co-chair of Joint Finance, "[The bill] doesn't have much fiscal effect. The eight or nine prisoners a year cumulative effect is smaller than most of the other things we're doing."[75]

That procedural hurdle surmounted, Rosenzweig's bill moved through the legislature like a runaway freight train. A week after its introduction, the bill reached the senate floor, where it passed by a 29–3 margin.[76] The very next day, the assembly concurred by an equally lopsided 91–8 margin.[77] Along the way, Rosenzweig had amended the bill so as to prohibit *any* juvenile offenses from counting as strikes.

Governor Thompson did not even wait for the bill to reach his desk before making his support clear. Once again sounding populist themes, he declared, "We need to throw away the key for career criminals, who have repeatedly proven they are a threat to the security of law-abiding citizens."[78] Indeed, in a year full of anticrime enactments, the three-strikes legislation had become the centerpiece of the governor's agenda, and he made a show of signing the bill in a key battleground senate district.[79] Left unexplained by Thompson or anyone else was how the three-strikes law—reaching not even a dozen offenders annually who likely would have had long prison terms anyway—would have any discernible impact on public safety. The new law truly seemed, in the words of one of the few legislators to vote against it, a "bumper-sticker bill."[80]

Given the bill's political value and lack of short-term fiscal impact, it should not be surprising that Wisconsin's version of a three-strikes law attracted such widespread support. The more difficult question may be why it was not tougher. After all, in the very same month that the legislature passed Rosenzweig's bill, California adopted a far more practically significant version of three-strikes legislation. The California bill, in fact, was tougher than any of the other comparable bills being adopted across the country in 1994, particularly in three respects: (1) it contained a *two*-strikes provision that doubled penalties for qualifying offenses; (2) it counted as strikes convictions for simple burglary, a relatively common, nonviolent offense; and (3) *any* felony could count as the third strike.[81]

Although the California law was available as a model—and was partly replicated in the two-strikes provision of the failed assembly bill—Wisconsin ultimately chose to stick much closer to the more narrowly targeted Washington law. The effect of the contrasting policy choices is evident in the dramatically different numbers of defendants sentenced under the various laws. One 1998 study, for instance, found that 40,511 defendants had been sentenced under California's law (including 36,043 two-strikers), while only 121 had been sentenced under Washington's law and only 3 under Wisconsin's—far below even the measly 9 per year projected for the original Rosenzweig bill.[82] Indeed, among the twenty-three three-strikes laws for which the researchers were able to obtain data, not one besides California's had been applied to even 1,000 defendants, and most (like Wisconsin's) had been applied to fewer than 100. Clearly, in the national context, California's law proved much more the outlier than Wisconsin's.

In retrospect, California's draconian measure seems to reflect the confluence of various distinctive aspects of the Golden State's history, politics, and culture. Of particular note, the California law was initially developed as a ballot initiative by outsiders to the legislative policymaking process; the proposal was then seized upon by a Republican governor facing an uncertain reelection campaign and looking to capitalize on public outrage over the Polly Klaas slaying in October 1993. Unwilling to let the governor claim the tough-on-crime high ground, Democrats in the legislature quickly acceded to the governor's position and adopted the extremist version of three-strikes legislation.[83]

Wisconsin, by contrast, had no comparable ballot initiative mechanism, and outsider, populist agitation played no discernible role in shaping the policy options considered by the legislature. Instead, Wisconsin's version of a three-strikes law emerged from within the legislature, with a lead role being played by Rosenzweig, a moderate, veteran lawmaker. Moreover, while crime was an important preoccupation of voters in 1994, no extraordinary incident like the Klaas murder served to raise public concerns in Wisconsin quite to California's fever pitch. Indeed, polling in early 1994 indicated that taxes, not crime rates, were far and away the preeminent concern of Wisconsin voters.[84] Finally, the reelection of Wisconsin's popular Republican governor, unlike California's, was never in any serious doubt.[85] Although it may have seemed politically important for Governor Thompson to create and deliver on an anticrime legislative agenda in 1994, desperate measures were not in order. The assembly's wild floor fight over the three-strikes bill did echo some of the California dynamics, but, in the end, Wisconsin's law did not emerge from the sort of political game of chicken that hijacked California's policymaking process. Given the range of policy options that were seriously in the mix, Wisconsin did not go to the furthest extreme, like California, but instead went with a middle-of-the-road option— one that could be presented to the public as tough by requiring LWOP, but that would apply only to a small group of defendants thanks to a number of relatively obscure technical choices, such as excluding juvenile offenses and declining a two-strikes sentence enhancement.

Notably, managerial concerns about the bill's impact on the prison population were always in view and, indeed, almost prevented the proposal from emerging from the Joint Finance Committee and reaching the senate floor. The final senate version implicitly made concessions to these concerns and was then quickly adopted by the assembly, which quietly abandoned its more extreme version of the legislation. Governor Thompson himself provided the "guiding hand" favoring the senate's bill over the assembly's. "We had built enough prisons," he recalls, and had to "look economically at the future of the state."[86]

As enacted, the Wisconsin three-strikes law seemed far more a political than a policy triumph. And, indeed, it did not take long for the law to begin paying political dividends. Touting her support for the three-strikes law and other tough-on-crime measures, Rosenzweig won a resounding 63 percent of the vote in November 1994—eleven points above her total in April 1993, before the three-strikes bill became law.

The three-strikes law was only the most publicized component of a much broader wave of populist crime legislation adopted after the 1993 Republican takeover of the senate. Some of the other reforms also reflected the populist distrust of official discretion. For instance, repeat serious sex or violent crimes became subject to a five-year mandatory minimum,[87] while certain assaults in juvenile detention facilities became subject to three- or five-year minimums.[88] Such provisions, however, did nothing to change the essentially equivocal character of the long-term challenge to discretion in Wisconsin. Not only were the new laws narrowly targeted, as the three-strikes bill was, but the new minimums for assault in a juvenile facility were made presumptive, not mandatory.[89]

Importantly, the legislature more often expressed its tough-on-crime sensibilities through increased *maximums* rather than increased minimums. For instance, the 1993–94 legislature that adopted the three-strikes minimum also enhanced the maximum sentences available for gang-related crimes,[90] crimes involving terrorism,[91] and repeat child sex crimes.[92] The legislature also adopted an across-the-board doubling of the maximum for all Class B felonies.[93] Such enactments, of course, had the ironic effect of *increasing* judicial sentencing discretion, which might seem precisely the wrong direction if one took the view that bleeding-heart judges were to blame for record-setting crime rates. However, populist energies in Wisconsin were strategically channeled in ways that expressed anger over crime without significantly reducing the overall discretion in the system. As discussed in the next two chapters, this discretion was becoming an increasingly vital buffer between populist pressures for more imprisonment and the realities of an already-overcrowded prison system. Thus, the wide sentencing and parole discretion of the seventies synthesis was preserved largely intact as policymakers struggled to triangulate between the poles of populism and managerialism.

4

The Quest for Improved
Community Corrections,
1980–1997

The seventies synthesis included both a high level of judicial sentencing discretion and a strong managerial preference for community-based alternatives to imprisonment. There was always a certain amount of tension between these two components of the synthesis, for sentencing judges might or might not share the managerial agenda. Given a great deal of discretion, judges who were quick to pull the imprisonment trigger might well fill the prisons with low-risk offenders who could be managed more cost-effectively in the community. The latent tensions between high discretion (a *procedural* preference) and managerialism (largely a set of ideas about *outcomes*) became more manifest in the 1980s and 1990s as crime and punishment became more politicized, average sentence lengths increased, and prisons became chronically overcrowded. To observers with a managerial bent, it seemed that something had to be done to get judges to rely less on prison and more on community corrections.

Broadly speaking, there are two possible strategies for changing judicial behavior. First, the judges might simply be ordered to do things differently. This strategy was exemplified by the McClain Committee's failed proposal for presumptive sentencing guidelines. Second, the nature of the judicial decision might be altered. If new options are put on the table, new information provided, or incentives restructured, then judges might produce different outcomes even though, as a formal matter, their discretion is preserved intact. It was this latter strategy that became a focal point for managerial reformers in the 1980s and 1990s. They aimed to improve community corrections, including by the creation of new "intermediate sanctions" between conventional probation and full-blown imprisonment. With more attractive community-based sentencing options available, perhaps judges would be slower to send marginal offenders to prison.

The Legislative Council's Special Committee on Community Corrections Programs, 1980–1982

The Legislative Council launched a Special Committee on Community Corrections Programs in May 1980. As discussed in chapter 2, such Legislative Council special committees are deliberative policymaking bodies comprising legislators, executive officials, and other interested citizens. Given an open-ended mandate to study "innovative correctional programs," the new special committee met seventeen times over the next two years, covering a great deal of ground in its discussions but ultimately proposing only seven rather modest bills on a hodge-podge of different topics.[1] A review of the committee's detailed minutes reveals that state budgetary pressures were a persistent concern. In the summer of 1980, as the committee was getting started, Governor Lee Dreyfus ordered all state agencies to reduce their budgets by 4.4 percent.[2] The fiscal climate doubtlessly discouraged the proposal of any major new correctional programs.

Like the McClain Committee, the Community Corrections Special Committee presents an intriguing "path not followed" story. As discussed in chapter 2, Minnesota and Wisconsin had very similar imprisonment rates for decades, but Wisconsin's grew much more quickly in the era of mass incarceration and has consistently been about twice as high as Minnesota's since the early 1980s. Minnesota's presumptive sentencing guidelines are sometimes cited as an explanation for the Gopher State's smaller imprisonment boom, but another important factor may be Minnesota's Community Corrections Act of 1973. The law effectively decentralized community corrections, giving county governments the option to take control of probation and other alternatives to incarceration. The counties wishing to exercise this option were given state subsidies to pay for new community-based programs but faced a stick if sentencing judges did not actually use the new options: the state would charge the counties for sending low-level offenders to prison. The carrot and stick, it was hoped, would lead to the development and use of more effective community-based alternatives designed to fit local needs and circumstances. The Wisconsin Legislature was sufficiently intrigued that it adopted the Minnesota model for *juvenile* corrections in 1979, transferring financial responsibility to the counties for sending young offenders to state institutions.[3] The decentralized, incentive-based system for juvenile corrections remains in place as of this writing.[4]

Wisconsin has never extended this model to *adult* corrections but considered doing so in the early 1980s through the Community Corrections Special Committee. A staff memo prepared for the committee's first meeting described the Minnesota law in detail. Championing the decentralization concept on the committee was Austin McClendon, a longtime staffer of the Council on Criminal Justice (CCJ) who had worked a decade earlier on Governor Lucey's Committee on Offender Rehabilitation (the group that had advised shutting down the entire state prison system). In 1980, CCJ funds were secured, presumably by McClendon, to bring corrections officials from Minnesota to address the Community Corrections Committee.[5] However, the Minnesota officials delivered a mixed report.[6] Although more offenders were being kept out of prison as a result of the Community Corrections Act, the total cost of corrections in the state up to that time had actually increased. This resulted from heavier use of local jails. As hoped, sentencing judges were responding to the economic incentives and diverting offenders from prison, but the offenders were largely going into another form of incarceration (jail), not community supervision. Indeed, some of the "diverted" offenders were actually spending *more* time behind bars than they would have if they had gone to a state institution.

In the fiscal climate of the early 1980s, the possibility of increased costs may have been enough in itself to doom the chances of a community corrections act in Wisconsin. Further undermining McClendon was the opposition of Elmer Cady, head of Wisconsin's Division of Corrections.[7] Cady was a DOC careerist and protégé of Sanger Powers, the corrections head in the early 1970s who had grown to distrust the corrections reformers around Governor Lucey. Like other DOC careerists, Cady tended to be skeptical of the CCJ in general and of McClendon in particular—in the mid-1970s, McClendon had sought closure of the Green Bay Reformatory, where Cady had been warden.[8] Quite apart from such personal considerations, though, Cady was already struggling to keep programs alive through a time of budget cuts, and the last thing he wanted was the diversion of more state corrections money to the counties, as would have been likely if the counties were going to take over responsibility for probation. In the background, too, was the pending, controversial construction of a new prison in centrally located Portage, Wisconsin. Cady argued that the Portage facility was necessary to ease overcrowding in the existing institutions.[9] However, a community corrections act would be premised on the contrary view that many prisoners could be handled better in the community than in the prisons. Cady asserted that Wisconsin was near the "community corrections saturation point," where it would no longer have good candidates to move out of the prisons.[10]

Despite the opposition, McClendon continued to push for the Minnesota model, and a subcommittee was formed to draft legislation. A proposed bill was then presented at one of the full committee's last meetings in January 1982. The proposal went nowhere.[11] Some of its critics recalled the Minnesota experience of increased overall costs. Additionally, it turned out that the counties did not want more correctional responsibilities; indeed, some were already balking at the juvenile decentralization initiative. The counties suspected that the new proposal was really just a ploy to get them to absorb a projected 14 percent shortfall in the state's community corrections budget. Even some who were sympathetic to the Minnesota model argued that the time was not right. Milwaukee's Representative Dismas Becker, for instance, said that he did not want a community corrections bill "simply for the purpose of experimenting with a concept that could never work under the present financial situation, because, later on, people could say that the concept itself had failed."[12]

If Becker thought the concept might come back in better fiscal times, he proved mistaken. Little serious consideration has been given since the early 1980s to the possibility of a community corrections act for Wisconsin. However, as discussed in chapter 6, experiences since 2000 indicate that local officials, if properly supported and incentivized, can indeed achieve significant decarceration.

The Intensive Sanctions Program

Despite the absence of a community corrections act, criminal justice officials still worked to develop and maintain alternatives to imprisonment in the 1970s and 1980s. In 1978, for instance, Kenosha County used CCJ funds to establish a deferred prosecution program.[13] Low-level offenders with a drug or alcohol problem could enter into a contract with the district attorney's office to undergo treatment; upon completion, the charges would be dismissed. Other counties developed similar programs.

Local judges and prosecutors were drawn to such presentencing programs because they could control how the programs were designed and run. Once a case got to sentencing, the path to community supervision was through probation, and probation was administered by the Division of Corrections, not local officials. The judge and prosecutor lost much of their control over the offender. In some counties, the state probation agents developed good collaborative relationships with the judges, but in others the judges might perceive probation as a mysterious black box or worse. Of course, sentencing judges were less inclined to grant probation if they lacked confidence that the agents would provide appropriate supervision and treatment.

The Division of Corrections was trying to improve what it was doing with probation. In 1975, the DOC implemented a uniform risk-needs scale to determine how much supervision to provide each probationer.[14] For instance, offenders at the top of scale had to be seen by an agent at least once every fourteen days, while offenders at the bottom might get a meeting only once every ninety days. The DOC also developed a revocation diversion program in Milwaukee; struggling probationers who might otherwise have been sent to prison were instead held in a local facility and given programming to help get them back on track.[15] Still, none of this fundamentally altered the picture for the local judges and prosecutors who were skeptical of the state corrections bureaucracy.

In 1991, the legislature attempted a more profound change, formally providing sentencing judges with an intermediate penal option between straight probation and imprisonment. This new Intensive Sanctions Program (ISP) was intended to relieve the fiscal pressures created by the state's still-burgeoning prison population. The Portage facility had not proven anything like a long-term fix, and additional prisons were becoming necessary. The ISP helped to moderate growth in the state's prison population through the mid-1990s but then fell prey to a populist political backlash after two offenders under ISP supervision were accused of murder in 1997. Even before then, however, the ISP had never fully lived up to expectations. In some respects, the ISP did provide more rigorous and transparent supervision than traditional probation, yet few judges and prosecutors were persuaded to take advantage of the new option.

The Path to Intensive Sanctions, 1984–1991

The years leading up to passage of the Intensive Sanctions Program were a time of swelling crime and imprisonment in Wisconsin, as indicated in figure 4.1.[16] In 1991, when the legislature adopted the ISP, violent crime was up about 75 percent from 1979. Meanwhile, Wisconsin's prison population had almost exactly doubled. Prison capacity also grew but could not keep pace with demand. By 1992, the prison population stood at nearly 130 percent of capacity.[17] Corrections spending also increased swiftly, more than doubling from $137 million in 1984 to $291 million in 1992.[18]

These trends erupted into political controversy with Governor Tommy Thompson's State of the State address in 1991, which included a proposal for 4,500 new prison beds, with projected construction costs of $583 million.[19] Thompson's construction plan was consistent with his long-standing populist

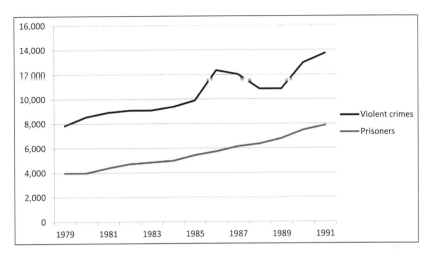

Figure 4.1. Violent crime and imprisonment, 1979–1991

political stance, but it may also have had an aspect of pork-barrel politics. He appreciated that prisons were desired for economic reasons in depressed rural areas. He thus modified site-selection procedures so as to ensure that new facilities would only go to communities that welcomed them[20]—even if that meant inmates would be sent far from their families in the urban centers from which most came. With this administrative change effected, Thompson could be confident that his prison-expansion plans would not only burnish his tough-on-crime credentials but also enhance his political support in the communities where the construction would occur.

Notwithstanding Thompson's reelection in 1990, Democrats still controlled both legislative chambers as the governor proposed the new prison-building plan. Party liberals were concerned that the state's swelling corrections budget would drain resources from social services. They sought to develop a counterproposal that would accommodate increasing demand for punishment without giving Thompson the full increase in prison capacity he requested. Thus, in April 1991, assembly Speaker Walter Kunicki, a Milwaukee Democrat, appointed a small blue-ribbon commission to study alternatives to Thompson's prison-building plan. Chaired by eminent law professor Frank Remington, the Wisconsin Correctional System Review Panel also included Remington's colleague Walter Dickey, a fixture in Wisconsin sentencing and corrections reform efforts in the 1980s and 1990s. Outspoken in his managerial views, Dickey could be a polarizing figure, but he had led a successful effort in the 1980s to modernize Wisconsin's homicide laws. He had also served as Democratic governor Anthony

Earl's administrator of corrections. He and Remington were joined on the Correctional System Review Panel by a jail administrator, two judges, a business executive, and a social worker.[21]

By comparison with earlier deliberative policymaking efforts, the panel's final report was a rush job; Kunicki had given the panel only two months to do its work. Fortunately, the panel had the benefit of Dickey's correctional expertise, including his acquaintance with intermediate sanctions experiments taking place in other states.[22] He drew on this expertise in developing what would become known as the Intensive Sanctions Program.

In its report, the panel noted that Wisconsin's prison population was on track to triple in size to twenty thousand by the decade's end—a remarkably accurate forecast—and that prison construction could not keep up with this burgeoning demand without "severe interference with the state's ability to furnish other important services."[23] The panel thus proposed the creation of a new intermediate sentencing option in order to divert more nonviolent offenders from prison. The intermediate option would be more rigorous (and more expensive) than straight probation, but much less expensive than imprisonment. Key features included a short period of incarceration and an individually customized package of supervision and treatment requirements in the community, which might involve electronic monitoring, community service, and restitution. As a model, the panel invoked an existing experiment in the Department of Corrections known as the Community Structured Supervision Program (CSSP).[24] Implemented in 1989, the CSSP provided an opportunity for early release from prison for inmates who required more intensive supervision than was available through conventional parole.[25] While emphasizing prison construction, Governor Thompson's corrections proposal to the legislature had also included a significant expansion in resources for the CSSP and another similar community supervision program—a characteristic blending by Thompson of populist and managerial initiatives. The key conceptual leap made by the panel from these existing programs was to envision intensive supervision in the community as a *sentencing* option, not merely a supplement to parole at the back end of the corrections system.

The panel expected the new sentencing option to diminish, but not entirely eliminate, the need for new prison beds. The panel thus endorsed the immediate development of 750 new beds and the initiation of planning for another new facility. However, the lion's share of projected increases in demand for punishment would be satisfied by the creation of 3,500 intermediate sanction slots by 1995 and 5,000 by 1997. These slots, the panel specified, were not to be used as an alternative to probation but as a diversion for those who would otherwise be prison-bound. This was an ambitious plan that might have fundamentally altered the corrections picture in Wisconsin; the 5,000 intermediate sanctions slots would have amounted to more than one-third of the total projected prison population in 1997.

Democratic legislative leaders embraced the panel's idea of an intermediate sentencing option, and Thompson also proved receptive. Although the governor remained wedded to imprisonment as the preferred sentence for all violent offenders, he was drawn to the restitution and work requirements of the Intensive Sanctions Program; these gibed with his view that work "might just be the best [crime] preventive measure around."[26] Thompson was to achieve national prominence in the 1990s for his aggressive efforts to move welfare recipients into the workforce,[27] and the governor himself invited comparisons between the ISP and his welfare reforms.[28] In any event, whatever the ideological resonance, Thompson was at least willing to accept the ISP as the political price for new prison beds, and the deal became law as part of the state budget in August 1991.[29] The CSSP and other existing enhanced supervision programs were simply rolled into the new program.[30] In addition to the ISP, Thompson got 1,600 of the 4,500 prison beds he had requested.[31]

Under the new law, judges could begin sentencing offenders to the ISP on July 1, 1992, but judges were not in any circumstances required to use it. In principle, any felon could be sentenced to the ISP as long as he had not been convicted of a crime punishable by life imprisonment.[32] However, the statute directed the Sentencing Commission to develop guidelines for the identification of cases in which the ISP would be presumptively appropriate. Moreover, the Department of Corrections could veto an ISP sentence in cases in which the guidelines called for probation as the presumptive sentence; this was intended to prevent "net-widening," that is, to prevent the ISP from becoming a diversion from regular probation, rather than from prison.

However, the most important limitation on judicial discretion lay not with the initial decision to send an offender to the ISP but with the practical significance of what it meant to receive such a sentence. The DOC was almost entirely in control of the ISP's structure; the department could select as it saw fit from a statutory menu of penal options for offenders and even add to the menu at its discretion. Moreover, while the judge could determine the *maximum* period of incarceration that would be included in an ISP sentence, the DOC could freely provide less and had the authority to discharge ISP participants from custody "at any time."[33] This was a period, however, in which sentencing judges were increasingly fearful of catastrophic supervision failures, like those involving Willie Horton and Jeffrey Dahmer. Against this backdrop, the willingness of judges to use the ISP sentence would depend on their trust in the ability and willingness of the DOC to identify and closely supervise potentially violent offenders. As we will see, such trust proved lacking.

Importantly, though, the statute envisioned that the ISP might also be used independently of the judges, specifying three different nonsentencing mechanisms by which an offender might be placed in the ISP: as a condition of discretionary parole release, as an alternative to revocation of parole or probation (ATR), or through administrative transfer from prison by the DOC.[34] The Remington Panel had also contemplated that some ISP participants might come from the back end of the correctional system, but it recommended that only about one-third of ISP slots be used for this purpose.[35] In actual operation, the ratio would be much higher, which had important implications for the ISP's character and political viability.

The ISP in Practice,
1991–1997

Shortly before the adoption of the Intensive Sanctions Program, the Division of Corrections had been removed from the Department of Health and Social Services and rechristened as the new Department of Corrections. Attorney Patrick Fiedler, serving as Governor Thompson's secretary of corrections in 1991, was initially quite skeptical of the ISP.[36] As he saw it, the ISP was a Democratic program, and Republicans like him were generally opposed to it. But, once the ISP became law, Fiedler thought his department should try to make it a success. He and his deputy, Michael Sullivan, traveled to newspapers around the state to try to "sell" them on intermediate sanctions. They also spoke to prosecutors and judges, educating them about the new sentencing option and emphasizing that it was supposed to be a diversion from prison, and not from straight probation.

In addition to the need to build awareness of the ISP, Fiedler and his staff also faced the challenge of giving more precise meaning to the vague legislative language that created the program. They formed an advisory group of judges and lawyers to help. What emerged was a complicated, four-stage program for offenders, who would progress from confinement (Phase I) through electronic monitoring in the community with strict travel limitations and programming requirements (Phase II) to progressively greater freedom (Phases III and IV).[37] The DOC further determined that the ISP should be limited to offenders convicted of nonviolent, non-drug-dealing property offenses whose prison sentences would otherwise be four years or less. Although this decision was not technically binding on sentencing judges, the law did require the DOC to

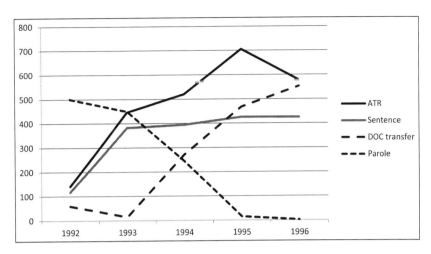

Figure 4.2. Admissions to the Intensive Sanctions Program, 1992–1996

provide its views before a person could be sentenced to the ISP, and risk-averse judges were not likely to divert offenders from prison over the DOC's objections very often.

Once an ISP offender was released to the community, he faced much closer supervision than he would have in conventional probation or parole. While community corrections agents normally juggled staggering caseloads of about seventy-six offenders apiece, the ISP agents had their caseloads capped at twenty-five.[38] As a result, the ISP's per-offender administrative costs ran much higher than regular probation and parole ($22.22 per day versus $3.28). The ISP, however, was supposed to be an alternative to imprisonment (averaging $53.51 per offender per day), not conventional community supervision; viewed from that standpoint, the ISP seemed to be delivering significant cost savings.

By 1996, the ISP was sufficiently established and successful that Governor Thompson touted it in his political autobiography as one of his leading criminal justice achievements.[39] Yet, upon closer inspection, the ISP in practice seemed to look quite different from what had been envisioned by the Remington Panel.

For one thing, the overall size of the program remained smaller than anticipated. As of July 1, 1996, the DOC supervised only 1,533 offenders in the community in the ISP,[40] which was far short of the 3,500 projected for 1995, let alone the 5,000 for 1997. But even these numbers greatly overstate the significance of the ISP as a *sentencing* option. Of those in the ISP, only about one-quarter got there through a judge's sentencing decision, with the balance coming from back-end decisions[41]—a nearly complete reversal of the ratio contemplated by the Remington Panel. Figure 4.2 tells the year-by-year ISP admissions story.[42]

When the ISP went into operation in 1992, the DOC combed the prison population to find parole-eligible inmates who could be released into the new supervision program via the Parole Commission (which was administratively attached to the DOC); this population, which presumably would have been regarded as not appropriate for release to regular parole, initially dominated the ISP.[43] However, since the DOC limited ISP participation to nonviolent, non-drug-dealing offenders, the volume of inmates who could be paroled to the program was not large, and the numbers dropped off precipitously to almost nothing between 1993 and 1995. The DOC's efforts to change its rules so as to permit ISP release for drug dealers met with resistance from the Milwaukee County district attorney's office, which was deploying a get-tough response to the city's crack cocaine problems. The DOC then increasingly resorted to administrative transfers, which were available even for inmates who were not yet parole-eligible, in order to keep moving inmates out of prison into the ISP.[44] But, after 1993, the program really came to be dominated by the final back-end mechanism: alternatives to revocation (ATR). Meanwhile, the number of ISP sentences remained essentially stuck year after year.

These developments had important consequences. As the Remington Panel had envisioned things, the typical ISP participant would be a drug-involved property offender with no significant criminal history; an important premise was that drug treatment would be administered more swiftly and effectively in the ISP than in prison.[45] But, instead of these greenhorn offenders with little or no record of prior failure under supervision, the ISP was actually filled with offenders who faced revocation—by definition, offenders with a track record of failure under supervision—or were only recently out of prison and trying to deal with the difficult transition from institutional life. Had the ISP's population resembled more closely what the panel described, it seems likely that success rates would have been higher and the program's reputation among practitioners more positive. As it was, the ISP came to be seen simply as "a dumping ground for an overburdened prison system."[46]

Why did judges not make more extensive use of the ISP? For one thing, the program suffered by its association with the DOC. The department's community supervision efforts were widely distrusted by judges in the 1990s, especially in Milwaukee—the single most important place in which the ISP had to take hold if it was going to have a real impact. Supervision in Milwaukee posed unusually strong challenges for the DOC, not only because of the obvious difficulties posed by a high-crime, high-poverty urban environment but also because of a chronic inability to keep experienced agents on the job there; agents tended to start their careers in Milwaukee and then transfer elsewhere in the system as soon as possible.[47] As one trial judge from Milwaukee put it in explaining the ISP's failure to gain traction, "This was at a time when you did not trust the agents."[48] The ISP's reduced caseloads failed to overcome this entrenched judicial skepticism.

Distrust of the agents, of course, fed into the general risk aversion of sentencing judges, who had to be concerned about the implications of a high-profile failure, especially in the political and media environment of the 1990s. In the words of a leading private defense attorney who tried without success to get ISP sentences for his clients, "Willie Horton changed the landscape."[49] As against this risk aversion, the prison crowding and expense concerns that fueled the ISP's adoption counted for little with the judges.

With some judges, general distrust of the DOC was amplified by particular knowledge of ISP failures, which were not uncommon. By mid-1997, the DOC was reporting that 1,328 participants had failed out of the ISP, as compared to 4,065 "graduates."[50] Although many of these failures might be quietly returned to prison through DOC administrative processes, fresh crimes could land an ISP participant in front of a judge, who would thereby be left with a negative impression of the ISP's effectiveness. Moreover, judges were well aware of the DOC's overcrowding problems, which heightened concerns that the department might not "bust someone back to prison" quickly enough when they started to show signs of failure.[51] Judges ultimately perceived the disciplining of ISP participants as inconsistent and overly lenient.[52] Supervision, in the words of one judge, "was 'intensive' in name only."[53] Given such perceptions, judges might well fear the potential negative consequence—both for community safety and for their reelection prospects—of sentencing an offender to the ISP.

Thus, as the ISP entered its sixth year of operation in mid-1997, it faced a set of challenges that, ominously, echoed those that had faced the Sentencing Commission and guidelines two years earlier on the eve of their extinction. The ISP was perceived, not entirely fairly, as a "Democratic thing" at a time when Republican power was at a zenith. The ISP was perceived as a soft penal option at a time when judges and other public officials were especially oriented to getting tough. The ISP was associated with a widely distrusted state agency, and support among practitioners was disappointingly thin. Much as these sorts of difficulties had heightened the Sentencing Commission's vulnerability to budget-cutting pressures, they also left the ISP poorly positioned to survive a high-profile Willie Horton–type failure.

The ISP's Demise, 1997

The long-dreaded catastrophic failure finally occurred on August 21, 1997, when a troubled Milwaukee teenager named Patrick Neal Rucker fired a pistol into a crowd following a neighborhood disturbance, killing two.[54] At the time, he was wearing an Intensive Sanctions Program electronic monitoring bracelet around his ankle. As details about Rucker's background emerged in the press—the story was front-page news in Milwaukee—the ISP looked more and more ineffectual. Rucker, nineteen, had been convicted a year earlier of auto theft and, unusually, was sentenced directly to the ISP.[55] After serving about five months in prison as his upfront confinement time, he was released to the ISP's electronic monitoring phase, where he was hardly a model of compliance; DOC logs revealed that Rucker was responsible for 158 alerts over the ensuing seven months, indicating that he had strayed beyond permissible areas or did not come home when required. Apparently, the only sanction he suffered was a month-long suspension of the privilege to leave his home for recreational purposes. Although Rucker was able to obtain three jobs during his time in the ISP, he was fired from two of the jobs for poor performance. Agents visited his home only about once per month.

Rucker's double-homicide charges produced an immediate firestorm of political controversy, which was soon exacerbated by news that a second ISP participant had confessed to an unrelated killing in Milwaukee the same summer.[56] Prominent Democrats, including Attorney General Jim Doyle, senate majority leader Chuck Chvala, and Milwaukee mayor John Norquist, were quick to demand a review of the ISP.[57] They doubtlessly hoped that shortcomings in the program would be blamed on Governor Thompson. "It's his responsibility to manage it," Chvala asserted. "They've dropped the ball."

The ever-nimble Thompson, however, moved promptly to distance himself from the ISP. A spokesman declared, "It's never been a program [Thompson's] been enthusiastic about," and blamed Democrats for forcing the governor to accept the ISP as the price of prison expansion in 1991. Thompson appointed an independent panel to review the ISP; yet, at about the same time, Michael Sullivan, Patrick Fiedler's successor as secretary of corrections, administratively suspended the ISP.[58] Although this move left the ISP technically intact as a *sentencing* option, it had never been popular as such, and judicial confidence in the ISP could be expected to plummet even further after the Rucker incident. In any event, because the ISP's chief importance was as an administrative tool for the DOC, its suspension by the department effectively constituted the program's demise. The number of participants fell from a high of 1,628 offenders in the community on September 5, 1997, to a mere 627 on January 1, 1999.[59]

The ISP's last hope for a comeback was through the work of the governor's Intensive Sanctions Review Panel. With no staff and only three members, none of whom had much direct experience with the ISP, the panel only dimly resembled earlier exercises in deliberative policymaking. Given less than four months in which to do its work, the panel produced a report that was mostly a compilation of DOC guidelines and data and a catalog of criticisms of the ISP. Chief among these were the lack of consequences, or of adequately severe consequences, for program violations, and the DOC's purported failure to keep dangerous offenders out of the program. Although the panel noted that some judges supported the ISP, and that the program's recidivism rates were somewhat lower than the norms for probation or parole, the report's negative comments far outweighed the positive. Authored by the panel chair, Judge Elsa Lamelas of Milwaukee, the report's tone reflected the Milwaukee judicial perspective. While not ultimately condemning the ISP in so many words, the report concluded, "[T]here are serious questions as to whether the Department should place felons on Intensive Sanctions. The shortage of prison beds creates such a powerful pressure on the Department to make room for incoming inmates that its placement decisions would remain suspect."[60] The report thus fell far short of the unequivocal endorsement of the ISP concept that was probably necessary for the program to have any chance for a revival.

The panel's nod to the "powerful pressures" facing the DOC highlighted the ISP's fundamental problem from a judicial perspective: the program primarily seemed to serve the state's interest in restraining imprisonment growth, but the locally elected and accountable judges had little reason to share that interest. Indeed, the very pressures that led to the ISP's creation made it inherently suspect in the eyes of judges who cared more about the intensity of supervision and the avoidance of catastrophic failures than about keeping the state corrections budget under control.

From the DOC's perspective, by contrast, the ISP was a successful, useful program. Indeed, Corrections Secretary Sullivan still regrets his decision to pull the plug.[61] In doing so, he felt himself to be following the cues of the governor's chief of staff, who was likely focused on the imminent 1998 reelection campaign. As a member of Thompson's cabinet, Sullivan was hardly in a position to disregard the fact that the ISP had become a political liability for the governor. Thompson's interest in distancing himself from the ISP thus prevailed over the department's administrative concerns over what to do with all of the offenders who were being moved into the program. But this calculus, in turn, may have depended on the failure of the ISP to achieve the originally projected scale. If the program had the 5,000 participants by 1997 that Frank Remington's panel called for, it may well have been like Bank of America and Citibank in the Great Recession—"too big to fail." As it was, new prison capacity was in the works, and another option for dealing with overcrowding was becoming available at just the time that the ISP ran into problems: the DOC had recently received authority to send 700 prisoners to jails in Texas, and a request for 500 additional "export" slots was already pending.[62] Given the ISP's modest scale, the Texas option made the program's demise a manageable problem for the department. Indeed, as the ISP withered away, its funding was simply reallocated to contracts for out-of-state beds.[63]

The Governor's Task Force
on Sentencing and Corrections

Even before the ISP's demise, it was clear that the program would only moderate, not eliminate, the continued demand for more prison beds. The prison population had doubled in the twelve years from 1979 to 1991, and then doubled again in only six years from 1991 to 1997. Once again displaying a managerial streak, Governor Thompson turned in 1995 to Professor Walter Dickey to head a new deliberative policymaking effort. Dickey had played a lead role on the panel that proposed the ISP in 1991. Now, he and his colleagues on the Governor's Task Force on Sentencing and Corrections would be asked once again to consider alternatives to the endless construction of new prisons—this time at the behest of a Republican. In the election year of 1994, Governor Thompson had signed the three-strikes bill and a host of other populist measures into law, and his campaign had emphasized tough-on-crime themes. One memorable television ad featured the governor hitting a punching bag in a gym while talking about crime.[64] The following year, however, at the start of a new term, Thompson had some political breathing room to pursue managerial initiatives.

Long on businesspeople and notably short on system insiders, Dickey's task force threw itself into its work with remarkable energy—a revival, it seemed, of the deliberative policymaking of the 1970s. The task force held eight meetings at which dozens of experts presented testimony, commissioned a public opinion survey, and developed a computer model to allocate and track correctional resources.[65] Finally, in December 1996, almost two full years after its creation, the task force issued its report, which included no fewer than twenty-nine separate recommendations for the sentencing and corrections system.

Despite the breadth and complexity of the task force's proposal, its centerpiece was essentially a vast expansion of the Intensive Sanctions Program, now renamed Community Confinement and Control. Like the Intensive Sanctions Program, CCC was a multifaceted intermediate sanction—an alternative to incarceration in a state prison but considerably more rigorous than traditional probation or parole. As with the ISP, an offender's CCC supervision would begin with a period of incarceration in a jail or other community-based detention facility, which would be followed by home detention and electronic monitoring, during which time the offender would have regular contact with an agent.

Additionally, the offender would be required to work, go to school, or provide community service. Finally, as with the ISP, an offender might be sentenced directly to CCC or be placed on CCC after imprisonment.

Notwithstanding the disappointing numbers of the Intensive Sanctions Program, the task force contemplated that there would be nearly twelve thousand offenders on Community Confinement and Control by November 2001. This was feasible because the task force contemplated a network of other reforms that would effectively require greater use of the intermediate sanction. For instance, the task force called for the abolition of traditional probation for felonies; if a sentencing judge wanted any substantial supervision for a felon, but did not think that prison was warranted, then CCC would be the only option.[66] Additionally, the task force would have required that *all* prisoners serve time in CCC before release (with the potential for eventual graduation into traditional parole).

The task force's bold, thoughtful proposal went nowhere. It was, in the words of one reporter, "effectively dead on arrival."[67] Truth in sentencing, not CCC, was the leading criminal justice reform when Governor Thompson unveiled his new budget in January 1997, just one month after the task force issued its final report.[68] Thompson's one nod to the task force was a limited enhanced-supervision pilot program in Racine and Dane Counties. Although the pilot produced promising results, the program was never rolled out more extensively.[69]

At first blush, the failure of the task force to have a greater impact may simply seem a function of Democrats' declining fortunes in state politics. In 1991, Democrats still had substantial majorities in both chambers of the legislature and were thus in a position to make adoption of the Intensive Sanctions Program a condition for funding Governor Thompson's prison-building plans. In December 1996, by contrast, Republicans controlled the assembly, while Democrats clung to a tenuous one-vote majority in the senate. Thompson, in short, had far more leverage in 1996 than in 1991 to pursue an imprisonment-prioritizing correctional policy. However, this explanation for the limited impact of the task force's proposal assumes that Thompson never had any genuine interest in enhanced alternatives to imprisonment but had to be forced into accepting them by Democrats. Yet Thompson put up little resistance when the Democrats proposed the ISP, and seemed supportive until the Rucker incident. Moreover, Thompson surely had a sense of what he was going to get when he appointed Walter Dickey to head his task force; Dickey had been a prominent figure in state criminal justice policymaking for many years, and his skepticism of throw-away-the-key sentencing policies was no secret.

The task force's failure must be attributed not only to a changing balance of power between the parties but also to changes within each party, which altered the political context in which Governor Thompson was operating. On the Republican side, the changes were exemplified by the rise of a young Scott Walker as one of the assembly's leading voices on criminal justice. Walker, the future governor and presidential candidate, represented the increasingly Republican western suburbs of Milwaukee. Still just in his twenties when the task force released its report, Walker had from the start built his career on tough-on-crime politics. "Tired of the violence?" queried a newspaper ad in his first campaign for public office. "Scott Walker has a plan."[70] In his rhetoric, Walker echoed Governor Thompson's populism but seemed to lack the counterbalancing managerial sensibility that Thompson often displayed. Walker was among a new generation of harder-line conservatives in the legislature—another was John Gard, the initiator of Wisconsin's three-strikes law—that was pushing aside the moderate Republicans like Senator Peggy Rosenzweig.

For their part, state Democrats, following the lead of President Bill Clinton on the national level, were also sounding quite populist and were trying aggressively to neutralize crime as a wedge issue for Republicans. Leading the way was Attorney General Jim Doyle, the state's highest-ranking elected Democrat, who was pushing for the abolition of discretionary parole and who had no interest in the task force's reform proposal. Doyle, a Harvard-trained lawyer and former Dane County district attorney, was emerging as a significant political threat to Governor Thompson in the 1990s and would eventually serve two terms as governor in the early 2000s.

Other Democrats were no less dismissive of Walter Dickey's task force. Milwaukee mayor John Norquist, for instance, wasted no time in publicly attacking the task force's report, labeling the proposed new CCC facilities as "bed and breakfast prisons."[71] Norquist had earlier appeared before the task force to argue that all Milwaukee prisoners should serve their full sentences regardless of parole eligibility.[72]

In addition to the increased pressure from both Democrats and Republicans to get tough on crime, there was also another key difference between 1991 and 1996: in 1991, policymakers did not know that the Intensive Sanctions Program would prove a disappointment. Although the task force did not frame its proposal as an expansion of the ISP, it was hard to miss the similarities. Indeed, one member of the commission, the conservative author and activist George Mitchell, dissented from its recommendations based, in part, on the ISP connection.[73] Attorney General Doyle, an outspoken opponent of the ISP, also noted the similarities.[74]

Longtime Republican senator Mike Ellis offered this epitaph for the task force's proposal: "It was a too-liberal set of recommendations at a time when the Legislature and the governor and the public in general want to hang 'em by their heels and never let 'em go. . . . It was the right recommendations at the wrong time, politically."[75] To be sure, the task force could, and did, argue that its proposal *was* tough. By contrast to existing probation and parole practices, CCC offered considerably more rigorous supervision. Seen from that perspective, CCC "was anything but a soft-on-crime approach," as one Task Force member put it.[76] But there was no getting around that CCC was also intended to hold down the prison population. The penal populist mindset did not readily see beyond the basic dichotomy between prison and community supervision; from this perspective, differences in the quality of community supervision might seem of little moment. Doyle, for instance, characterized the phrase "community confinement" as "nonsense": "You're either confined or you're in the community."[77] If you approached criminal justice policy with a resolute distrust of community corrections and a firm belief that the system should imprison more offenders for longer periods of time, then you were unlikely to find much appeal in CCC. Unfortunately for the task force, its report appeared at a time when these attitudes seemed especially influential among policymakers. These attitudes also fueled support for the crowning policy reform of this tough-on-crime era, truth in sentencing.

5

The Demise of Parole,
1994–2002

Over the entire mass-incarceration era, Wisconsin made its most consequential changes to state sentencing law in 1998 through the so-called truth-in-sentencing (TIS) legislation. Parole had long played a central part in the state criminal justice system, and it grew even further in importance in the early and mid-1990s as a desperately needed safety valve to relieve prison overcrowding. By the mid-1990s, about 90 percent of the offenders returning from Wisconsin's prisons were being released through discretionary parole. However, as the Parole Commission worked harder to keep the state prison population under control, it became more and more of a political lightning rod. Much like the Intensive Sanctions Program, parole was increasingly seen in the 1990s as a "soft" program that focused more on serving the administrative needs of the Department of Corrections than on protecting public safety. Indeed, the demise of discretionary parole was almost exactly contemporaneous with the demise of the ISP, and similar political dynamics surrounded both events, with Democrats leading the attack as much as, if not more than, Republicans.

As we will see, TIS represented a major victory for populism and judicialism, but managerialists did not go away entirely empty-handed. With an eye to the potential impact of TIS on the prison population, the legislature delayed the law's effective date so that an implementation committee could develop mitigating recommendations. In the end, however, the implementation law adopted in 2002 largely confirmed, rather than undermined, the populist and judicialist triumph of four years earlier.

Wisconsin Sentencing Policy and Politics
on the Eve of TIS

More than any other single event, the adoption of truth in sentencing marked the ultimate repudiation and collapse of the seventies synthesis. However, by the mid-1990s, on the eve of the adoption of truth in sentencing, it was already clear that the synthesis was under a great deal of strain. Let's reconsider the various elements of the synthesis.

First, judicial sentencing discretion remained high. As discussed in chapter 3, Wisconsin's first sentencing guidelines imposed little meaningful constraint on judges and, even at that, were eliminated in 1995. Meanwhile, mandatory minimums, like the three-strikes law, were few in number and narrowly focused. Indeed, in some respects, the judges had actually acquired *more* power over punishment. For instance, the life-means-life law gave judges control over the parole eligibility of the most serious offenders, while new "enhancers," such as the gang enhancer, gave judges the benefit of higher maximums within which to work.

Second, parole officials also retained a great deal of discretion in setting release dates from prison. This discretion effectively counterbalanced the judges' sentencing discretion. To be sure, a pair of 1984 statutes somewhat restricted the Parole Commission's discretion, but these limitations were of little practical importance. Previously, prisoners could be paroled at any time after serving six months. In 1984, though, parole eligibility was delayed until the one-quarter mark of the sentence (or six months if that was greater).[1] However, because few prisoners were released at the earliest possible opportunity, the DOC estimated that only about five inmates per year would be affected by the change.[2] A separate 1984 law also nominally reduced parole discretion at the other end of the prison term, imposing a new mandatory release (MR) requirement at the two-thirds mark of the sentence.[3] However, at the same time, the legislature eliminated "good time" credits, which had also established a mandatory release date based on good conduct in prison. In effect, the new law merely replaced a complicated, individually determined MR date with a simple, uniform MR rule. In any event, on the eve of TIS, the Parole Commission had the power to select a release date anywhere within the broad parameters of one-quarter to two-thirds of the imposed prison term.

Third, while discretion remained high, it seemed to be exercised in tougher ways, moving the system away from the restraint in imprisonment that was

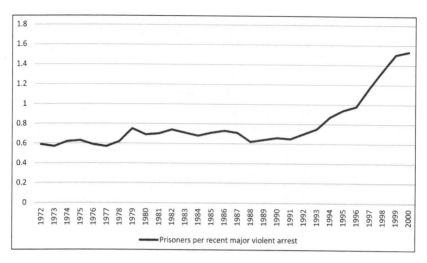

Figure 5.1. Wisconsin parsimony index, 1972–2000

embraced by the seventies synthesis. Sentencing scholars refer to such restraint as "parsimony." One way of measuring parsimony is by comparing the number of prisoners in a state with the number of recent arrests for serious violent crimes. Among the arrestees for such crimes, we would expect to find the core of serious offenders as to whom imprisonment is most clearly appropriate. If we see the ratio of prisoners to major violent arrests increase over time, that is an indication the system is either imprisoning more marginal offenders, imprisoning the serious offenders longer, or both—in other words, it is an indication of reduced parsimony. Measured this way, Wisconsin retained a remarkably consistent level of parsimony until the mid-1990s but then experienced a spike in toughness. Figure 5.1 illustrates the trend by comparing the number of prisoners per major violent arrest in the preceding two years.[4] A sustained and dramatic upward shift began in 1992.

Fourth, where managerialism had seemed the leading official ideology in the 1970s, populism had emerged as a strong challenger by the mid-1990s. This is not to say that populism had become dominant. Indeed, it seemed a rough equilibrium had been reached between populism and managerialism. Populism predominated in the political rhetoric, but populist enactments such as the three-strikes legislation tended to be more symbolic than operationally significant, reflecting the quiet influence of managerial concerns about the costs of imprisonment. Moreover, key managerial devices like probation and parole remained in place, and managerialists even won a notable legislative victory with the adoption of the Intensive Sanctions Program in 1991. Still, the abrupt abandonment of the ISP in 1997 in order to preempt populist election-year attacks demonstrated the fragility of managerial policies.

Fifth, rehabilitation had largely disappeared from official discourse by the mid-1990s. Even managerialists seemed to retreat from the rehabilitative ideal. For instance, neither the 1991 report by the Correctional System Review Panel—the body that proposed the ISP—nor the 1996 report of the Governor's Task Force on Sentencing and Corrections had much to say about treatment or programming except to a very limited extent with respect to drug-involved offenders. There seemed little of that confidence we saw in Governor Lucey's Council on Criminal Justice that offenders would "develop a non-criminal lifestyle with the aid and support of the professionals in corrections." Instead, the managerial emphasis in the 1990s was on enhanced surveillance and control of the community corrections population.

Finally, the tradition of deliberative sentencing lawmaking of the 1970s had withered away by the mid-1990s. For a decade, the legislature had adopted wave upon wave of sentencing changes—life means life, three strikes, the drug sentencing laws that are the subject of chapter 7, and many others—without the benefit of a transparent, inclusive, informed policy-development process. These were ad hoc enactments, often simply copied from other states without any serious attempt to evaluate their effectiveness. They tended, of course, to be merely symbolic, but the fact that they were adopted at all reflected an implicit rejection of deliberative lawmaking. Three additional developments in the mid-1990s demonstrated the collapse of the deliberative tradition. First, the cavalier elimination of the Sentencing Commission in 1995 deprived the state of its most comprehensive source of sentencing data—a prerequisite to truly informed lawmaking. Second, political leaders largely ignored the final report of the Governor's Task Force on Sentencing and Corrections after its release in 1996. Third, the ISP was effectively terminated in 1997 just two weeks after the Rucker shooting incident, subject only to a quick review by a small, under-resourced committee. By then, Wisconsin seemed to have committed itself to a new model of hasty, ill-informed, politicized lawmaking in the sentencing area.

Setting the Stage for TIS:
Imprisonment and Parole in the 1990s

Long-term growth in the state prison population, which had motivated the ISP's creation in 1991, not only continued in the ensuing years but actually accelerated. By the end of 1998, the prison population reached 18,613, more than doubling since the decade's start. Prison construction, held up by "not in

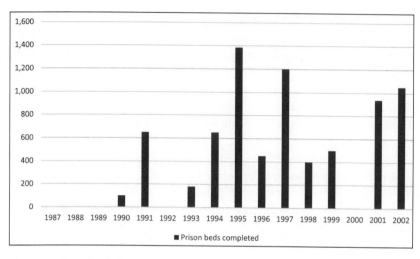

Figure 5.2. New prison beds, 1987–2002

my backyard" siting controversies in the 1980s, also grew explosively once Governor Thompson decided that new facilities should go to communities that would welcome them as sources of economic development. Figure 5.2 depicts the number of new adult prison beds created in each year of the Thompson era, adding up to 7,503 by 2002.[5] Yet this figure fell well short of the 15,990 net increase in prisoners over the same time period. Overcrowding thus remained a chronic problem throughout the 1990s, with the population officially standing at 134 percent of capacity in 1999.[6]

The Department of Corrections thus had an urgent need for safety valves. The Intensive Sanctions Program was one, and when the ISP was phased out, contracts with out-of-state institutions emerged as another. The most important, however, was parole. For most of the 1990s, Wisconsin's Parole Commission took a relatively aggressive approach to early release. The approach was particularly associated with the chairmanship of John Husz, who served from 1991 to 1998.

Governor Thompson's appointment of Husz as Parole Commission chair signaled that parole would be liberalized. (Although Wisconsin's Parole Commission had other members, they served only in an advisory capacity; as chair, Husz was free to exercise release authority without regard to the views of the other commissioners.[7]) In contrast to his predecessor, a judge, Husz was a DOC careerist. He had worked for two decades in probation and parole supervision and was a true believer in community corrections. He made this clear when he interviewed with Governor Thompson, and he understood when Thompson gave him the job that he was expected to do more than his predecessor had done to identify good candidates for parole and expedite their movement through the system. Corrections secretary Michael Sullivan also understood Husz's appointment in these terms.[8]

Husz recalls his efforts to identify and move along suitable parole candidates as exhaustive and exhausting. He took requests to review files "from anywhere," even from inmates' mothers. He regularly intervened with prison officials to ensure that inmates received the services they needed in order to enhance their parole prospects. "I inserted myself wherever I could," he says—all the while living in fear that there might be a Willie Horton on his watch.[9]

Facilitating Husz's more aggressive approach, the statutory criteria for parole release were vague and subjective, which effectively gave the Parole Commission chair wide discretion to decide when release was appropriate. Indeed, in 1993, Secretary of Corrections Patrick Fiedler (Sullivan's predecessor) published a law review article contending that prison overcrowding could be taken into account under the statutory criteria.[10]

Husz's efforts were soon reflected in the numbers. For instance, in 1990, more than 40 percent of the males released from prison had been required to wait until their mandatory release date (i.e., the two-thirds mark of the sentence).[11] In 1991 alone, Husz's first year, that figure dropped to less than 30 percent, and in 1992 to less than 15 percent. Mandatory releases eventually fell below 10 percent in 1994 and remained low through the mid-1990s.[12] As a result, the average prison time served before release dropped by 7 percent between 1990 and 1998, even though the average judge-imposed prison sentence *increased* by 8 percent in the same time period.[13]

The Path to TIS, 1994–1998

Wisconsin's 1998 TIS law might be seen as the culmination of reform efforts dating back two decades to the Legislative Council study of determinate sentencing in 1978. However, the defeat in 1980 of Ed McClain's comprehensive sentencing reform bill seemed to take the wind out of the sails of parole opponents for many years. Eventually, efforts to scale back parole reemerged in the form of more narrowly targeted reform bills, such as the life-means-life law (1988) and the three-strikes law (1994). In the same term as the three-strikes law, the legislature also gave sentencing judges the discretion to delay parole eligibility in certain serious felony cases, and the Parole Commission discretion to delay mandatory release beyond the two-thirds mark in a parallel set of cases.

It was not until the 1994 gubernatorial election campaign that Governor Thompson seemed to revive the broader attacks on parole of the 1970s. In the speech launching his candidacy for a third term, Thompson declared that "violent criminals should serve the full time period of their sentences."[14] It may seem odd that Thompson, now more than seven years into his governorship, would choose to target parole in this particular campaign. He recalls that the primary impetus was a number of cases of parolees committing "horrendous crimes."[15] However, John Husz, his parole chair, proudly maintains that there were no "Willie Hortons" on his watch.[16] For his part, Democrat Jim Doyle, then serving as Wisconsin's attorney general and thought to be a potential challenger for the governor's job, asserts that Thompson only began to press for truth in sentencing to divert attention from Doyle's attacks on the Intensive Sanctions Program.[17] Additionally, it may be significant that Thompson's 1994 promise to end parole for violent criminals coincided with the adoption of the three-strikes law the same year, which had confirmed the extraordinary political popularity of tough-on-crime laws. The 1994 election season accordingly featured a great deal of punitive rhetoric. Thompson's Democratic opponent, state senator Chuck Chvala, called for the elimination of parole for twenty-seven violent felonies, while Doyle's opponent claimed that parole was a "cruel joke."[18]

Although in keeping with the political mood of 1994, Thompson's proposal to restrict parole seemed out of step with his actions as governor. After all, Thompson's parole chair, who was reliably reappointed every two years, was liberalizing parole at that very same time, and Thompson's secretary of corrections was a grateful beneficiary. Given the disappointing performance of the Intensive Sanctions Program and steady increases in both prison admissions and average sentence lengths in the early and mid-1990s, Thompson arguably needed discretionary parole as a safety valve. Perhaps that helps to explain why his initial call for parole restrictions focused just on "violent criminals." Then, too, this relatively narrow focus was congruent with Thompson's avowed purpose in proposing the reform; he was responding to a few high-profile cases of catastrophic failure—"that was the justification, people on parole committing horrendous crimes."[19]

Whatever the underlying political and policy calculus, Thompson decided to move forward with his parole reforms after the campaign was over. (In Wisconsin, as in many other states in the 1990s, proposals to restrict parole went by the name "truth in sentencing," a term that had first appeared on the national scene in the 1980s.[20] The term alluded to the "truth-in-lending" laws of the 1970s, which required lenders to make various disclosures to their customers. Proponents of truth in sentencing thus made an implicit analogy between parole-eligible prison sentences and shady, hide-the-ball consumer-finance practices.) Thompson assigned the task of drafting a specific truth-in-sentencing plan to his new legal counsel, Stewart Simonson. Simonson prepared a series of proposals, but none of his initial efforts met with the governor's approval. According to Simonson, such back and forth was typical of policy development in the Thompson administration.[21] However, some of the governor's aides thought their boss was less than enthusiastic about the project.[22] Thompson himself recalls that Simonson's first attempts were too tough for his taste.[23] Much as he had with the three-strikes legislation, the governor seemed to be trying to find a way to deliver a popular sentencing policy change without generating a large increase in an already-swelling prison population.

As Thompson's TIS plan continued to develop slowly and quietly behind the scenes, his Democratic rival, Attorney General Jim Doyle, took the initiative. Building on his earlier criticisms of Thompson's management of corrections, including the Intensive Sanctions Program, Doyle announced his support for TIS in 1995 and then released a specific proposal in October 1996.[24]

Was truth in sentencing just another populist tough-on-crime measure, in the same spirit as the three-strikes law? Certainly, Doyle, Thompson, and other TIS supporters appealed to punitive sensibilities, but TIS differed from the three-strikes measure in that supporters also invoked severity-neutral process values, like democratic accountability and transparency. For instance, Doyle argued, "The current system has removed power [from the] elected judges and placed it in the hands of the corrections bureaucracy. . . . We elect judges to make sentencing decisions. . . . If the public doesn't like the job they do, new judges should be elected. It is difficult to make midlevel corrections officials accountable in the same way."[25] Such reasoning exalted the judiciary and resonated with judicialist sensibilities.

Whatever its primary ideological orientation, Doyle's proposal followed the lead of most TIS states in retaining an opportunity for inmates to earn a modestly earlier release date through good behavior in prison. The good-behavior credits could amount to at most 15 percent of the prison sentence. In Doyle's view, this aspect of his proposal would preserve incentives for inmates to behave well and take advantage of rehabilitative opportunities while incarcerated.[26] Ironically, of course, Wisconsin had eliminated good-time credits just a dozen years earlier. Good-time credits had not seemed to add much to the parole system—after all, the Parole Commission was supposed to take into account the same sorts of considerations that were rewarded through good conduct. However, the elimination of parole would give good behavior a clearer function to serve; for that reason, it was natural for a TIS proposal to include a good-time component.

Doyle's proposal also called for an increase in spending on child abuse prevention and for the creation of a commission to develop plans for implementing

TIS. He explains that his main hope for the committee was that it would create presumptive sentencing guidelines.[27] While serving as the district attorney of Dane County in the late 1970s and early 1980s, he had participated in some of the early judiciary-sponsored research on sentencing disparities in Wisconsin and remained convinced that it was important for judges across the state to have a more uniform starting point in determining sentences. Although he did not agree with the purely descriptive approach of the old Wisconsin guidelines, he favored the basic grid structure they employed, as well as the flexibility they preserved for judges to take into account case-specific considerations. Moreover, in his view, the need for uniformity in sentencing would grow under TIS, for the Parole Commission would no longer play its traditional role of evening out some of the disparities that occurred at sentencing. Yet Doyle also recognized that there would be resistance in the legislature to any scheme designed to push judges to reduce their nominal sentences, as they would have to do in order to prevent a large increase in the size of the prison population. (For example, a judge who gave out nine-year sentences to armed robbers pre-TIS would have to reduce the initial prison term in such cases to five or six years in the new system in order to have the same practical effect.) Doyle saw his implementation committee as a "buffer" that would give the legislature political cover for making the right policy choices—choices that might superficially appear to soften sentences, but that were really designed to maintain consistency in outcomes through the transition away from parole.

What followed Doyle's TIS proposal was a classic bit of tough-on-crime one-upmanship, with Republicans focusing on Doyle's proposal for good-time credits. Letting prisoners out after serving just 85 percent of their sentences, sniffed Governor Thompson's spokesman, is not truth in sentencing.[28] Within a couple of months, Thompson was privately vetting Stewart Simonson's latest TIS draft among advisers. Corrections secretary Sullivan expressed concerns about the impact on prison overcrowding, but he seemed a lone dissenter,[29] and the governor unveiled his TIS plan in the January 1997 proposed budget. The bill served notice that Thompson would not permit Democrats to outflank him to the right on crime issues. Gone was Thompson's original idea of limiting TIS to violent offenders; parole would be eliminated for *everyone*. The bill, moreover, rejected Doyle's proposal for good-time credits, thereby requiring inmates to serve 100 percent of their sentences. Perhaps most strikingly, though, the bill increased maximum sentences for nearly all felonies by 50 percent or more.[30]

According to Simonson, this across-the-board increase in maximum sentences was intended to prevent the bill from being attacked as soft on crime.[31] Because the bill contemplated that TIS sentences would include both a term of imprisonment and a term of community supervision after release, judges would no longer be able to impose a prison sentence equal to the statutory maximum. Both parts of the "bifurcated sentence" (initial term of confinement plus a term of "extended supervision") had to fit within the maximum. Thus, if maximums were not increased, some judges would not be able to announce prison terms as long as they had imposed in the past for the most aggravated offenses. Of course, this apparent softening would have been illusory; nearly all pre-TIS prisoners had to be released by the two-thirds mark of their sentences. Nonetheless, recalls Simonson, TIS would have been "dead on arrival" without the increases: "Had we not hiked maximums, the proposal would have never gone anywhere; it was very clear from the signals we got from members of both parties." However, there was some risk to Simonson's approach: if the judges did not adjust their sentences downward to reflect the elimination of parole and mandatory release, TIS might result in a massive expansion of the prison population. Simonson believed, though, that the across-the-board increase would never take effect as written. Faced with that hammer, legislators would have to agree to mitigating measures, which were expected to be proposed by the implementation committee.

The assembly, now controlled by Republicans, swiftly passed Thompson's proposal. However, in a replay of the assembly's efforts to restrict parole in 1980, the truth-in-sentencing measure became stalled in the Democrat-controlled senate, where the key committee was headed by a leading liberal, Senator Lynn Adelman. Chair of the Senate Judiciary Committee for most of the preceding two decades, Adelman had proven a tenacious and effective opponent of tough-on-crime legislation. Despite representing an increasingly conservative suburban Milwaukee district, Adelman—given the ironic nickname "Landslide Lynn"— managed to stay in office through a series of narrow reelection victories.[32] A graduate of Columbia Law School and the son of a prominent Milwaukee businessman, Adelman earned the admiration of liberals and the anger of conservatives by keeping tough-on-crime proposals bottled up for years without a hearing—some referred to his committee as "the Bermuda Triangle."

With the truth-in-sentencing bill stuck in Adelman's committee, Doyle and Thompson announced a new compromise bill in June 1997.[33] Doyle accepted the "100 percent truth" aspect of Thompson's proposal, while Thompson acceded to Doyle's wish for increased funding for child abuse prevention. Also included was a TIS implementation committee.

Yet senate inaction continued for several more months. Democrats in the upper chamber finally pushed through their own version of truth in sentencing in February 1998. They mostly followed the Doyle-Thompson compromise, but with one highly controversial modification: the senate bill did not include the assembly's across-the-board increases in maximum sentences.[34] The bill's sponsor, Senator Brian Burke, a fast-rising young Democrat from Milwaukee, explained that any changes in maximums should await the implementation committee's work. Notably, the senate bill specified that the implementation committee should make recommendations as to a new sentencing commission and new sentencing guidelines. Although it might seem surprising that the bill called for a new sentencing commission barely two years after the elimination of the first, Burke recalls, "I would have to say that we included it in the legislation because it was good public policy and the fact that it had been eliminated in the 1995 budget (when the GOP controlled both houses) probably added a special partisan twist."[35]

Attorney General Doyle endorsed the senate bill, but assembly Republicans castigated it as an effort "to put criminals back on the street faster."[36] Simonson's concerns about the political response to a more moderate TIS bill seemed validated. In any event, both sides awaited the outcome of an April special election to fill the seat of Senator Adelman, who had left the legislature at the end of 1997 in order to take a federal judgeship. In a curious twist, Governor Thompson had supported the appointment of the liberal Democrat Adelman to the bench.[37] However, given the conservative leanings of Adelman's district, Thompson likely assumed a Republican would win the special election, which would return the senate to GOP control.

In the meantime, another political development greatly diminished the immediate practical significance of truth in sentencing. With John Husz again renominated to continue his service as parole chair, the widening gap between nominal and real sentence lengths suddenly became a hot topic. Amid media exposés, Kenosha County's outspoken district attorney Robert Jambois publicly labeled Husz "the most dangerous man in Wisconsin."[38] The so-called parole scandal followed much the same script as the Intensive Sanctions Program controversy had a few months earlier. Sensing an opportunity to score points against Thompson, Democrats pounced. For instance, Ed Garvey, the Democratic challenger for governor in what was another election year, accused Thompson of "in essence cover[ing] up the fact that he's been dealing with overcrowding through very liberal parole policies."[39] Thompson's public defense of Husz was less than enthusiastic. The governor was quoted as saying that Husz "was doing OK" and "handling the situation" in an "extremely difficult job that burns people out." Meanwhile, Thompson's chief of staff privately tried to arrange Husz's removal.[40] Not wanting to subject himself and his family to a bruising confirmation battle, Husz chose to withdraw.[41]

As a practical matter, Husz's departure marked the end of robust parole in Wisconsin. With or without truth in sentencing, the scandal likely ensured that discretionary parole would be used only very conservatively, at least in the near term. And, indeed, even though TIS did not take effect until the very end of 1999, parole dropped off precipitously even before then. Where discretionary parole had accounted for 89 percent of first releases of male prisoners in the mid-1990s, that figure dipped to 75 percent in the 1997–98 biennium, and then to under 34 percent in 1999–2000.[42] Most prisoners were now required to wait until the legally maximum time before their release.

Yet political support for a truth-in-sentencing law remained high. When a Republican won the special election for Adelman's seat, shifting control of the senate to the GOP, it seemed only a matter of time before TIS became law. In short order, the senate finally took up consideration of the assembly version of TIS, amending it so as to conform to the Doyle–Thompson agreement of the previous summer. The bill included "100 percent truth," funding for child abuse prevention, an implementation committee, and across-the-board increases in maximum sentence lengths of 50 percent or more.[43] In order to give the implementation committee a chance to do its work, the bill would not apply to crimes occurring before December 31, 1999. This was all consistent with Simonson's political strategy: assuming the implementation committee could produce a credible mitigating proposal, leaders in both parties might sign on in time to prevent the across-the-board increase from taking effect.

In describing the implementation committee's mission, the amended bill largely tracked the language of Senator Brian Burke's TIS proposal, but with one notable change: the new sentencing guidelines to be created by the committee would now be "advisory" in nature. Ironically, just three years after the legislature abolished Wisconsin's first set of advisory guidelines amid widespread perceptions that the guidelines were almost entirely ineffectual in practice, the legislature committed itself to another advisory guidelines system — and did so without any apparent plan in mind for avoiding the proven pitfalls of the advisory approach. Legislators recognized that the guidelines might play an important, perhaps even necessary, role as a tool to bring down nominal sentences in a parole-free system, but they also feared the political fallout of *mandating* lower sentences. Said one Democrat, "I can't imagine some of the Republicans around here voting to lower sentences for criminals. They'll yell and scream that we're soft on crime just as they are now."[44]

Notwithstanding this unresolved conundrum, the senate passed the assembly bill as amended by a 28–4 vote in May 1998, and the assembly agreed to the amendments 80–17 within a week. The truth-in-sentencing bill ultimately reached Governor Thompson's desk amid an election-year flurry of thirty-two Republican-sponsored tough-on-crime measures, including bills providing for chemical castration of sex offenders and several new life-sentence provisions.[45] The governor joked that he could hardly keep track of all of the crime bills headed his way.[46] In signing TIS into law, Thompson again sounded the populist tough-on-crime theme that was so prominent in Madison in 1998, declaring that it was "not a good day for the bad guys in Wisconsin."[47]

Throughout the debates over TIS, proponents continued to press both democratic accountability and public safety arguments. Governor Thompson, for instance, argued that "elected judges, not unelected parole boards," should decide how much time criminals will serve behind bars, but he also asserted that criminals "no longer fear Wisconsin's prison system because they know they won't serve their full sentence in prison."[48] For their part, opponents high-lighted prison overcrowding and cost concerns, asserting that TIS might triple Wisconsin's prison population within a decade.[49] Proponents responded that judges would reduce sentences so as to take account of the parole changes. This view was in tension, though, with assurances that TIS would increase public safety by increasing the time some offenders served. Moreover, it seemed un-realistic in light of the democratic accountability that proponents touted. As Democratic senator Joe Wineke put it, "The judges are not going to reduce sentences because they have to run for office."[50] In the end, some proponents conceded the likelihood of an increase in imprisonment. For instance, Repre-sentative Scott Walker, the leading legislative advocate for TIS, predicted a 25 percent increase in corrections spending but asserted that the benefits to society in crime averted would outweigh the costs.[51]

The back-and-forth debate over the uncertain costs of TIS closely resembled the earlier debate over the three-strikes bill. Yet where cost concerns seemed to introduce some restraint into the development of the three-strikes provision in Wisconsin, the path of TIS seemed more in line with that of three-strikes legis-lation in California. As with the latter law, policymakers ultimately settled on the most extreme possible version of TIS. Parole was abolished for all felonies, not just violent crimes. There was no provision for good behavior, and maxi-mums were significantly increased across the board. Indeed, these provisions distinguished Wisconsin's version of truth in sentencing from the dozens of TIS laws adopted in other states in the 1990s: Wisconsin's version was likely the nation's single harshest and most inflexible.[52]

Why did Wisconsin's policymakers show so much less restraint with TIS in 1998 than they had with three-strikes legislation in 1994? The intensifying politi-cal rivalry between Thompson and Doyle seems an important factor. Both were determined to take the tough-on-crime high ground, and this dynamic seemed to drive some of the escalating severity in the TIS proposals. Additionally, Republicans controlled both legislative chambers in the spring of 1998, as they had not in 1994, and liberal Democrats like Senators Lynn Adelman and Fred Risser were either gone from the legislature or powerless to influence the final version of TIS. Meanwhile, the Republican legislative caucus was growing more conservative as it was growing more powerful. Finally, the harshness of Wisconsin's TIS law was somewhat obscured by the arguments based on transparency and democratic accountability and by the suggestion that judges would reduce their nominal sentences after the elimination of parole.

Against this backdrop, Thompson and Doyle seemed unable or unwilling to settle on a more moderate TIS proposal that would accommodate the transparency and accountability criticisms of parole without risking a massive increase in imprisonment. The last, best hope was the implementation committee, officially dubbed the Criminal Penalties Study Committee (CPSC), a throwback to the era of deliberative policymaking that might yet save the politicians from themselves.

Before turning to the CPSC, though, two persistently repeated stories about the origin of Wisconsin's truth-in-sentencing law should be addressed. First, it is sometimes said that Wisconsin adopted TIS in an effort to qualify for federal truth-in-sentencing grants. In 1994, Congress established a new grant program to help states pay for prison construction, and one condition for the grants was that states require violent offenders to serve at least 85 percent of their imposed sentences.[53] However, I have found no evidence that the federal initiative played any role in the thinking of Wisconsin's key TIS players. Moreover, the fact that Wisconsin's law was so much more stringent than the minimal federal requirements seems to confirm that the architects of TIS in Wisconsin were focused on other considerations beyond just qualifying for the federal program. This should not be surprising; a comprehensive 2002 study found that the federal program had been only a minor influence on the wave of TIS laws adopted in the United States in the 1990s.[54] Given the explosive growth of state corrections budgets in that decade, the federal money was simply not a very impressive carrot; the typical grant was projected to cover the construction costs for only fifty additional prisoners.[55] As indicated in figure 5.2, however, Wisconsin was averaging more than ten times that amount of construction *each year* in the 1990s. A federal TIS grant would have been only a drop in the bucket of Wisconsin's prison-building expenses.

Second, it is also sometimes said that Wisconsin adopted TIS at the behest of the American Legislative Exchange Council (ALEC), a well-funded national organization that develops and disseminates conservative, pro-business policy proposals to state legislators. ALEC supported truth-in-sentencing legislation in the 1990s, reflecting the economic interests of one of its corporate backers, the Corrections Corporation of America, which was the nation's leading operator of private prisons.[56] (CCA had contracts with Wisconsin in the late 1990s and early 2000s to house the state's excess prison population.) ALEC likely played a somewhat more important role in Wisconsin's adoption of TIS than did the federal grants. Representative Scott Walker, a leading proponent of TIS, was a member of ALEC and used information supplied by ALEC when arguing for the law.[57] Walker later praised ALEC's contributions: "ALEC had proposed model legislation, and probably more important than just the model legislation, they had actually put together reports and such that showed the benefits of truth-in-sentencing and showed the successes in other states. And those sorts of statistics were very helpful to us when we pushed it through, when we passed the final legislation."[58]

Still, it is easy to overstate ALEC's importance. Walker, the alleged key link between ALEC and Wisconsin's TIS law, was still only a junior legislator in the 1990s. When TIS was adopted, Walker had been in the assembly just five years and was still in his twenties. Figures like Tommy Thompson and Jim Doyle seem to loom larger in the policymaking process that produced TIS. Indeed, Wisconsin's version of TIS, in both its originally proposed and final, adopted form, was considerably tougher and more complicated than ALEC's model legislation, which, for instance, permitted the release of nonviolent offenders after they had served 85 percent of their sentences. Whatever ALEC's level of influence, there is more to the Wisconsin TIS story than simply a passive acquiescence to the wishes of wealthy corporate interests.

TIS in the Criminal Penalties Study Committee, 1998–1999

Charged with implementing TIS, the Criminal Penalties Study Committee included a large and diverse membership with considerable experience in the criminal justice system. The judiciary was particularly well represented, providing fully one-third of the CPSC's membership, including the chair. The committee was aided by two professional staffers, as well as many volunteers, but was given a wide-ranging mandate and less than a year to do its work. Most notably, the CPSC's statutory charges included developing a new penalties classification scheme and designing a new sentencing guidelines and commission system. The committee worked hard to accomplish these objectives, meeting nineteen times as a full body and at least forty times in various subcommittees.

Among the CPSC's biggest challenges was a basic philosophical divide over the importance of fiscal considerations in setting sentencing policy. This divide echoed a fundamental ambiguity in the statute itself: was TIS primarily a get-tough measure that was *intended* to increase imprisonment (and hence costs), or was it instead a severity-neutral procedural reform focused on transparency and democratic accountability? The more one saw and approved a populist get-tough agenda at the heart of TIS, the less likely one would be to elevate managerial cost containment as a central objective of the TIS implementation plan.

The cost debate also recalled the basic divergence in interests between the judges and the Department of Corrections that had been revealed through the failure of the Intensive Sanctions Program to catch on as a sentencing option. The judges had to focus on serving the needs and preferences of their local constituents. To them, the statewide interest in fitting sentences to match state penal resources was at best only a secondary concern. Indeed, a survey of Wisconsin judges at the time TIS was being debated found that 69 percent favored building more prisons.[59]

Two Milwaukee judges, Diane Sykes and Elsa Lamelas, were among the CPSC's most outspoken members, and neither saw cost containment as an especially important part of the committee's mandate.[60] "Judges thought that community protection, rehabilitation, and punishment should be the preeminent concerns," recalls Lamelas. "We thought it was up to someone else to figure out how to pay for it." Perhaps most vocal on the other side was attorney Stephen Hurley. The one question he tried to ask of every proposal before the CPSC was "how much will it cost?"[61] Given his role as a lawyer for defendants, though, some on the committee suspected that his emphasis on cost was somewhat disingenuous and actually motivated by a simple desire to reduce severity.[62]

For his part, Governor Thompson worked quietly behind the scenes to keep the CPSC focused on costs. He shared concerns regarding escalating prison costs with his handpicked chair, Judge Thomas Barland of Eau Claire, and requested that the committee do what it could to address the problem.[63] (This was the same Judge Barland who had headed the judicialist Courts Subcommittee of the CCJ in the mid-1970s.) An aide to Thompson also informed Barland that the governor was especially concerned that corrections spending might take money away from higher education. However, the committee's final report, issued in August 1999, did not explicitly embrace cost containment as a primary objective, and its recommendations seemed instead to reflect a compromise between conflicting ideological positions.

The CPSC's most important and enduring accomplishment was its systematic reclassification of penalties, an effort that was led by Marquette Law School's Professor Thomas Hammer, a former Milwaukee prosecutor who was widely respected by Wisconsin's judges and criminal lawyers. As discussed in chapter 2, Wisconsin's penal classification system had been created in the 1970s by a Legislative Council special committee. In effect, a quarter century later, the CPSC modified the original scheme so as to accommodate TIS and also clean up some of the messiness created by all of the ad hoc lawmaking of the 1980s and 1990s.[64] Under the committee's plan, Wisconsin's six classes of felonies were expanded to nine, each with its own maximum initial term of confinement and maximum term of postconfinement extended supervision (ES). The new felony classes permitted the committee to establish sensible distinctions between many offenses that had previously been lumped together in a single class. Additionally, the committee's proposal included the elimination of many of the penalty enhancers (increased maximums and mandatory or presumptive minimums) that had appeared in Wisconsin law since the 1970s.

There remained the massive undertaking of associating each of the hundreds of existing felonies with a new classification, from I (least serious) to A (most serious). The CPSC's overall reclassification proposal was based on a standard "converter" from the old system to the new.[65] The converter would assure at least a rough comparability with pre-TIS maximums. For instance, under the old system, a burglar would have had to wait at most six and two-thirds years before mandatory release to community supervision (that is, two-thirds of the ten-year statutory maximum for burglary). Under the new classification system, the burglar would have at most seven and a half years of initial confinement before release to ES.

The CPSC's reclassification proposal plainly brought greater order and rationality to Wisconsin's patchwork criminal code, and even some of the committee's biggest critics conceded that the reclassification was in some respects an improvement over the status quo.[66] However, contrary to managerialist hopes, the reclassification only partly undid the across-the-board increase in maximums that had been adopted in the initial TIS legislation, or TIS I. For one thing, the standard converter, while moving penalties much closer to the pre-TIS system, still shaded in the direction of greater severity. Thus, out of the six felony categories in the old system, total maximum supervision time (initial confinement plus post-imprisonment supervision) increased for four categories and decreased for none. Additionally, the CPSC's proposal did not uniformly stick to the converter but instead included many significant upward "adjustments." Thus, for instance, the maximum initial term of confinement for robbery went from six and two-thirds years in the pre-TIS system to ten in the committee's proposal, for first-degree sexual assault from twenty-six and two-thirds years to forty years, and for second-degree sexual assault from thirteen and one-third years to twenty-five years.[67] In effect, for these and dozens of other crimes, the CPSC preserved the increases of TIS I. Although the committee also recommended some *downward* adjustments from the standard conversion for some crimes, movement in that direction was less than half as common, and mostly confined to relatively low-level—often quite obscure—felonies that were unlikely to result in lengthy prison terms anyway.

Why so many upward adjustments? Among other things, the CPSC's final report noted "the political reality that its recommendations must ultimately survive the scrutiny of both the legislature and the governor in order to become law."[68] The committee thus seemed to indicate a sensitivity to populist, tough-on-crime dynamics in the legislature. Much as such a sensitivity had played a role in the addition of the across-the-board increase to Governor Thompson's TIS bill, it also helped to ensure that some of that increase would be perpetuated in TIS II.

Thus, for all of the accomplishments of the reclassification proposal, one thing that it did not do was to fully preempt the imprisonment increases that seemed implicit in TIS I. The other potential firewall against imprisonment increases lay in the new guidelines and commission system that a different group of CPSC members was devising at the same time that the reclassification work was going on. In theory, the new guidelines might have pushed judges to adhere to their past sentencing practices notwithstanding TIS I. As we will see in the next chapter, however, the guidelines that were actually adopted by the CPSC ultimately offered little hope of substantially restraining imprisonment growth.

In addition to detailing the reclassification and guidelines proposals, the CPSC's final report also highlighted concerns with the viability of probation as an alternative to imprisonment, especially in Milwaukee.[69] The committee's meetings with judges revealed that about one-third lacked confidence in the quality of probation supervision, which likely contributed to the flow of defendants into prison. The concerns were especially pronounced in the state's largest city, which helped account for the fact that Milwaukee County, with only 18 percent of the state population, accounted for 40 percent of its prisoners and more than half of the prison admissions for drug offenses. However, the committee did not develop a specific legislative proposal to address the probation problem but instead offered general support for intermediate sanctions and more rigorous forms of community supervision. This, of course, had been precisely the aim of the now-discredited Intensive Sanctions Program and of the Walter Dickey–led Governor's Task Force on Sentencing and Corrections. Following up on this aspect of the CPSC's report, a new Governor's Task Force to Enhance Probation, also chaired by Judge Barland, produced yet another call for beefed-up probation supervision and treatment, but this recommendation went as unheeded as that of the earlier task force.[70]

As might be expected in light of the prominent role of judges on the CPSC, the committee's final report seemed primarily judicialist in its orientation. This approach was hardly inconsistent with the underlying truth-in-sentencing legislation, which had been premised, in part, on the inherent superiority of judges over corrections officials as punishment deciders. Yet the CPSC's proposal took this judicialism to a higher level, for instance, in the elimination of many mandatory and presumptive minimums. Notably, too, the CPSC gave judges authority over ES revocations, letting them determine for how long struggling offenders would be returned to prison. The populism that had seemed an equally important impetus for the underlying legislation took a back seat to judicialism on the CPSC. A degree of managerialism was also apparent, for instance, in the repeal of certain sentence enhancers. Still, the CPSC's proposals hardly amounted to a complete reversal of the populist victories of 1998.

TIS Returns to the Legislature, 1999–2002

The CPSC's proposals required legislative approval, which was quickly forthcoming in the assembly. However, the senate, now back in Democratic hands, failed to act before TIS took effect on December 31, 1999. Passage of the implementing legislation, often referred to as TIS II, would not happen until after two more years of contentious debate.

At the heart of the debate was the proposal of Senator Gary George, a leading African American Democrat from Milwaukee, to authorize sentence modification by judges. More specifically, his proposal would have permitted judges "at any time" to reduce the confinement portion of a sentence in exchange for a longer extended supervision term.[71] In effect, George would have restored the back-end discretion that had existed in the parole system but placed that discretion in the hands of the judges rather than the Parole Commission. Occupying Lynn Adelman's former seat as Judiciary Committee chair, George was in a position to block the assembly version of TIS II if judicial modification were not included.

Republicans charged that George's proposal "gutted" truth in sentencing.[72] This charge required some creative reimagination of the TIS law. George's proposal kept release authority in the hands of the elected judges, so it was perfectly consistent with the arguments for democratic accountability that seemed so prominent when TIS was adopted. Nor did there seem much reason to think that judges would with any frequency revise their sentences so as to threaten public safety by releasing violent criminals. Rather, Republicans criticized George's proposal for undermining the certainty of sentences. In the words of Representative Scott Walker, George's most outspoken critic, "Truth in sentencing wasn't necessarily to make sentences longer, it was to make them certain."[73] Walker and other assembly Republicans thus proclaimed that there was a "line in the sand" when it came to sentence modification.[74]

In order to pressure George and the senate Democrats to back down, Walker invoked the threat of a rapidly escalating prison population under the now-effective TIS I, with its across-the-board sentence increases. "Every day that goes by I think you're going to see a trend toward lengthier and lengthier sentences," said Walker.[75] However, George was unimpressed by the potential of TIS II to address the problem: "Whether you do it under the current system [TIS I] or under this modified sentencing system [the CPSC proposal]," he declared, "you're going to have the same problem: massive overcrowding."[76] George echoed the views of Professor Walter Dickey, the lone dissenter from the CPSC's final report, who had argued that doing nothing might indeed be preferable to adopting the committee's recommendations.[77]

Although some of George's Democratic colleagues may not have been persuaded on this score, they nonetheless backed him up in his confrontation with Walker and the assembly Republicans. Then-senate majority leader Chuck Chvala identifies three reasons for the solid Democratic front.[78] First, there was a strong tradition in the senate of deferring to committee chairs on matters within the jurisdiction of their committees. (This was the tradition that had helped Lynn Adelman stall so many tough-on-crime bills over the years.) Second, with Democrats clinging to a very tenuous 17-16 advantage in the senate, "every man [was] a king"; Democrats were not likely to undermine a colleague whose position was critical to their majority status. Finally, other senators tended to defer to George on sentencing issues because he was an African American legislator representing an inner-city district, and everyone recognized that his constituents were disproportionately affected by the sentencing laws.

Whatever the calculus, TIS II remained caught in the legislative impasse until 2002. By then, more than a year into the TIS regime, evidence was mounting that punishment was indeed growing harsher. In April, for instance, the DOC released data showing longer real sentences under TIS for all offense types, including a *doubling* of sentence lengths for violent and sexual offenses.[79] One reporter, in a front-page story on the data, referred to TIS as a "ticking financial time bomb." The news was all the more alarming in light of the state's fiscal woes in the wake of the 2001 recession, which left Wisconsin scrambling to address a $1.1 billion deficit. These financial pressures revived legislative interest in the CPSC proposal, which, accurately or not, was consistently portrayed in the media as a way to bring sentences down and thereby save corrections costs. It was no coincidence that the proposal was inserted into Governor Scott McCallum's budget repair bill. McCallum, who was elevated from lieutenant governor when Thompson became President George W. Bush's secretary of health and human services, observed, "I'm trying to kick start this whole thing. And it does make sense to do it with the budget because of the fiscal implications."[80]

In addition to mounting fiscal pressures, TIS II also benefited from personnel changes in the legislature. Scott Walker, who had drawn the "line in the sand" on sentence modification, departed after his election as Milwaukee County executive, while Gary George decided to focus his attention on a run for governor.[81] With these hardliners out of the picture, senate and assembly negotiators finally reconciled the competing versions of TIS II. Judicial sentence modification made it into the final bill, but in a much weaker form than George had envisioned. Defendants convicted of the lowest grades of felonies could petition for modification after serving 75 percent of their prison terms, while defendants convicted of midgrade felonies would have to wait until the 85 percent mark. The most serious classes of felons were excluded altogether. Moreover, district attorneys and victims were given a veto, offenders were limited to one sentence-modification petition, and no appeal was available from an adverse decision.[82] While the bill allowed George to save some face, the sentence-modification provision ultimately seemed a rather feeble gesture in the direction of back-end sentencing flexibility. Indeed, later research found an almost microscopically low success rate of 0.8 percent for sentence-modification petitions in three of the state's largest counties (Milwaukee, Racine, and Kenosha), and only a 15 percent success rate in the rest of the state.[83] Moreover, only a fraction of eligible inmates even bothered to file petitions.[84]

When Governor McCallum signed TIS II into law in July 2002, including essentially the entire package of CPSC recommendations plus the watered-down sentence modification proposal, he brought to a conclusion the four-year legislative implementation process for truth in sentencing in Wisconsin. This process threw into sharp relief the fractured and dysfunctional character of sentencing lawmaking in the state. The legislature adopted a draconian across-the-board sentence increase that was not intended to take effect as written. The committee that was supposed to correct this only partly did so. Meanwhile, the critical problems with probation identified by the committee went unaddressed. Moreover, with lingering doubts that the committee's recommendations offered a real advance over the unadulterated TIS I regime, the legislature allowed that regime to operate for a year and a half before finally passing TIS II. The court and corrections systems were then forced to adapt to a new sentencing system for a second time in a little over three years, with many transitional questions left unanswered in the statutes.

Throughout, the process suffered not only from a deep-rooted mistrust across party lines and a crude politicization of penal policy—Attorney General Doyle, running to unseat McCallum, immediately blasted the governor for signing the weak sentence modification provision into law, claiming that it allowed "prisoners to take the truth out of their sentences"[85]—but also from the wide gap in interests separating state-level policymakers and the locally elected judges who played a central role on the CPSC. Neither on the committee nor in their courtrooms were judges willing, as Walter Dickey put it, to "take the fall" for the legislature's extreme approach in TIS I.[86] As everyone recognized, TIS would inevitably result in increased lengths of stay in prison unless the judges carefully and systematically altered their sentencing practices to account for the elimination of parole. However, the judges' adjustment to TIS was slow and erratic. Expected confinement time initially spiked after TIS, then temporarily returned to pre-TIS levels before resuming an upward climb.[87] Overall, between 2000 and 2007, judges increased the confinement portion of their sentences from an average of thirty-one to forty months.[88] Post-prison supervision periods increased even more dramatically, from twenty-three to fifty-four months on average, which helped to fuel a growing tide of returns to prison for violations of the conditions of release. (The longer an offender serves on ES, the more likely it is that he will eventually trip up and be revoked.) Total sentence length (imprisonment plus postprison supervision) for new inmates climbed from a pre-TIS average of 6.9 years to 8.7 years in 2005–6.[89] Closer analysis of the inmate population shows increases in average sentence lengths between 1997 and 2006 for every broad offense category—violent, property, and drug.[90] Notwithstanding some managerial aspects to the CPSC report and TIS II, the net effect of two waves of truth-in-sentencing legislation seemed a real advance in Wisconsin's punitiveness.

6

Managerialism's
Modest Comeback,
the Early 2000s

If this book had been written at precisely the millennium, its overarching story would have been "the triumph of penal populism." In 1980, populism had first revealed its power through the defeat of Ed McClain's sentencing-guidelines proposal, but few populist sentencing laws were adopted in the ensuing decade. In the 1990s, though, the populist legislation came fast and furious. Initially, the laws were like the three-strikes legislation—more symbolically than practically significant. Truth in sentencing was the great breakthrough. Populism had at last achieved a profound change in the day-to-day operation of Wisconsin's sentencing system.

If you were a true believer in toughness, then you might well have felt triumphant as the 1990s gave way to the early 2000s. TIS took effect on December 31, 1999. Parole was on the way out. Maximum sentences had been increased across the board by 50 percent. The pre-TIS mandatory minimums were all still in place. Even apart from the statutory changes, average sentence lengths had been inching up for years. And more toughness was also apparent in the way those longer sentences were being served. In 1999, Wisconsin completed its new "supermax" prison in rural Boscobel. Inmates there would spend twenty-three hours per day in their windowless cells, with no in-person communication permitted with visitors or other inmates.[1] "The supermax will be a criminal's worst nightmare," crowed Governor Thompson.[2] At the same time, Wisconsin had become the nation's number one exporter of prisoners.[3] "If keeping criminals off our streets means sending our prisoners to Texas—bye, bye," Thompson declared. The state had even implemented a new system of civil commitment to keep violent sexual offenders behind bars after they had completed their prison terms. At the millennium, about two hundred inmates languished in this indefinite confinement, with the number continuing to increase every year.[4]

Populism's high-water mark proved short-lived. As we have already seen, fiscal pressures created by the 2001 recession finally led to the passage of TIS II, which repealed most of the existing minimums and undid much of the across-the-board increase in maximums. TIS II was hardly a grand managerial triumph, but it did dispel the notion that sentencing legislation could only push in the direction of greater toughness. TIS II thus opened the door for a decade of managerial initiatives intended to bring corrections costs under control. These efforts culminated in the adoption of a complex "earned release" reform package in 2009. However, while populism was thrown on the defensive through much of the early 2000s, it was hardly expelled from the ring. Populism demonstrated its continuing vitality when the 2009 reforms were repealed just two years later. This repeal made clear the real story of Wisconsin sentencing policy since the 1970s—not a populist triumph but a back-and-forth tug-of-war between populism and managerialism in which (aside from truth in sentencing) neither side has been able to score significant, durable victories over the other.

Wisconsin's Second Commission and Guidelines

The 1998 TIS law set Wisconsin on a path to create a second sentencing commission and adopt a second set of advisory guidelines. These proved no more successful than the first. For a brief period of time, the guidelines were the focus of reformers who hoped to rein in Wisconsin's still-burgeoning prison population. However, the second guidelines were brought down even more quickly than the first, done in by an even higher level of judicial resistance.

Adoption of the Second Commission and Guidelines, 1998–2002

As discussed in chapter 5, the new guidelines and commission system had its origins in Democratic senator Brian Burke's truth-in-sentencing bill, which was offered as an alternative to Governor Thompson's plan. Burke knew that Thompson and the Republicans had killed the first Wisconsin Sentencing Commission, and thus saw some partisan appeal in trying to revive the commission idea.[5] However, there seems no evidence that the Republicans resisted, or even noticed, the partisan tweak, and this aspect of Burke's proposal survived the process of reconciling the assembly and senate versions of TIS without apparent controversy. Perhaps it was lost as a small part of a complex bill. Or perhaps the implementation of the new guidelines and commission seemed too distant and uncertain to be worth fighting over in the spring of 1998. After all, TIS I did not directly establish guidelines and a commission but merely ordered the Criminal Penalties Study Committee to develop a more specific guidelines and commission proposal, which would have to be submitted to the legislature for approval.

In spite of the legislature's seemingly offhand approach to reviving the guidelines, the new system's structure proved the single most contentious point of controversy within the Criminal Penalties Study Committee. The committee's vague statutory charge ("development of temporary advisory sentencing guidelines for use by judges when imposing a bifurcated sentence"[6]) provided plenty of room for different designs. Walter Dickey and his UW Law School colleague Michael Smith took advantage of this freedom in proposing a refreshingly original approach to sentencing guidelines, which they called "rule-of-law" guidance.[7] Dickey and Smith envisioned a more explicitly principled (and managerial) sentencing process: "The rule of law requires that a court first determine what facts are relevant in light of the purpose for which a penal sanction is being imposed and then, by inference from those facts, reason to the type and amount of penal measure." Their approach involved an individualized determination in each case of whether public safety and just-punishment needs required imprisonment.[8] Significantly, and in contrast to the first Wisconsin guidelines and most other guidelines systems, rule-of-law sentencing was not built around a formulaic grid.

Dickey and Smith won the support of criminal defense attorney Stephen Hurley, another CPSC member, but drew strong opposition from others. Many of the criticisms of rule-of-law sentencing focused on its "amorphous" character and the risk that it would lead to disparate outcomes.[9] However, these criticisms need to be taken with a grain of salt; there was little or no support on the CPSC for a fully objective or truly constraining guidelines model.[10] Perhaps more significant was the criticism that rule-of-law sentencing would be "too long and unwieldy."[11] In a grid-based system, the grid does much of the analytical work in connecting sentencing factors to sentencing outcomes; rule-of-law sentencing would ask more of judges. Additionally, there were the deadline pressures under which the CPSC labored: it had only about a year to produce the temporary guidelines demanded by the legislature. As the committee pointedly observed in its final report, "It should be noted that the former Wisconsin Sentencing Commission, with a staff of 5 people, took 11 years to develop 16 guidelines."[12] To some, including chair Thomas Barland, the rule-of-law sentencing model required much more elaboration than could be realistically accomplished within the statutory timetable.[13]

While the CPSC did not accept the Dickey–Smith proposal in full, it also declined to adopt a formulaic system that assigned predetermined weights to specific offense and offender characteristics, as the first Wisconsin guidelines had done. Instead, the committee's final proposal sought to blend a grid with aspects of the rule-of-law approach.[14] Rather than calculate a numerical criminal history score and offense severity score, as in the old guidelines, the sentencing judge would instead rank the offender's risk as lesser, medium, or high and the offense severity as mitigated, intermediate, or aggravated, thereby placing the offender in one cell in a three-by-three matrix. To assist with the ranking, the committee developed checklists of sentencing factors and twenty-two pages of narrative guidance. Matrices were developed for eleven high-volume crimes that accounted for about 72 percent of the corrections resources devoted to prisoners.

Once the basic blended approach had been decided on, the real challenge was figuring out what ranges to place within each of the matrix cells. The CPSC considered adapting the numbers from the old guidelines, "but the resulting ranges were so low as to cause concern among some members that the ranges were insufficiently punitive and would not adequately protect the public."[15]

Rather than rely on the too-lenient old guidelines, the CPSC convened a one-day meeting of eighteen judges from around the state in order to help formulate the new ranges. Participants discussed what they felt to be the significant offense and offender characteristics for sentencing each of the eleven covered crimes, and then they individually wrote a range into each cell in each matrix. After further discussion, the judges were given an opportunity to revise their ranges, after which the numbers were compiled so as to generate the final ranges. Many of the resulting final ranges were quite broad, such as probation to four years in prison (burglary matrix), three years to twelve years (second-degree sexual assault of a child), and fifteen to thirty years (first-degree sexual assault), while other ranges, typically involving less serious offenses, were considerably narrower, such as probation to one year in prison (forgery). On the whole, the guidelines reflected that the "consensus among all who worked with the monthly ranges was that they wished to see relatively broad ranges in each cell to maintain flexibility."[16]

The CPSC maintained flexibility and discretion to an even greater extent with the extended supervision (ES) component of sentences. (ES was the portion of the "bifurcated" sentence to be served in the community following release from prison.) At the one-day guidelines meeting, "the judges were surveyed as to whether or not they would recommend that the standard term of extended supervision be presumptively set at 25 percent of the confinement term. The judges' responses to that inquiry [were] overwhelmingly 'no.'"[17] The guidelines ultimately made *no* recommendations as to ES. Thus, for instance, an armed robber might get an eight-year term of initial confinement. ES might then be anywhere from two to fifteen years in length, and the guidelines had nothing to say about where to sentence within this very wide range. This was an invitation to some highly consequential disparities—after all, the longer an offender spent on ES, the more likely he was to run afoul of one of the many conditions of ES and be returned to prison.

Nor, beyond simply identifying probation as an option within some cells in the matrices, did the guidelines make any recommendations or provide any information as to alternatives to imprisonment. Such cursory treatment of alternatives risked reinforcing the tendency to view all non-imprisonment sentences in an undifferentiated way as a proverbial slap on the wrist.

Also reflecting a tough-on-crime approach, "it was concluded that the cell for the high-risk offenders committing the most severe version of the crime had to include the statutory maximum time in prison."[18] This decision ensured wide ranges of as much as fifteen years in the "worst of the worst" box of each matrix.

Figure 6.1 presents the key components of a representative guideline, that for armed robbery.[19] It is striking to compare this matrix with that in figure 3.1, the old Wisconsin armed robbery guideline. The ranges in each cell of the new guideline were considerably wider, thus supporting greater judicial discretion, and the recommended maximums generally more severe.

In sum, an intriguing new guidelines structure, offering a more principled approach to sentencing than the descriptive, numbers-driven first guidelines, was undermined at the latter stages of its development. With the CPSC facing pressures to finish its work in haste, maintain severity, and maximize flexibility, the committee produced guidelines that were markedly short on guidance: ranges were wide, ES and alternatives to imprisonment went unaddressed, and judges were left largely to their own devices in translating the checklist of offense and offender characteristics into a cell on the matrix. The managerial spirit that had animated the original Dickey–Smith proposal has been wholly supplanted by judicialism. Nor did basing the new guidelines on a single meeting with eighteen judges seem likely to inspire much confidence. The CPSC's proposed guidelines thus offered little hope of changing actual sentencing outcomes, whether the ultimate goal was to reduce disparity, contain costs, or enhance public safety. Indeed, CPSC chair Thomas Barland recalls the guidelines as the biggest disappointment in all of the committee's work; the guidelines required a "major study," he contends, but were instead largely put together in a single day.[20]

Perhaps the best that could be said of the new advisory guidelines was that they were intended only as a temporary measure, subject to modification by the new Sentencing Commission once it was established.

The CPSC had quite a bit to say about this new commission, articulating an ambitious agenda for it that went beyond oversight of the guidelines. If elsewhere the CPSC had seemed reluctant to address cost or the overuse of imprisonment, these managerial considerations seemed paramount in its discussion of the new commission. Consistent with the CPSC's general tendency to leave judicial discretion untouched, though, the commission was presented as a body that would focus its efforts on the executive and legislative branches of government: "The Committee envisions a Sentencing Commission as a large, broad-based group that will review sentencing policy for the state." "Frequently," the committee chided, "the legislature feels pressure to pass criminal penalty laws in response to notorious crimes, without the benefit of a cost analysis of the impact of that new law on the court system or the prison population. . . . A Sentencing Commission can review proposed criminal legislation as to its impact on the court system, the probation and prison population, and cost to the state."[21]

In terms of composition, the "Committee decided that the new Sentencing Commission should have a make-up similar to the Criminal Penalties Study Committee," including seventeen voting and three nonvoting members appointed by various authorities and representing a wide range of stakeholders.[22] Of course, this decision by a divided CPSC to replicate itself in the new body may have made inevitable the contentiousness that we will see in the second commission, and its failure to develop an alternative to the CPSC's highly judicialist guidelines model. In any event, under the CPSC's proposal, the commission would have six professional staffers to help with the research and analysis. On the other hand, the CPSC recommended a five-year sunset (expiration) provision for the commission—an odd move for an agency that was supposed to be keeping sentencing policymakers up to date with the latest research and trends in sentencing practice.

As enacted, TIS II largely embraced the CPSC's recommendations with respect to the Sentencing Commission and guidelines. However, the 2002 law did modify the CPSC's vision for the new commission in at least two notable respects. First, Governor Scott McCallum exercised his partial veto power to reduce the size of the commission staff from six to just two, citing the very postrecession budget crisis that had finally motivated the legislature to pass TIS II.[23] Second, the law authorized a new Joint Review Committee on Criminal Penalties, which was to perform the same analysis of proposed criminal laws that the CPSC had envisioned for the Sentencing Commission.[24] In practice, the

Offense Severity Assessment

1. Determine factors affecting severity of the armed robbery:
    ____ Extreme degree of force
    ____ Threats
    ____ Abduction or restraint of victim

2. Assess harm caused by the offense:
    Consider the victim's statement and needs and impact of crime on victim
    ____ Offender targeted vulnerable victim
    ____ Victim suffered bodily harm
    ____ Victim otherwise harmed
           How? _____
    ____ Vulnerable victim
    ____ Other

3. Assess the offender's role in the offense. If more than one offender, determine:
    ____ Leader or organizer of criminal activity
    ____ Involvement manipulated or pressured (but less than statutory coercion)
    ____ Minimal role
    ____ Other

4. Statutory aggravating factors and penalty enhancers:
    Statutory aggravating factors. *See Stat. §973.017*
           ____ Committed against an elder (62 or over) person
           ____ Committed in connection with a gang
           ____ Concealed, disguised, altered appearance to hinder identification
           ____ Wore a bulletproof garment
           ____ Other

Penalty enhancers.	Pleaded and Proved	Uncharged/Dismissed
Hate crime Stat. §939.645	____	____
School zone Stat. §939.632	____	____
Other	____	____

5. Other factors related to offense severity:
    ____ Defendant abused a position of trust or authority
    ____ Conduct reflects more serious conduct than offense of conviction
    ____ Other

Risk Assessment Evaluation

Determine the defendant's risk to public safety or to re-offend. Consider the nature of the risk that the defendant poses and conditions necessary to reduce risk.

1. Factors that may suggest heightened/lesser risk:
    ____ Previous acts (whether or not convictions/adjudications)
    ____ Employment history

(*continued*)

Figure 6.1. Armed robbery revised sentencing guidelines, 2002

_____ Mental health

_____ Dependence on controlled substances

_____ Dependence on alcohol

_____ Performance on bail

_____ Age

_____ Physical condition

_____ Mental health treatment/counseling

_____ Drug treatment

_____ Alcohol treatment

_____ Other

2. Criminal history

In assessing criminal history consider whether it overstates or understates future risk to public safety. Juvenile adjudications for acts that are crimes if committed by an adult should ordinarily be treated the same as criminal convictions. Assess criminal history with caution. Consider whether it fairly reflects risk to public safety or to re-offend. Consider if applicable:

_____ Convictions old

_____ Multiple convictions same as (or similar to) previous offenses

_____ Other circumstances indicate conviction/adjudication an inappropriate indicator of risk

Armed Robbery Chart

Risk assessment

Offense severity		Lesser	Medium	High
	Mitigated	Probation to 3 yrs Prison	Probation to 6 yrs Prison	5 yrs Prison to 10 yrs Prison
	Intermediate	Probation to 6 yrs Prison	5 yrs Prison to 10 yrs Prison	10 yrs Prison to 17 yrs Prison
	Aggravated	4 yrs Prison to 10 yrs Prison	8 yrs Prison to 15 yrs Prison	15 yrs Prison to 25 yrs Prison

*Choose the cell reflecting correct offense severity and risk assessment.

*A period of Extended Supervision must be assigned in all sentences; that period must be at least 25% of the prison component of the bifurcated sentence.

legislature proved no more enthusiastic about making cost-informed criminal justice policy decisions in the early 2000s than it had been in the 1990s; it took years for the legislature to get around to appointing members to the Joint Review Committee, which never had much impact.[25] But its creation in 2002 nonetheless cast a shadow over what had been projected as a core function of the new Sentencing Commission.

The Second Commission and Guidelines in Operation, 2003–2009

Democratic attorney general Jim Doyle was elected governor in 2002, just a few months after the legislature adopted the CPSC's guidelines and commission plan, and it would fall to Doyle to launch the new agency. This seemed a suitable responsibility; after all, it was Doyle who had initially pressed for the creation of an "implementation committee," and he had done so with the hope that a new system of presumptive sentencing guidelines would emerge.[26] He was particularly keen to deal with the issue of judge-to-judge sentencing disparities. He had been disappointed with the CPSC for its failure to address this more effectively, which he attributed to the influence of the committee's judicial members. To this day, Doyle still calls the CPSC effort "the moment that was lost." In August 2003, as he worked on filling out the membership of the new Wisconsin Sentencing Commission, Doyle felt that he had been given a second chance to accomplish what had always seemed to him an integral part of the overall TIS plan. The Parole Commission's discretion had been brought under control; now, it was the judges' turn.

Yet, even in 2003, the new commission already had several strikes against it. It would be permitted a staff (not yet hired) of only one-third of the recommended size. Moreover, with a large and unwieldy membership that, by design, roughly mirrored that of the CPSC, the Sentencing Commission was unlikely to take bold action in support of any policy objectives, especially if that meant challenging judicial sentencing discretion or reining in severity. Additionally, the commission had no clearly structured role besides superintending and perhaps eventually refining the advisory sentencing guidelines. Yet, based on the state's historical experience, there were good reasons to doubt that the judiciary would pay much attention to the guidelines. Complicating matters, the guidelines had already gone into effect six months earlier; the commission thus lost the opportunity to manage judges' first impressions of the new guidelines, which must have struck many users as an unloved orphan right from the start. And, if all of that were not a sufficient challenge, the clock was ticking on the commission's sunset clause; less than four and a half years remained before the clock would expire.

In January 2004, the commission finally had its undersized staff on board. Leading the enterprise was Executive Director Michael Connelly, a nationally known figure in the sentencing commission field who had previously led Maryland's commission and served as research director for Oklahoma's. In short order, Connelly succeeded in multiplying the research capacity of his tiny agency through grants, internships, and partnerships with academic institutions. Connelly's efforts were reflected in a steady stream of analytic reports on Wisconsin sentencing trends.

Yet the new commission and guidelines made little headway with the judiciary. Between February 2003, when the guidelines officially took effect, and September 2006, judges submitted worksheets to the Sentencing Commission for only 14 percent of the offenses nominally covered by the guidelines.[27] In the vast majority of cases, it was impossible to say whether judges were paying any attention at all to the guidelines. And even in the cases with submitted worksheets, nearly half of the sentences were outside the recommended ranges.[28] These numbers are consistent with what I heard in my interviews with judges and lawyers, who were unanimous in saying that the second guidelines had little or no impact in practice.

At one point, the Wisconsin Supreme Court seemed to provide a boost for the guidelines, but the support proved illusory. Generally silent in the sentencing field, the court issued its most significant statement on sentencing in decades in 2004. The case, *Gallion v. State*, involved a twenty-one-year prison term for a fatal drunk-driving accident.[29] Challenging this sentence in the Wisconsin Supreme Court, Gallion argued that the new TIS system demanded more rigorous justification of sentences by trial judges. No longer would the Parole Commission be able to correct thoughtlessly excessive sentences. The high court agreed that TIS changed the landscape. Judges *should* explain the purposes of their sentences, whether that be deterrence, rehabilitation, or something else. They should also show how the sentence imposed in each case would advance the stated purposes, and do so by reference to the specific facts of the case.[30] How to draw this connection between facts and sentence was left open, though. The court vaguely referred to a number of benchmarks that might be consulted, one of which was the new sentencing guidelines.[31] Optimistic supporters of the guidelines read *Gallion* to signal a more aggressive approach to the appellate review of sentences in Wisconsin, in which adherence to the guidelines would be favored. In truth, though, the *Gallion* opinion sent mixed messages.[32] For instance, the supreme court affirmed Gallion's own sentence rather summarily and without reference to the guidelines or any other benchmark. In any event, the court proved to have no enduring interest in strengthening the appellate review of sentences, and *Gallion* largely withered on the vine as precedent.

Meanwhile, the commission was considering revisions to the "temporary" guidelines that it inherited. In November 2003, Governor Doyle had given the commission a charge that, if taken seriously, would have resulted in the creation of something quite different from the CPSC's handiwork.[33] First, Doyle urged a focus on uniformity: "[A]s you evaluate new guidelines . . . I ask that you take into account whether sentences are consistently applied throughout the state. . . . [I]t is incumbent on us to ensure, to the greatest extent possible, that those found guilty of similar crimes and have similar criminal histories receive similar sentences, regardless of where in the state they may have committed that crime." Second, Doyle also pushed consideration of costs: "As you strive . . . to create guidelines, the Commission should take into account the overall costs and effectiveness of sentencing practices." Finally, Doyle urged, "Any permanent guidelines that you create should include guidelines for the use of alternative sanctions. . . . [R]esearch demonstrates that taxpayer investment in alternative programs . . . results in lower crime rates and lower taxpayer expenditures."

In theory, Doyle could have exerted considerable influence over the commission through his power to appoint seven of its eighteen members, including the chair. As a whole, though, his appointees did not seem to provide consistently strong support for his managerial agenda. Instead, the commission's most outspoken and influential members were two judges appointed by the Wisconsin Supreme Court, and they seemed particularly focused on protecting judicial sentencing discretion.[34] As Connelly saw it, they had little interest in strengthening the guidelines in the ways that Doyle had urged, which might have impinged on the discretion of their fellow judges. For his part, Doyle believes that his agenda for the commission was hampered by the fact that Republicans controlled both houses of the legislature throughout his entire first term. Those who opposed the governor's agenda knew that the legislature would do nothing to back him up.[35] The commission seemed to dissolve into contentiousness. Kristi Waits, initially Connelly's deputy and then his successor as executive director, recalls that it was "incredibly difficult to move things forward"; it might take three or four meetings for the Commission to make a decision about a single document.[36] As the perception grew that the commission was not actually going to accomplish anything, some members simply drifted away, and the commission struggled even to get a quorum for its meetings.[37]

In Connelly's mind, there was one particular moment when it finally became clear to him that the commission would fail. In light of resistance on the commission to the idea of new "guidelines," Connelly had developed a set of nonbinding "principles" for cost-effective sentencing, hoping that this terminology would appear less threatening. In October 2005, the commission met to discuss Connelly's principles, which had been derived from what he understood to be established best practices in the field. Some judicial members nonetheless offered stiff criticism, including one who called the principles "a defense counsel's dream." In the end, three members, all from the judiciary, voted against the principles. Coupled with three abstentions, the nays were sufficient to kill the proposal. Returning to his office after the meeting, Connelly decided it was time to return a call he had received earlier about another commission job in Oklahoma, which he eventually took. "There was no point in staying," he recalls.[38]

Ultimately, the commission did little to improve the CPSC's temporary guidelines, providing just a few tweaks for the worksheets in 2005. Nor did the commission do much advising of the legislature. In 2004, the commission's first full year of operation, the commission noted that it received no requests from the legislature,[39] while in 2005, the commission provided an assessment of only one bill.[40] Like the first commission, the second never really established itself in the policymaking process.

After Connelly left in 2006 and Waits took the helm, the commission continued to issue reports, including a lengthy analysis of racial disparities that received considerable media attention,[41] but it was clear the commission's days were numbered. As one assembly member recalls, the commission simply had no constituency, made no impression on policymakers, and had no defenders in the legislature.[42] Sure enough, the legislature eliminated the commission in its 2007–9 budget and then formally axed the guidelines shortly thereafter. As he watched this story unfold with disappointment, it seemed to CPSC chair Thomas Barland that the commission and guidelines had been killed by a "judicial revolt."[43]

Would things have played out any differently if the commission had been able to achieve consensus on new guidelines to replace the CPSC's slapdash effort? It is conceivable that the judges might have felt it more worthwhile to use genuinely research-based guidelines, but long-term success for any advisory guidelines introduced in the early 2000s seems unlikely. Governor Doyle was pushing for more rigorous guidelines that would emphasize uniformity and cost-effectiveness. However, Wisconsin's experience with the first guidelines and the Intensive Sanctions Program indicates that judges were not especially responsive to appeals based on uniformity or cost. Then, too, the second commission and guidelines had history working against them. Connelly, for instance, maintains, "The reason the second Commission failed was the first Commission"; "the water was really poisoned."[44] I heard this view echoed in many of my conversations with judges and lawyers: for many judges, it "was hard to take the second guidelines seriously after the failure of the first";[45] the first guidelines "left a bad taste" when the second came around;[46] judges did not "get on board" with the second commission because it was "seen just like the first";[47] and so forth. Given the historical baggage, it may well be that the second guidelines were doomed regardless of their content.

The Increasing Prominence
of Racial Disparity Concerns

Before the Civil War, Wisconsin had been known as a center of antislavery sentiment. In one celebrated 1854 incident, a Milwaukee mob freed Joshua Glover, an imprisoned fugitive slave, and aided his escape to Canada.[48] The Wisconsin Supreme Court then defied federal authorities in protecting the mob's instigator, the fiery abolitionist Sherman Booth. Still, as we have seen, this history did not protect Wisconsin from escalating racial tensions as Milwaukee's black population exploded in the decades after World War II. The tensions reached a climax of sorts in 1967 with Father Groppi's fair-housing marches and a bloody inner-city riot.[49]

Though not normally expressed with such violence, racial resentments have persisted, and racial disparities in the state prison population have been a particular point of concern. Racial disparities were hardly new or unique to the era of mass incarceration. In 1965, the Division of Corrections reported that "negroes" accounted for 19 percent of Wisconsin's prison population, even though they constituted less than 3 percent of the overall population.[50] Five years later, in 1970, blacks had grown to more than 30 percent of the prison population, but remained less than 3 percent of the overall population.[51] Nor did the beginning of the imprisonment boom soften the disparities; in 1980, blacks accounted for nearly 40 percent of the prison population but less than 4 percent of the overall population.[52]

These trends did not escape the attention of the new generation of black, Milwaukee-based political leaders who emerged in the 1960s and 1970s. A major point of focus was the disparity between the black percentage of the correctional population and the black percentage of the correctional workforce. State senator Monroe Swan, for instance, drew attention to the issue in 1979 when he co-chaired a special legislative committee on the state prisons. Swan embodied many aspects of the black experience in Milwaukee. Like many black Milwaukeeans of his generation, he was born in the Jim Crow South (rural Belzoni, Mississippi), then moved North with his family.[53] He settled in Milwaukee after high school, earning a college degree and becoming a community activist. In 1972, he became Wisconsin's first black state senator, unseating a white incumbent in an inner-city district that had just recently become majority-black. As he took office, only two other black politicians served in the legislature—both Milwaukee Democrats, like Swan. Swan proved outspoken and controversial in office, feuding with Democratic governor Pat Lucey, among others. Prison conditions were a particular focus of Swan's, so it was natural for him to lead a special committee established by the legislature in the wake of a disturbance at the Fox Lake Correctional Institution. In a statement accompanying the release of the special committee's final report, Swan attributed conflicts in the prisons to the "cultural and ethnic" insensitivities of prison staff and charged that the DOC had made little progress with affirmative action in hiring.[54] "The hiring of minority individuals in percentages reflective of the prison population should become a priority," Swan declared. He also opposed construction of the proposed new prison in Portage. Citing the controversial 1972 report of the Committee on Offender Rehabilitation, Swan affirmed that "a careful review of [the] current inmate population will show that incarceration is not the proper remedy in all cases."

However, the senator was soon out of office, brought down in part by a federal corruption indictment in 1980.[55] With Swan gone, race seemed to figure less prominently in the political debates surrounding sentencing and corrections in the 1980s and 1990s. It was probably no accident, though, that the man who held Swan's former inner-city seat, Senator Gary George, played the lead role in pushing for a sentence-modification provision in TIS II. Race was at least implicitly part of the political dynamics surrounding TIS II. As senate majority leader Chuck Chvala observed, other Democrats tended to defer to Gary George on sentencing legislation because they knew that George's constituents were disproportionately affected by such laws.[56]

Although Senator George's critique of truth in sentencing focused more on cost than race, he simultaneously raised racial issues more directly by supporting legislation that would require police to collect data on the race of drivers they stopped.[57] This requirement, directed at the increasingly controversial practice of "racial profiling" by police, was included in the 1999–2001 state budget but was vetoed by Governor Tommy Thompson. Recognizing the resonance of the issue, though, Thompson announced at the same time that he would form a task force to determine whether racial profiling occurred in Wisconsin. The task force issued its report in 2000, concluding that racial profiling was a reality in Wisconsin, but that its frequency could not be determined. The task force urged police departments to adopt policies expressly prohibiting racial profiling and to begin collecting racial data on a voluntary basis.

Notwithstanding the tepid character of its conclusions and recommendations, the Task Force on Racial Profiling marked a turning point; the first decade of the 2000s would witness several notable initiatives to study the role of race in the criminal justice system. Indeed, at precisely the same time that the Task

Force was conducting its research, the Criminal Penalties Study Committee was including within its massive legislative proposal a requirement for the new Sentencing Commission to "[s]tudy whether race is a basis for imposing sentences in criminal cases."[58] The provision was then quietly enacted three years later along with the rest of TIS II.

The understaffed Sentencing Commission was hardly quick to comply, but its race report finally emerged in 2007.[59] Guarded in its language and qualified in its conclusions, the commission's report nonetheless drew considerable media and political attention to race and sentencing. The commission calculated that Wisconsin's blacks were imprisoned at a rate nearly twelve times higher than whites—the sixth-worst such disparity in the nation. Analyzing five criminal offense areas in more detail, the commission found that disparities were most pronounced in the "in/out" decisions (that is, whether to grant probation in lieu of imprisonment) for low- and middle-grade felonies, especially in the drug area. However, among those who were sent to prison, the commission could find little evidence of disparity in the length of terms.

State senator Lena Taylor, a member of the Sentencing Commission, dissented. Taylor, an African American from Milwaukee whose outspoken views on racial issues sometimes recalled Monroe Swan, criticized the commission's report for its tone and emphasis. "The report has minimized every area of disparities with an inconclusive defense," she charged. "The language of persuasion and change is laid aside for the language of comfort and status quo." Like Swan three decades earlier, Taylor urged greater use of treatment and community-based alternatives to imprisonment. She suggested that such reforms were especially urgent in drug cases. Taylor's dissent neatly illustrates how concerns about racial disparities might dovetail with a managerial agenda and the growing backlash against the War on Drugs.

Even before the commission issued its report, another body, the National Council on Crime and Delinquency, drew media attention with a study showing that young blacks in Wisconsin were imprisoned at 18.4 times the rate of young whites; the state's incarceration rate for young blacks was third highest in the nation.[60] Governor Jim Doyle, fresh off his 2006 reelection victory, responded with an announcement that he would establish a Commission on Reducing Racial Disparities in the Wisconsin justice system. Co-chairing the effort were Noble Wray, Madison's African American police chief, and another African American senator from Milwaukee, Spencer Coggs, who represented the same inner-city district as had Monroe Swan and Gary George. (Coggs unseated George in a 2003 recall election; shortly thereafter, in an eerie replay of the ignominious end of Swan's political career, George found himself the target of a federal corruption investigation and would later serve time in prison.)

With a broad, open-ended mandate, the Racial Disparities Commission engaged in a year-long deliberative process that included a dozen public meetings around the state and presentations by twenty-five experts and public officials.[61] The commission's *Final Report*, issued in 2008, recalled the work of Governor Lucey's Committee on Offender Rehabilitation a generation earlier in its attempt to address unfairness across the entire criminal justice system, although its fifty-seven recommendations included nothing so pointed or radical as the earlier committee's call to close down all of the state prisons. For the most part, the commission's recommendations took the form of encouragement for certain vaguely specified initiatives to be undertaken. As foreshadowed by Senator Taylor's dissent a year earlier, the commission's recommendations in the sentencing area had a clear managerial bent. For instance, the commission advised, "Judges should recommend and encourage the use of new adjudicative methods, including community-based sentencing alternatives." The commission also urged that "every effort should be made" to provide the Department of Corrections with funding for "necessary" rehabilitative programs.

Shortly after the commission finished its work, outside groups again issued much-publicized reports that drew further attention to racial disparities in Wisconsin. In one report, Human Rights Watch determined that blacks in Wisconsin were forty-two times more likely than whites to receive a prison term for a drug conviction—the highest such disparity in the nation.[62] In the second report, the Sentencing Project determined that blacks in Milwaukee were seven times more likely than whites to be arrested for a drug offense—the second-highest such disparity among the forty-three major American cities analyzed.[63] Governor Doyle and local leaders responded in good managerial fashion by promising that Milwaukee would get a drug treatment court (discussed in more detail in chapter 7).[64]

Beyond the adoption of legislation requiring the collection of data on the race of individuals stopped by the police (since repealed),[65] it was hard to see much direct effect on state law from all of the public hand-wringing over racial disparities in the early 2000s. There may have been more of an impact on *local* practices, such as the development of the Milwaukee drug treatment court, and on the internal policies and priorities of state agencies. In 2008, Governor Doyle created a Racial Disparity Oversight Commission in order to follow up on the recommendations of the Racial Disparities Commission.[66] Two years later, the Oversight Commission reported progress on several fronts, particularly in efforts by the Department of Corrections to develop better support for prisoner reentry.

Racial disparity concerns gained prominence in the early 2000s, but they were ultimately subsumed into the efforts by Governor Doyle and other state and local leaders to reduce corrections costs and recidivism rates. Why did a more radical racial justice agenda not emerge? The answer may lie in the fact that the same neighborhoods that suffered the most from racial disparities in imprisonment also suffered the most from crime. Community leaders were understandably reluctant to press for radical changes that might result in less effective crime control. As the Racial Disparities Commission put it, "Just as it was important that questions of discrimination and disparity be addressed, it was also important that a part of the Commission's deliberations and recommendations include considerations of community safety. The Commission recognized that overall respect for and faith in the fairness of the justice system requires that it not only treat all of its citizens fairly, but also that it provides protection for these citizens. One ongoing form of discrimination in United States history has been the under-protection of minorities in the criminal justice system. The Commission notes that progress in avoiding over-incarceration of minorities should not be made at the expense of victims of crimes. Protection must also remain for those victims who live in challenged neighborhoods."[67] A managerial agenda seemed to offer a way through the conundrum, reducing the number of African Americans who were locked up by keeping nonviolent offenders out of prison and delivering treatment to those who would benefit from it, while at the same time preserving tough responses to violent crime.

Despite various managerial advances in the Doyle era, the steady flow of dispiriting news about racial imbalance in the criminal justice system has not abated. Most attention getting was a report by two University of Wisconsin–Milwaukee researchers in 2013 showing that Wisconsin had the highest incarceration rate in the nation for African American men.[68] The same report also revealed that a *majority* of Milwaukee's black men in their thirties and forties were either in prison or had been in prison. The hand-wringing continues.

The Rise and Fall of Earned Release

In 2003, in his first year in office, Governor Jim Doyle urged the new Sentencing Commission to adopt guidelines that would promote more cost-effective sentencing, including the use of more alternatives to imprisonment for nonviolent offenders. This mandate reflected Doyle's belief that "whether corrections was going to continue to be one of the fastest-growing parts of the budget was one of the most serious long-term issues [he] faced" when he became governor.[69] By 2007, as Doyle was beginning his second, and final, term in office, it was clear that the commission would not deliver what he had requested. Yet Wisconsin continued to face chronic budgetary pressures that were due in no small measure to burgeoning corrections costs. Following the commission's failure, Doyle sought to contain costs through a new strategy, quietly developing a complex legislative package that, to a remarkable extent, seemed to restore Wisconsin's pre-TIS system of flexible prisoner release.

Adoption of Earned Release, 2009

Contrary to the dire predictions of its opponents, TIS I did not produce an explosion in the size of Wisconsin's prison population after it took effect at the end of 1999, as indicated in figure 6.2.[70] In part, this was because the system had already absorbed the impact of eliminating discretionary parole; recall that Parole Commissioner John Husz stepped down in 1998 under fire for his liberal approach to discretionary release and that his successor promptly turned down the parole tap. Additionally, Wisconsin benefited from a long-term decline in violent crime that continued for about four years after TIS I went into effect; this may also have helped to conceal the impact of the new law on imprisonment rates. Curiously, admissions to prison continued to rise even as violent crime fell, but this was largely driven by revocations from probation and parole, not original sentences. Between 2000 and 2010, revocations rose from 12 percent of prison admissions to 40 percent.[71] A rise in revocations followed predictably from a massive increase in the number of prisoners released to community

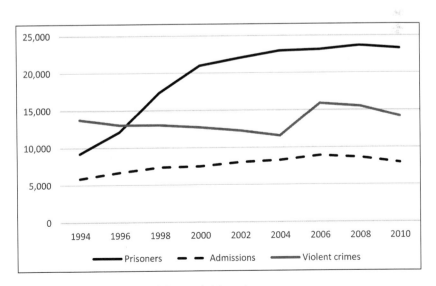

Figure 6.2. Prisoners, prison admissions, and violent crimes, 1994–2010

supervision—an ongoing legacy of the imprisonment boom of the 1990s. Releases from prison doubled between 1999 and 2010. Of course, more releases to
community supervision inevitably meant more revocations. However, the rising
tide of revocations produced relatively short periods of imprisonment and hence
contributed little to the size of the prison population at any given time; thus, for
instance, only about 8 percent of prisoners on July 1, 2008, were behind bars
as a result of revocation. If revocations are subtracted from the equation, admissions *fell* by 28 percent between 2000 and 2010, which offset much of the
increased real severity of the TIS sentences. Although violence spiked again
after 2004, the impact was softened by a sharp reduction in revocations between
2006 and 2012 and by a comparable drop in felony drug arrests over the same
time period, which is discussed in more detail in the next chapter.

Yet, despite the relative stability of the state prison population over the first
decade of the 2000s, the costs of maintaining this population continued to sky-
rocket. The budget for the DOC's Division of Adult Institutions nearly doubled
from $489 million in the 2000–2001 biennium to $838 million in 2010–11, even
though the prison population experienced only a modest increase from 20,976
to 23,250. A comparison of budget line items reveals a key difference: in 2010–11,
the DOC was paying for five additional facilities that were not part of the 2000–
2001 budget, accounting for an additional $120 million in operating expenses.
Additionally, most existing facilities experienced increases in inmate numbers
and budgetary allocations. In effect, Wisconsin had temporarily suppressed the
costs of a burgeoning prison population in the late 1990s through relatively
cheap contracts with the Corrections Corporation of America to house Wisconsin prisoners in out-of-state institutions. On January 5, 2001, CCA held 4,359
Wisconsin prisoners at a cost to the state of $44 per inmate per day, which was
one-third less than the average cost of housing inmates in the state's own institutions.[72] However, as new facilities came on line, Wisconsin gradually repatriated
its prisoners and assumed correspondingly greater costs.

Health care constituted another notable source of increased corrections
costs, growing from $28 million to $87 million over the course of the decade. This
was likely driven to some extent by an aging prison population, as the percentage
of prisoners fifty and older grew from only 5 percent in 1998 to 14 percent in
2010.[73]

Thus, notwithstanding a relative stabilization in the size of the prison
population, Wisconsin faced continued imprisonment-related fiscal pressures
throughout Governor Doyle's time in office, and those pressures were expected
to grow even more intense in the near future. For instance, a 2009 study projected that the DOC would have to spend an additional $2.5 billion in the
coming decade to deal with overcrowding and expected increases in the prison

population.[74] Some observers focused particularly on the extended supervision "time-bomb."[75] Thanks to the across-the-board increases of TIS I and the lack of much limitation or guidance on the length of extended supervision within the high statutory maximums, the average period of postconfinement supervision more than doubled from twenty-three to fifty-four months between 2000 and 2007.[76] Coupled with growing numbers of prisoners being released, these longer periods of postrelease supervision would inevitably mean swelling revocations and returns to prison in the coming years.

These fiscal challenges became increasingly urgent in the wake of the 2007 recession, which caused Wisconsin to face a nearly $7 billion budgetary shortfall in 2009.[77] Much as the shortfall following the 2001 recession helped to motivate passage of TIS II, the later shortfall also played a role in fueling support for the "earned release" reforms, which Doyle added to his proposed state budget in 2009. The complex reform package included a variety of provisions that added some new release mechanisms and liberalized some existing mechanisms.[78] Passage was projected to make three thousand prisoners eligible for release and lift supervision from an additional seven thousand offenders on probation.[79]

Key provisions of Doyle's proposal included the following. First, the bill renamed the Parole Commission the Earned Release Review Commission (ERRC). The Parole Commission had continued in existence under TIS because thousands of prisoners sentenced under the pre-TIS system were still theoretically eligible for parole. The new ERRC would carry on the Parole Commission's responsibility to review the cases of these "old law" prisoners but would also be given authority over a variety of new early-release opportunities. Second, Doyle's bill restored time off for good behavior, given the new label positive adjustment time (PAT). The amount of credit that might be earned by an inmate for good behavior varied depending on the severity of his offense, whether he was a violent or sex offender, and whether he was classified by the Department of Corrections as high risk. At the most generous level, an inmate might earn one day of positive adjustment time for every two days he or she was incarcerated without violating a prison rule or regulation. The more serious or higher-risk offenders would accrue PAT credit at a slower rate and would also have to petition the ERRC to use the credit. The bill also established analogous good-time credits for early discharge from extended supervision. Third, the bill shifted responsibility for handling TIS II sentence adjustment petitions from the judiciary to the ERRC. This included both the general sentence-adjustment petitions that Senator Gary George had fought so hard to add to TIS II and "compassionate release" petitions for inmates who were elderly or ill. Fourth, the bill authorized the Department of Corrections to release nonviolent inmates up to twelve months early. Fifth, the bill eliminated the judiciary's role in revocations of extended supervision. Under TIS II, when an offender violated a condition of release, there would be an administrative process to decide whether to revoke ES and then a return to court to determine how long the offender would have to spend behind bars. Doyle now proposed that the length of reconfinement also be determined through an out-of-court administrative process—the judges would be wholly cut out of the picture. Sixth, the bill eliminated supervision of certain probationers determined by the Department of Corrections to present low risk. Seventh, the bill authorized the department to release certain inmates who successfully completed a substance abuse, boot camp, or other rehabilitation program in prison.

Doyle's package of reforms reflected not only the exigencies of a budget crisis but also a much higher level of confidence in the ability of corrections officials to assess risk and protect public safety than he displayed a decade earlier when he sought to dismantle parole and the Intensive Sanctions Program. In part, this change of heart no doubt resulted from Doyle's ascension to the governor's office; it was his appointees, not Tommy Thompson's, who now ran the Department of Corrections and the Parole Commission, and there was no political benefit to his bashing them. But, in part, the new faith in corrections also reflected the department's changing culture and improving risk assessment capacity. The DOC had been consulting with the University of Cincinnati's Edward Latessa, a leading national authority on evidence-based decision-making in corrections. Also, in 2009, the DOC was in the final stages of a multiyear evaluation of its risk assessment tool—the first such study it had undertaken since 1984.[80]

Paralleling these developments within the department and the drafting of Governor Doyle's earned-release reforms, the Council of State Governments Justice Center was undertaking a "justice reinvestment" study in Wisconsin at the joint request of Doyle, Chief Justice Shirley Abrahamson of the Supreme Court, and leaders in the legislature; the idea was to reduce corrections spending and reinvest the savings in new strategies that would more effectively protect public safety.[81] In collaboration with a variety of other private and public agencies, the Justice Center, a national nonprofit, has undertaken similar justice reinvestment studies in more than twenty other states since 2000. In Wisconsin, the Legislative Council—the body that had played such a prominent role in criminal justice reforms in Wisconsin prior to the 1990s—appointed a special committee to oversee the justice-reinvestment initiative. Chairing the special committee was Senator Lena Taylor, the African American Milwaukee Democrat who had objected so forcefully to the Sentencing Commission's work on racial disparities.

The Justice Center issued its final report in May 2009, three months after Doyle unveiled his earned-release proposals. Senator Taylor's special committee then endorsed four draft bills that were intended to implement Justice Center recommendations.[82] These bills would have capped extended supervision at 75 percent of the term of confinement for most offenders, set six months as a standard period of reconfinement after revocation of ES, appropriated $20 million for services for offenders in community supervision with an express goal of reducing recidivism rates by 25 percent, and created a new "risk reduction" sentencing option that would have permitted release at the 75 percent mark of a prison term if the offender had completed certain programming recommended by the Department of Corrections. These proposals were added to Doyle's budget bill at Taylor's behest. Using the budget was, of course, a time-honored strategy for getting potentially controversial proposals through the legislature—a strategy that we have already seen in use with the TIS II reforms.

Doyle's budget barreled through the legislature, as might be expected with the governor's party now back in control of both houses. No hearings were conducted on earned release, but the proposals drew bitter criticism from Republicans. Representative Mark Gundrum from suburban Milwaukee, a leading Republican voice on criminal justice issues, accused Doyle of "a complete gutting of truth in sentencing"[83]—using precisely the same phrase that Republicans had used in attacking Senator George's sentence-adjustment proposal a decade earlier. Indeed, the criticisms of Doyle's package echoed both of the major themes that had been sounded by TIS proponents (including Doyle himself) in the 1990s. First, there was the theme of democratic accountability; as Gundrum put it, "With judges you have accountability. Judges are elected and they're re-elected by the people. The nameless faceless bureaucrats on this parole commission will be able to release whoever they want with no accountability." Second, there was the theme of public safety: "We're not talking about Boy Scouts here. We're talking about some dangerous people that are going to be released," warned senate minority leader Scott Fitzgerald.

Despite such criticisms, both reform packages—Doyle's original earned-release provisions and the later-added justice reinvestment proposals—passed the legislature and reached Doyle's desk in July 2009. However, Doyle vetoed most of the justice-reinvestment proposals,[84] as well as provisions that would have provided for judicial review of sentence reductions and given judges the authority to order early discharge from probation.[85]

If truth in sentencing had largely stripped from the corrections bureaucracy the power to manage the size of the prison population and to determine the real severity of punishment in most cases, Doyle's earned-release reforms marked a striking comeback for the DOC and the (renamed) Parole Commission. To be sure, the reform package did not fully re-create the Parole Commission's pre-TIS ability to release inmates after only one-quarter of the prison term had been served. Moreover, certain categories of the more serious offenders were largely excluded from the new opportunities for early release. Still, the DOC and the ERRC—both to be run by Doyle appointees and presumably to function in sync—now had a plethora of new tools available to manage the use of correctional resources. Doyle's vetoes, moreover, tended to reinforce the empowerment of the corrections bureaucracy and the limitation of judicial discretion: Senator Taylor's cap on DOC-ordered reconfinement time was lifted, judicial review of sentence reductions was diminished, and judges lost the ability to order early discharge from probation. The earned-release reforms also reflected the DOC's ascendance in a more procedural sense: the reforms were developed within the DOC and received little systematic review by external stakeholders in the short time between their announcement and their adoption.

Although Doyle vetoed many of the specific proposals that emerged from Wisconsin's justice-reinvestment initiative, the earned-release package none-theless broadly reflected justice-reinvestment ideals, which, in turn, embodied managerial principles and a renewed interest in rehabilitation. As Doyle put it, earned release "implements a smarter criminal justice policy that holds individuals accountable for their crimes, but also better prepares and supports those individuals when they reenter the community so that they do not return to the criminal justice system."[86] Better incentivizing rehabilitation played a central role in this "smarter" policy. For instance, Doyle noted that the DOC's power to discharge offenders early from extended supervision "creates an incentive for an offender to comply with the rules of their supervision and earn discharge through rehabilitation, which better protects public safety."[87] Although the 2009 budget crisis helped to propel earned release to the top of the legislative agenda, with its alleged potential to "save millions of dollars,"[88] the reforms were not an indiscriminate population-reduction strategy but instead embodied a relatively coherent approach to restraining and rationalizing imprisonment based on risk assessment, rehabilitation, and much enhanced bureaucratic discretion. Whatever the merits of this approach, however, it flew in the face of Wisconsin's now well-established preference for judicial control over punishment, as well as the populist unwillingness to take seriously the possibility that prison might be counterproductive to public safety in some cases. Since Doyle himself had supported these points of view in the 1990s, there was at least some poetic justice in the role they played in bringing down his earned-release reforms a decade later.

Operation and Demise of Earned Release,
2009–2011

Earned release proved to have much less impact in practice than proponents promised or opponents feared. By July 2010, nine months after the reforms had taken effect, only 158 inmates had been released early.[89] Savings to the Department of Corrections were only $900,000, well off track from the $30 million projected through the end of 2011. Al Graham, a former police officer appointed by Governor Doyle to chair the Earned Release Review Commission, attributes the slower-than-expected pace of releases from his agency to all of the work that was necessary to adjust the Parole Commission's policies and procedures in light of the earned-release law—it was "meeting after meeting after meeting," he recalls; "there was no way we could operate fast at the beginning"—as well as to his own unwillingness to make any releases with which he felt uncomfortable.[90] "My concern was public safety," says Graham. He "lost a lot of sleep" in those days worrying that he might read in the newspaper about a terrible crime committed by someone released on his watch.

Despite the quiet start, Republican representative Scott Suder, earned release's most outspoken critic, kept public attention focused on the program through monthly records requests for release data. Some felt that the legislative and media scrutiny promoted by Suder discouraged the DOC and the ERRC from using their new release authority more aggressively. However, if the go-slow approach was indeed a calculated decision by corrections officials to head off public criticism, the strategy backfired: opponents began to argue that the reforms were a failure because they were not living up to Doyle's cost-saving promises.[91]

Eventually, the pace of releases did pick up, with 666 prisoners coming out by the time the program was axed in 2011.[92] ERRC chair Graham gives much of the credit to an increase in personnel, as several former parole commissioners were rehired on a part-time basis to help review the flood of new inmate applications. Yet the acceleration of releases may have come too late to reverse the perception, trumpeted in front-page headlines, that "sentencing reform results fall short."[93] Moreover, the raw number of inmates released may give an exaggerated sense of the program's impact, for many were within weeks or even days of when they would have been let out anyway.[94] At about the time of the program's demise, earned release was calculated to have saved 65,948 "bed days," or only about 100 days per release.[95] On the positive side, though, the state's cautiousness with early release successfully avoided any catastrophic failures. As of July 2011, only four inmates released under the reforms had been returned to prison for the commission of new crimes, and none of these were violent offenses.

There was a particular poignancy to the fate of the 2009 compassionate-release reforms. Compassionate release had become part of Wisconsin law through a little-noticed, narrowly focused provision of the Criminal Penalty Study Committee's massive legislative proposal. In its original form, as enacted in TIS II, compassionate release had to be ordered by a judge and could be made only on the basis of age or terminal illness. Doyle's 2009 law made three modifications, all of which were intended to facilitate releases. First, the terminal illness criterion was broadened to include any "extraordinary health condition." Second, prior exclusions for Class B felons and life-sentenced inmates were lifted. And, finally, authority over compassionate release was transferred from judges to the ERRC. However, in the nearly two years that these reforms were in place, the ERRC ordered only eight compassionate releases.[96] All were re-leased under the "extraordinary health condition" prong; age-based releases remained merely a theoretical possibility. Moreover, five of the eight died within four months of release,[97] suggesting that the standards for a qualifying health condition remained very dire indeed. Meanwhile, as against this paltry number of releases, seventy-three Wisconsin prisoners died in custody in 2010 and 2011,[98] and more than three hundred prisoners were aged sixty-five or older,[99] which would have qualified them for age-based release assuming they had served at least five years of their sentence.

Despite the difficulty of obtaining compassionate release, the program still became a lightning rod when the very first release was granted to Paula Harris—a "convicted murderer" and "dangerous criminal" in the words of Representative Suder.[100] However, Harris, who was convicted of reckless—not intentional—homicide, suffered from congestive heart failure and had trouble walking.[101] She died in early 2013. Yet, following the controversy, Harris proved to be the first and last Class B felon to obtain compassionate release in Wisconsin under the 2009 reforms.

Representative Suder and his fellow Republicans continued to focus critical attention on earned release throughout the election year of 2010. At one point, Suder introduced a bill that would have repealed what he called the "Demo-crats' 'Let Em' Loose Early' Program."[102] Also joining the criticism was guber-natorial candidate Scott Walker, formerly the chief legislative proponent of TIS I in the 1990s and now serving, incongruously for such a hard-line Repub-lican, as county executive in deep-blue Milwaukee. On the campaign trail, Walker promised to eliminate earned release if elected.[103] Ultimately, as part of the national wave of Republican victories in 2010, Walker swept to power in Wisconsin, carrying with him both chambers of the legislature. Suder himself became assembly majority leader. At that point, repeal of earned release seemed only a matter of time.

In the new legislative session, political partisanship reached what may have been an unprecedented high in Wisconsin's modern history. The focal point of controversy was Governor Walker's efforts to undermine the state's Democratic-leaning public employees' unions; this prompted mass protests by tens of thousands of demonstrators at the State Capitol, the flight of fourteen Democratic senators to Illinois in order to break quorum, and threats by Republicans to have the absent Democrats arrested.[104] Walker eventually secured passage of his collective bargaining reforms, as well as a number of other measures that were perceived as ideologically extreme by Democrats. Walker and several senators found themselves targeted by recall efforts. After a series of expensive political campaigns, two Republicans were removed from office in 2011, but Democrats were unable to take back the senate that year.[105]

With such goings-on in the background, the repeal of earned release received relatively little attention but was effectuated by Republicans in July 2011.[106] Reflecting the partisan spirit of the time, Governor Walker was joined by Suder and two other Republican legislators at the signing ceremony.[107] "Early release has allowed hundreds of high-risk inmates to get out of jail before serving their time," declared Suder, "and Wisconsin will undoubtedly be a safer place to live, work, and raise a family now that dangerous criminals will be kept behind bars."

Sentencing Policy and Politics after Earned Release: Managerialism Flowers on the Local Level

The repeal of earned release demonstrated the continuing vitality of penal-populist rhetoric, while also restoring the strongly judicialist TIS system. Yet, in other respects, the Scott Walker era has also witnessed a continuation of the managerial revival of the early 2000s. This revival has been more clearly visible at the local than the state level of government, but it is significant that many local initiatives have been financially supported by the state's Treatment Alternatives Diversion (TAD) grant program. TAD was first established in 2005, when Jim Doyle was governor, but the program was maintained and then eventually expanded in the Walker era. TAD is considered in more detail in chapter 7, as is a related grassroots campaign to cut Wisconsin's prison population in half. Even apart from TAD, though, managerialism has been flourishing in some individual counties. The Milwaukee experience provides a notable illustration.

As discussed in chapter 4, one important distinction between the Minnesota and Wisconsin criminal justice systems has been Minnesota's greater decentralization, with counties given the option of running their own community corrections programs. This sort of decentralization may, in theory, promote greater use of probation and reduced incarceration for a number of reasons. First, judges and prosecutors may have a greater sense of control over, and hence confidence in, locally administered alternatives to incarceration, especially if they are given a formal oversight role over community corrections programs. Second, locally administered programs may be better designed to fit local needs and circumstances. Third, with less bureaucratic red tape, it may be easier for local officials to implement promising new programs quickly. Indeed, some entrepreneurial judges and prosecutors may welcome the opportunity to get out of the rut of routine case processing and play a more prominent role in institutional leadership. Moreover, judges and prosecutors who establish new alternatives to incarceration will presumably want to use them and will also naturally want to promote their use by colleagues. Finally, if local control is accompanied by local financial responsibility for corrections, then judges and prosecutors will have another incentive to employ sanctions that are less costly than incarceration. Although the salaries of judges and prosecutors are paid by the state, these local officials have an interest in the health of county finances because it is county government that foots the bill for their support staff and other administrative expenses. Furthermore, judges and DAs can hardly relish the thought of facing the voters if their profligate use of incarceration has resulted in local property tax increases.

It has been hard for these managerial dynamics to take hold in Wisconsin because probation is administered by the distant and distrusted DOC and because the costs of imprisonment are borne by state government. *Jail* expenses, however, remain a county responsibility, and, in several Wisconsin counties, concerns over these expenses have catalyzed the development of new, locally administered alternatives to jailing. In order to understand these dynamics, it will be helpful to recall that jails traditionally hold two different groups of offenders: those awaiting trial or sentencing, and those who have been sentenced to short terms of incarceration. Jails are the responsibility of county sheriffs. In Milwaukee County, the two basic jailing functions are performed by two facilities, the County Jail (downtown) and the House of Correction (in suburban Franklin). The "House" traditionally focused on the postsentencing population, but the two facilities have not consistently maintained separate identities.

In Milwaukee, recent reform initiatives have been led by a so-called Community Justice Council (CJC), a quasi-official forum for key criminal justice stakeholders to share ideas and coordinate policies. Founded in 2007, the Milwaukee CJC grew out of litigation over chronic overcrowding in the Jail and the House. Five years of litigation over jail conditions eventually resulted in a

2001 consent decree, which specified certain remedial measures that would have to be undertaken if various overcrowding thresholds were met, including increased administrative releases to electronic monitoring in the community.[108] Compliance, however, proved less than satisfactory. For instance, in the midst of renewed litigation in 2006, the county itself acknowledged approximately sixteen thousand violations of one provision of the consent decree.[109] In 2005, the county's average daily inmate population exceeded the combined design capacity of the Jail and House by more than 10 percent.[110] In order to address this overcrowding and resolve the litigation, the county requested assistance from the National Institute for Corrections. Among other recommendations, the NIC advised the county to establish a cross-agency coordinating committee to manage correctional resources more effectively. A similar recommendation emerged from the jail settlement negotiations, and the Milwaukee County Board obliged by creating the CJC.[111]

Comprising twenty-seven members representing a diverse array of stakeholders, the Milwaukee CJC began to meet in early 2008. Its stated mission was "to efficiently and collaboratively coordinate services and to effectively allocate financial resources to ensure crime reduction, victim support, offender accountability, and restorative community-based programs." Controlling the CJC's agenda was a smaller executive committee comprising the county sheriff, Milwaukee chief of police, chief judge of the Milwaukee County Circuit Court, district attorney, first assistant state public defender, county executive, mayor, chair of the County Board Judiciary Committee, and the leader a local nonprofit. Neither the full CJC nor the executive committee could issue binding directives to participating agencies, but there was an expectation, in the words of the executive committee's Guidelines, that members would make "a good faith effort" to implement collective decisions.[112]

Since the CJC's founding, Milwaukee has experienced a flowering of initiatives intended to reduce its locally incarcerated population. In some cases, new programs have been created, while in others existing programs have been reinvigorated through institutional restructuring. Key components of the incarceration-reduction strategy have included:

- Universal pretrial screening—a standard risk assessment tool is used to inform pretrial detention decisions in the hope that bail amounts will not be set unnecessarily high
- Enhanced opportunities for deferred prosecution agreements conditioned on alcohol or drug treatment
- Specialized drug treatment court
- Specialized veterans court

- Electronic monitoring options for pretrial and postsentencing detainees
- Day reporting center as an alternative sentencing option.[113]

The reforms seem to have had an impact. Between 2005 and 2012, the average daily population of the Jail and House dropped from 2,950 to 2,445 — finally, if barely, within the combined design capacity of the two institutions.[114] To some extent, this decline reflected sustained reductions in Milwaukee's crime rate beginning in 2007, but there was widespread agreement among those in the system that alternatives to incarceration were also playing a significant role.[115] In all, between 2007 and 2010, some 2,264 offenders were admitted to diversion or deferred prosecution. Meanwhile, the drug treatment court has been consistently at or near its capacity of eighty participants.

The Milwaukee experience demonstrates the ability of locally led managerial initiatives to gain buy-in from judges and prosecutors—a striking contrast with the history of the state-led Intensive Sanctions Program. Moreover, this has occurred notwithstanding a populist pushback. In particular, Milwaukee County sheriff David Clarke, although a founding member of the CJC, has become harshly critical of many incarceration-reducing measures. His rhetoric echoes that of former representative Suder. For instance, he has castigated universal screening as "universal jail break,"[116] and railed against "criminal sympathizers" and "academic elites" who "indoctrinate the public with their soft-on-crime agenda."[117] Nor did he limit his opposition to words; in 2011, he used his administrative discretion to eliminate most releases to electronic monitoring.[118] In response, the county board removed the House of Correction from Clarke's control, which paved the way for a revival of electronic monitoring.[119] Meanwhile, the district attorney and leading judges have continued to make the case publicly for evidence-based, cost-sensitive reforms.[120]

The Millennial Synthesis

Despite ferment at the local level in some counties, the overall sentencing and incarceration picture in Wisconsin since 2000 seems to be one of stabilization and the achievement of a new equilibrium. From 2001 through the mid-2010s, the state prison population inched up and down within the relatively narrow range of 21,000 to 23,000. Local initiatives have drawn down local jail populations but have had little discernible effect on the state prison population. This is not surprising: the local fiscal pressures that drive local reforms may create incentives for reduced jail usage but not for reduced prison usage.

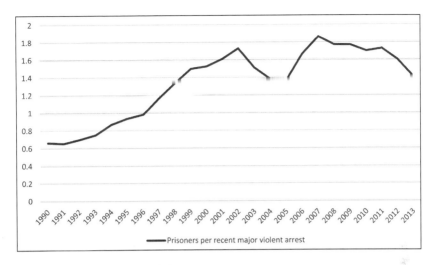

Figure 6.3. Wisconsin parsimony index, 1990–2013

Along with the new imprisonment equilibrium, there seems to be a stable new synthesis of sentencing policy, practice, and ideology. The millennial synthesis is most clearly marked by these features:

- Wide judicial sentencing discretion—even more so than in the seventies synthesis
- No discretionary parole and very limited flexibility otherwise regarding release dates from prison
- More aggressive use of imprisonment than in the seventies synthesis.

In chapter 5, we saw a dramatic increase in Wisconsin's parsimony index (number of prisoners divided by recent arrests for major violent crimes) in the 1990s, following what had been a long period of stability in the 1970s and 1980s. Figure 6.3 indicates what happened after the index finally reached a peak in 2002: there has been some up and down, but the number has consistently remained at least twice the established norm of the 1970s and 1980s.[121] This is the sign of a much-toughened system.

The millennial synthesis does not include a clearly dominant ideology of sentencing. We have seen a long-running tug-of-war between populism and managerialism, with no clear victor. In some respects, we might see judicialism as the ideology most clearly embraced by state sentencing policy, even if politicians rarely articulate or defend judicialist ideas. Judicial power over punishment has expanded dramatically since the 1970s, most importantly through the elimination of the traditional check and balance of parole. Judges have vast discretion in determining how long offenders will spend in prison but no meaningful accountability when it comes to exercising that discretion. This is judicialism in spades. However, it is hard to characterize judicialism as truly dominant when it is largely absent from the rhetoric of political leaders.

How did the system become so judicialist when the politicians and policymakers seem much more oriented to populism or managerialism? A metaphor hangs on the wall of my office. After a trip to Europe, my in-laws returned home with a piece of Slovenian folk art they thought a lawyer would enjoy. The simple painting depicts two farmers disputing the ownership of a cow. One tugs the cow by the tail, while the other attempts to pull the animal's head in the opposite direction. Neither is getting anywhere. Meanwhile, a third man quietly sits between the two, milking the cow for his own benefit. The man who capitalizes on the fruitless conflict is, of course, identified as an attorney. Similarly, as the proponents of populism and managerialism have continued their indecisive struggle in Madison, it is the legal establishment that has benefited.

A high-discretion system is common ground where the competing demands of populism and managerialism can both be partially accommodated. Politicians can appeal to tough-on-crime sensibilities by increasing maximum sentence lengths but at the same time hold onto the hope that sentences will not actually get much longer in practice. TIS also reflected this dynamic, with politicians promising both increased toughness and little impact on the corrections budget. This sort of "have-it-both-ways" strategy for dealing with the intractable conflict between populism and managerialism has the incidental effect of greatly augmenting judicial power. Moreover, judges serving on policymaking bodies— most importantly, the Criminal Penalties Study Committee charged with implementing TIS—have warmly embraced the judicialist turn and ensured there would be no retreat from it.

If the millennial synthesis includes no clearly dominant ideology, it similarly includes no clearly dominant model for making sentencing policy. There has been no shortage of special commissions, but their record of achieving durable policy change is quite thin. At the same time, the wave of ad hoc policymaking that dominated the 1990s has largely abated. As policy has been caught in stasis between the poles of populism and managerialism, there has been little opportunity for either type of policymaking *process* to establish itself as the norm.

One final notable aspect of the millennial synthesis has been the reemergence of interest in rehabilitation, albeit not in as strong and generalized a fashion as had been the case in the early 1970s. The new rehabilitationism has focused particularly on drug offenders, and its significance is best appreciated within the context of Wisconsin's longer history of drug enforcement and sentencing, which is the subject of the next chapter.

Looking Ahead:
Should Wisconsinites Be Satisfied
with Another Decade Like the Last?

Wisconsin's prison population has remained steady at about 22,000 for more than a decade. Existing policies offer little hope for significant reductions from that level, and the state political establishment seems wholly disinterested in the sort of bold criminal justice reforms that might make meaningful decarceration a possibility. All signs point to another decade of imprisonment at or near record highs. Should Wisconsinites be satisfied with that prospect?

The status quo is costly in many respects. Wisconsin spends more on corrections than it does on its university system. Moreover, even with stable prison numbers, the state corrections budget has continued to grow, and burgeoning health-care costs for an aging inmate population may ensure further growth for many years to come. But the fiscal costs of mass incarceration are only the beginning. The National Research Council recently sponsored a comprehensive assessment of the consequences of high imprisonment rates in the United States.[122] Although the existing research has some limitations, the NRC study found evidence pointing to significant negative short- and long-term effects of incarceration on the health, mental health, employment, and earnings of prisoners.[123] The evidence of costs to families and children is even clearer. The researchers concluded: "We find consistent evidence, in both the ethnographic and quantitative studies, of a link between men's incarceration and instability in male-female unions. We find a strong and consistent link between fathers' incarceration and family economic hardship, including housing insecurity, difficulty meeting basic needs, and use of public assistance. Incarceration tends to reduce fathers' involvement in the lives of their children after release, in large part because it undermines the coparenting relationship with the child's mother. Finally, both ethnographic and quantitative studies indicate that fathers' incarceration increases children's behavioral problems, notably aggression and delinquency."[124]

As against such costs of mass incarceration, there may be some crime-reduction benefits. However, there are good reasons to think that Wisconsin might be able to achieve large (50 percent or more) reductions in its prison population over the coming decade with little or no loss of public safety. For one thing, the state's crime-rate trends over the past generation make clear

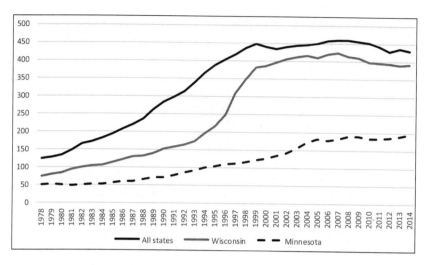

Figure 6.4. Imprisonment rates in the U.S., Wisconsin, and Minnesota, 1978–2014

there is no simple relationship between crime and incarceration. Figures 6.4 and 6.5 provide the long view. Sharply increasing imprisonment rates in the 1970s and 1980s did not prevent the state from reaching a then-record violent crime rate in 1986. Nor did continued growth in imprisonment over the following decade produce any sustained reduction in violence. Although violence finally did drop in the late 1990s and early 2000s, it then spiked back up to a new record high in 2007, even though imprisonment rates remained stable. At no time have rates of violence in Wisconsin returned to the levels of the 1960s and 1970s, when imprisonment rates were a fraction of the current numbers. Figures 6.4 and 6.5 reveal a similarly erratic crime-imprisonment relationship at the national level.[125]

The Minnesota trends depicted in Figures 6.4 and 6.5 provide further evidence that Wisconsin might be able to achieve large reductions in imprisonment without offsetting public safety costs. Since 1980, Minnesota has consistently maintained an imprisonment rate that is half or less of Wisconsin's, but the two states have followed a remarkably similar path when it comes to violent crime. This suggests that Wisconsin's dramatic divergence from Minnesota on the imprisonment front after the 1970s may have yielded few public safety benefits.

Recent experiences in New York, New Jersey, and California may also be instructive. Nationally, these three states have achieved the most significant reductions in imprisonment in recent years, but without any apparent diminution in public safety.[126] New York reduced its prison population by 26 percent between 1999 and 2012, while its rate of violent crime fell even more sharply by

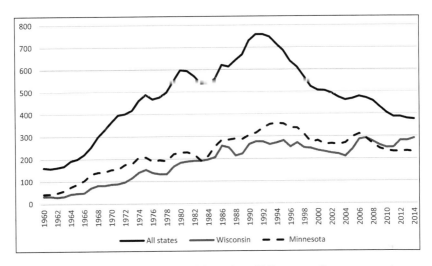

Figure 6.5. Violent crime rates in the U.S., Wisconsin, and Minnesota, 1960–2014

31 percent. New Jersey's figures over the same time period are almost identical. Meanwhile, California reduced its prison population by 23 percent between 2006 and 2012, while its rate of violent crime dropped by 21 percent. In all three states, the drop in violent crime was greater than the national average over the relevant time period.

More rigorous, multivariate regression analyses have consistently found that the great national imprisonment boom made only modest contributions to public safety and that the marginal benefits essentially disappeared over time.[127] The most recent and comprehensive analysis comes from the Brennan Center for Justice at New York University. The Brennan Center researchers concluded that the effectiveness of incarceration "has been decreasing as a crime fighting tactic since at least 1980. Since approximately 1990, the effectiveness of increased incarceration on bringing down crime has been essentially zero."[128]

The National Research Council study makes clear some of the underlying dynamics that have undermined the effectiveness of increasingly punitive sentencing policies and practices. Incapacitation and deterrence are the two potential mechanisms by which increased imprisonment might plausibly reduce crime. However, decades of research on these mechanisms have found only quite limited benefits from enhanced penal severity. The NRC report observed, "Because recidivism rates decline markedly with age, lengthy prison sentences, unless they specifically target very high-rate or extremely dangerous offenders, are an inefficient approach to preventing crime by incapacitation."[129] Likewise, the researchers concluded that "the incremental deterrent effect of increases in lengthy prison sentences is modest at best."[130] As against these small benefits, other research suggests that imprisonment may tend to have a criminogenic effect on offenders, that is, the experience of imprisonment may make them *more* likely, for a variety of reasons, to reoffend than they would have been otherwise.[131] Thus, at some point, escalating severity may even become worse than useless—it may actually diminish public safety. This risk appears even greater if one considers the possibility that increased imprisonment costs may be draining tax dollars from other types of public spending that might be more effective at reducing crime over the long run, including spending on police, probation, schools, vocational training, economic development in impoverished communities, and treatment of addiction and other mental health disorders.

Cumulatively, the evidence seems clear that Wisconsin could safely reduce its prison population over the coming decade by several thousand *if* there were a political will to do so.

7

Wisconsin's War on Drugs

During the era of mass incarceration, drug sentencing laws nationally took a sharply punitive turn, with tough new mandatory minimums playing a prominent role in many jurisdictions. Drug sentencing policies were developed in a politicized environment heavily influenced by penal populism, often emerging as ad hoc responses to specific cases or as election-year gambits for partisan advantage. Notwithstanding this fragmentary process of policy development, most changes in the 1980s and 1990s seemed to point in one direction: tougher sentences. And the new policies did indeed contribute to the imprisonment boom nationally: between 1985 and 2000, drug offenses accounted for more than one-quarter of the increase in state prisoners.[1]

In some respects, Wisconsin's War on Drugs closely paralleled the national experience. Between 1986 and 2000, Wisconsin added a host of new drug sentencing enhancements. For the most part, these were ad hoc, copycat reforms, much like the three-strikes law of 1994. Yet, even at the height of the War on Drugs, Wisconsin preserved more discretion in drug sentencing than many other jurisdictions. This helped to moderate the growth in Wisconsin's drug imprisonment in the 1990s and set the stage for a sharp drop in the state's drug imprisonment in the new millennium. Drug imprisonment has thus contributed much less to mass incarceration in Wisconsin than it has nationally. The common perception that our prisons are stuffed with nonviolent drug offenders simply does not hold true in Wisconsin.

This chapter recounts the history of drug enforcement and sentencing in Wisconsin from even before the imprisonment boom. In many respects, the drug story serves as a microcosm and recapitulation of the wider sentencing story. However, taking one particular offense area in depth permits a consideration of some topics that have been passed over glancingly in earlier chapters, such as the role of police discretion in contributing to imprisonment patterns.

Drug Sentencing in Wisconsin
before the Imprisonment Boom

Wisconsin adopted its first systematic drug control law in 1935, largely copying a federally sponsored model law, the Uniform Narcotic Drug Act.[2] The act regulated the possession, manufacturing, and selling of "any narcotic drug," including heroin, cocaine, and marijuana.[3] By later standards, penalties were relatively light: imprisonment for no more than three months for a first conviction and no more than five years for any subsequent conviction. The act also authorized judges to commit the unlawful user "to an institution for the treatment of drug addicts, for not less than six months, or until cured of his addiction to the use of narcotic drugs, but not exceeding one year."[4] Such provision for treatment in lieu of conventional incarceration would prove an enduring feature of Wisconsin law.

By 1967, Wisconsin's law had grown considerably harsher, with the addition of mandatory minimums, enhanced maximums, and additional penalties for sales to minors under age twenty-one. The penalty regime, which still did not distinguish marijuana from heroin or cocaine, is set forth in table 7.1.[5] As with Wisconsin's initial adoption of the Uniform Act, the subsequent shift to much tougher penalties also reflected the influence of federal models. Indeed, other than for sales to minors, Wisconsin's minimum and maximum penalties simply replicated the so-called Boggs Act, adopted by Congress in 1951.[6] "The premise [of the federal law]," observed President Lyndon Johnson's crime commission in 1967, "has been that the more certain and severe the punishment, the more it would serve as a deterrent."[7] The federal mandatory minimums reflected the long-held, zero-tolerance views of the head of the Federal Bureau of Narcotics, Harry Anslinger. Indeed, Anslinger, a former Prohibition agent, had advocated for mandatory minimum prison terms for *alcohol* purchases in the 1920s.[8] Yet the desire for a tough deterrent message did not entirely take rehabilitation out of the sentencing picture in Wisconsin. As under Wisconsin's original version of the Uniform Narcotic Drug Act, sentencing judges retained the discretion to sentence users to commitment in a state institution for addiction treatment.[9]

In 1972, Wisconsin entirely replaced the old Uniform Act with the new Uniform Controlled Substances Act (UCSA). As with the old law, the UCSA was a model state act developed with the close involvement of the federal government, this time on the orders of President Richard Nixon.[10] On the one hand, the UCSA flatly rejected the indiscriminate toughness of the Boggs Act mandatory minimums. Into state sentencing law came important distinctions between simple possession and distribution of drugs, and between soft and hard drugs. Yet, in other respects, the UCSA also reflected some of the strong antidrug

Table 7.1. Drug offense penalties, 1967

Offense	Sale to minor	Other violation (possession, distribution, manufacturing)
1st offense	Probation to 25 years of imprisonment	Probation to 10 years of imprisonment
2nd offense	20 years to life	5–10 years
3rd offense	Life	10–20 years

attitudes of President Nixon, who was elected in 1968 on a law-and-order platform that particularly targeted drug abuse. "No President has equaled Nixon's antagonism to drug abuse," observes a leading historian of drug control,[11] and he became the first to declare a "War on Drugs." Thus, while the UCSA rejected mandatory minimums, drug use and distribution remained decidedly criminal matters, and prison sentences could still be quite lengthy. The sentencing ranges in Wisconsin's version of the uniform law are summarized in table 7.2.[12] Notably, the maximum sentences for heroin distribution—a particular bête noir of Nixon's in this era of *The French Connection*—*increased* under the UCSA, even as the maximum cocaine and marijuana sentences went down.

Beyond the general liberalization of sentencing ranges, the UCSA model offered an even better deal in first-time possession cases: deferred prosecution and the possibility of a dismissal of charges and no criminal record upon the successful completion of probation. Here, again, Wisconsin simply followed the new model act. Additionally, in Wisconsin, court-supervised treatment also remained an option for *all* simple possession cases; this provision was not part of the national UCSA but was instead carried over from Wisconsin's pre-UCSA law. Notably, where Wisconsin chose to deviate from the national model, it was to provide for more rehabilitation.

Wisconsin's drug code also now included a "declaration of intent"—another unique feature that was not part of the generic national model and that still remains part of Wisconsin law.[13] The declaration particularly calls for differentiated sentencing approaches for different categories of drug offenders. For those who "traffic commercially" in illicit controlled substances, the approach should be a continuation of the severe sentences of the 1950s and 1960s: "The possibility of lengthy terms of imprisonment must exist as a deterrent to trafficking by such persons. . . . Persons who habitually or professionally engage in commercial trafficking in controlled substances and prescription drugs should, upon

Table 7.2. Drug offense penalties, 1972

Offense	Distribution to minor	Other distribution	Possession
Heroin (1st offense)	Up to 30 years in prison	Up to 15 years	Up to 1 year
Heroin (2nd offense)	Up to 60 years	Up to 30 years	Up to 2 years
Cocaine and marijuana (1st offense)	Up to 10 years	Up to 5 years	Up to 30 days
Cocaine and marijuana (2nd offense)	Up to 20 years	Up to 10 years	Up to 30 days

conviction, be sentenced to substantial terms of imprisonment to shield the public from their predatory acts." Contrasted with the commercial traffickers were the addicts and casual users. The legislature declared that they should "be sentenced in a manner most likely to produce rehabilitation." The dramatic reduction in penalties for simple possession obviously supported this objective, as did the new diversion option.

As Wisconsin stood on the threshold of three full decades of imprisonment growth, several enduring features of its drug sentencing system had emerged. First, the legislature had abandoned Harry Anslinger's vision of indiscriminate, mandatory, severe sentences for all drug crimes. Second, the legislature increasingly differentiated dealers from users, and heroin from cocaine and marijuana. Third, the legislature left sentencing judges with wide discretion when it came to implementing its basic deterrence and rehabilitation plan. Finally, the legislature had established a pattern of deferring to federal leadership on drug control and adopting federally endorsed models.

Rise and Fall of the War on Marijuana, 1972–1986

Once Wisconsin adopted the Uniform Controlled Substances Act template in 1972, the legislature made few changes to drug sentencing law over the next fourteen years. The only addition of note occurred in 1980, when the legislature doubled the maximum penalties for drug distribution to prisoners in correctional facilities. This narrowly targeted reform had no discernible impact on drug imprisonment rates, which remained remarkably consistent and low throughout the time period. Although the raw number of drug prisoners inched up year by year, the pace of growth almost exactly mirrored that of the prison population as a whole. Thus, by the end of 1985, the proportion of drug prisoners remained below 5 percent,[14] which was only slightly higher than it had been in the early 1970s. Wisconsin's prison population more than doubled over the time period, but drug imprisonment did not play a role of any particular prominence in fueling the imprisonment boom.

To be sure, drug *arrests* jumped sharply in the 1970s, reaching 12,835 in 1978—more than double what the number had been just six years earlier. However, the surge was almost entirely accounted for by a dramatic increase in the number of *juveniles* arrested for drug offenses, and their arrests were overwhelmingly (88 percent) for simple possession of marijuana. Given this population of arrestees, it should not be surprising that few were even charged and convicted, let alone imprisoned.[15] By the late 1970s, a decade after President Nixon had declared a national War on Drugs, action in the Wisconsin theater seemed largely confined to establishing a modest deterrent—a ride to the police station and perhaps a short stint in custody—for juvenile marijuana use.

Even as marijuana arrests climbed, the idea of decriminalizing the drug became increasingly popular nationally in the 1970s. A dozen states went this route,[16] and the Uniform Law Commission even amended the Uniform Controlled Substances Act in 1973 to decriminalize simple possession and not-for-profit distribution. Although Nixon remained bitterly opposed to any softening of the marijuana prohibition,[17] President Jimmy Carter endorsed decriminalization for possession of small amounts.[18]

Wisconsin came closest to decriminalization in the legislature's 1977 session, when a bill pushed by the National Organization for the Reform of Marijuana Laws drew significant support in the assembly. The NORML bill cleared the assembly's Health and Social Services Committee, as well as the powerful Joint Finance Committee.[19] However, the bill was effectively killed by a 54–41 vote in favor of further review by the State Affairs Committee. In the next legislative session, the NORML bill would not get even that far.

Nationally, too, the tide was turning against liberalization in the late 1970s, just as drug use was hitting its all-time peak. In 1978, more than 10 percent of high school seniors reported using marijuana *daily*.[20] Alarmed parents got organized and pushed legislators to take a tougher stance. Echoing their concerns, Ronald Reagan, running for president in 1980, painted Carter as soft on drugs. His election and, a few years later, his wife's energetic "Just Say No" campaign as First Lady signaled a national revival of Harry Anslinger's hard line on drugs and an eclipse of the UCSA's more nuanced, rehabilitation-supporting approach.

Despite the national political shift, as the 1970s gave way to the 1980s, Wisconsin's drug sentencing laws remained essentially frozen in their 1972 form. Arrest data, however, pointed to major changes in the way that Wisconsin's law enforcement agencies were fighting the War on Drugs. Drug arrests dropped sharply between 1978 and 1985, largely resulting from a two-thirds decrease in juvenile arrests.[21] As drug enforcement focused more squarely on adults, the composition of drug cases entering the criminal justice system shifted markedly. Marijuana cases remained easily the most common, but the number of cocaine and heroin arrests more than doubled. Similarly, distribution arrests remained a minority but also increased significantly. In short, over the early 1980s, Wisconsin's War on Drugs started to shift from an assault on juvenile marijuana use to an attack on heroin and cocaine distribution. This shift, moreover, had significant racial implications. While blacks always supplied a small and roughly proportionate segment of the marijuana arrests, they represented an increasingly large share of those arrested for more serious drug offenses. For instance, by 1985, while blacks constituted only 7 percent of those arrested for marijuana possession, they accounted for fully 42 percent of those arrested for heroin or cocaine distribution. Overall, the black proportion of drug arrests more than doubled between 1978 and 1985.

All of the Wisconsin drug-arrest trends (less white, less juvenile, less possession, less marijuana) mirrored national trends. It is not entirely clear what drove these trends, either nationally or in Wisconsin. Indeed, there is a certain irony that at precisely the time that marijuana decriminalization ceased to be a politically viable policy option, police shifted their law enforcement focus from marijuana possession. Part of the story, no doubt, was a decrease in drug use; all else being equal, reduced usage should naturally translate into fewer drug arrests. And indications were that the parents' movement was having an impact on attitudes. For instance, in 1978, only 35 percent of high school seniors agreed that smoking marijuana regularly was harmful, but that number climbed to 70 percent over the next seven years. Rates of reported use by high school seniors declined accordingly.[22]

Was there a conscious reorientation of law enforcement resources from marijuana to the "hard" drugs? Probably not. Most of the reduction in marijuana arrests occurred in Milwaukee, but there was no corresponding increase in the number of arrests for hard drugs or distribution in Wisconsin's largest city. Rather, the evidence suggests that police and prosecutors in Milwaukee had their hands full with a wave of violent crime. Between 1978 and 1981, the city's robbery rate exploded from 194 per 100,000 residents to 284, and then continued to grow to 341 in 1985. Police struggled to keep up. The robbery clearance rate (that is, the proportion of robberies resulting in an arrest) plummeted from 66 percent to 32 percent over the same time period. With such a crisis of "real" crime, the Milwaukee Police Department can hardly be blamed for deciding that it simply wasn't worth the bother to continue busting juveniles for marijuana possession.

Data generated for the first Wisconsin sentencing guidelines project give an unusually clear picture of drug sentencing during this transitional period, as the war on marijuana peaked and then started to decline. As described in chapter 3, in connection with the development of the guidelines, Sandra Shane-DuBow and her colleagues undertook a comprehensive analysis of felony sentencing between 1977 and 1981, including hundreds of drug cases. Of course, since simple possession of marijuana and cocaine were misdemeanors, these offenses were not included in the study, which was accordingly skewed toward distribution and heroin. Yet, even at that, more than three-quarters of the defendants received probation sentences.[23] Among those sent to prison, the average term was slightly over three years—subject to the highly discretionary parole system that existed before 1984.[24] Multivariate regression analysis found that the factors that tended to add the most to sentence length, holding all else constant, were drug type, with narcotics (heroin) producing the longest sentences; sale to a minor or a prisoner; incarceration at the time of conviction; and membership in a minority racial group.[25] As we saw in chapter 6, there have been recurring concerns in Wisconsin that the War on Drugs has particularly targeted African Americans for disproportionately harsh treatment.

The War on Cocaine, 1986–2002

In the 1970s, Wisconsin's War on Drugs was really a war on marijuana—a police action that came and went without much impact on imprisonment. The surge of several thousand additional drug arrests per year simply did not translate into many additional prisoners. By the mid-1980s, though, the first signs of a new war on cocaine were apparent. This new emphasis on cocaine would result in much greater changes to Wisconsin's drug sentencing laws and would produce many more inmates for Wisconsin's prisons. The UCSA, as originally drafted and then adopted by Wisconsin, had placed cocaine into the same severity class as marijuana. However, the war on cocaine effectively resulted in the substance's recategorization as a hard drug in the same class as heroin.

Changes in Wisconsin largely mirrored changes nationally. The United States of the mid and late 1980s was in full-blown panic mode when it came to cocaine. Historian David Musto has noted the cyclical nature of American attitudes toward cocaine, in which "the perception of cocaine [changes] from that of an apparently harmless, perhaps ideal, tonic for one's spirits or to get more work done, to that of a fearful substance whose seductiveness in its early stages of ingestion only heightens the necessity of denouncing it."[26] In the 1970s and early 1980s, cocaine's reputation was going through one of its positive phases.

The cocaine-related death of actor John Belushi in 1982 may have served as something of a wakeup call, but it also reinforced cocaine's reputation as a glamorous, celebrity drug. Within a few years, though, crack changed everything. Cocaine came to be seen as an insidious drug of the black underclass, linked to a national surge in violent crime and the deepening of ghetto misery.

The crack form of cocaine offered a high that was particularly quick, intense, and cheap. It first appeared in several American cities in the mid-1980s.[27] Hard-core crack users tended to be young, unemployed blacks.[28] Violent gangs handled much of the lucrative distribution business, and their armed confrontations became regular headline fodder beginning in 1985. Public concern seemed to reach a peak in the summer of 1986 in the wake of the overdose death of college basketball star Len Bias, which was repeatedly and incorrectly attributed to crack.

Following Bias's death, national politicians almost immediately put anti-crack legislation on a fast track in Congress, aiming to produce a new law before the November elections.[29] Mandatory minimums for dealing crack would be the centerpiece. There was broad agreement that crack sentences should be tougher than regular ("powder") cocaine sentences, but how much tougher defied logical analysis. One aide described the legislative process as simply "pulling numbers out of the air."[30] Congress ultimately settled on the now-notorious 100:1 ratio—the mandatory minimums for crack would be triggered by quantities that were only 1/100 of the quantities of powder cocaine associated with the same minimums. Thus, for instance, 500 grams of powder would net you a five-year minimum, but you would face the same punishment for a mere five grams of crack.

Wisconsin lawmakers moved even more quickly, albeit with much less harsh results. In May 1986, Democratic governor Anthony Earl, facing reelection in the fall, called a special session of the legislature for various specific purposes, including "increasing the penalties for the possession, manufacture, or delivery of cocaine." The Democratic legislature complied with stunning rapidity, passing Earl's bill just two days after it was introduced.

The path had been paved by the work of Wisconsin's Cocaine Task Force, which was sponsored by the State Council on Alcohol and Other Drug Abuse and chaired by assembly Democrat John Medinger. Following its creation in 1985, the task force consulted with national experts on drug abuse and conducted five public hearings across the state, at which participants repeatedly called for tougher penalties.[31] The task force issued its alarmist *Final Report* in April 1986, a month before Governor Earl introduced his cocaine bill. "[C]ocaine," the task force declared, "is an extremely serious problem that has reached epidemic proportions. . . . Instead of being the benign substance which is commonly believed, cocaine is one of the most addictive substances known."[32] The task force insisted that "drug abuse must be treated as a public health problem" and drew analogies to communicable diseases.[33] Yet the task force's first policy recommendation was to increase penalties for both distribution and simple possession. In part, this reflected the task force's comparative assessment of cocaine penalties across the United States, which revealed that Wisconsin's were among the nation's most lenient; the thirty-day maximum for simple possession, for instance, ranked fiftieth out of fifty states and paled by comparison to the national average of nearly six years.[34] The task force concluded that Wisconsin needed tougher sentences to achieve greater deterrence.

Largely following the task force's lead, Governor Earl's cocaine bill, as introduced, contained three key sentencing features. First, the bill revived the concept of mandatory minimums, which had been abandoned only fourteen years earlier with passage of the Uniform Controlled Substances Act. Earl's minimums were comparatively modest—just six months or one year, depending on the volume involved—but established a precedent for the tougher minimums that would be adopted in subsequent years. Second, the bill introduced into Wisconsin law the concept of weight-based sentence enhancements for drug distribution. While distributing as much as thirteen grams of cocaine could result in any sentence up to five years, more than thirteen grams would trigger a six-month mandatory minimum, and more than fifty-five grams a one-year minimum. Exceeding fifty-five grams also triggered an enhanced, fifteen-year *maximum*. Such a weight-based sentencing system had precedent in the federal Controlled Substances Penalties Amendments Act of 1984. Third, and finally, the maximum penalty for simple possession of cocaine was raised from thirty days to one year. The overall effect of these three features was to sharply distinguish cocaine from marijuana, which had been lumped together under the Uniform Controlled Substances Act, and to move cocaine much closer to heroin.

With its proud tradition of wide judicial sentencing discretion, Wisconsin did not adopt Earl's mandatory minimums without a fight. Introduced into the senate, the governor's bill was referred to the Committee on Judiciary and

Consumer Affairs, chaired by Lynn Adelman, the liberal senator with an impressive track record of quietly killing or watering down tough-on-crime proposals. Adelman likely would have been happy to keep Earl's bill in his committee indefinitely, but the closer media scrutiny and political pressures of a special session made simple neglect a problematic strategy. Adelman thus adopted a more direct plan of attack. At his behest, the Judiciary Committee simply stripped the mandatory minimums from the bill. At the same time, however, perhaps reflecting a compromise within the committee, the triggering weight for the fifteen-year maximum was reduced from fifty-five to thirty grams. Thus modified, the cocaine bill then swiftly passed the full senate.

Although Adelman and his fellow senate liberals were often quite successful in the 1980s in holding in check the assembly's tougher-on-crime inclinations, it was the assembly that prevailed on the 1986 cocaine bill. First, conservative Democrats led by Milwaukee's Louise Tesmer restored Governor Earl's mandatory minimums. Then, Tommy Thompson, the minority leader and soon to be anointed as Earl's opponent in the gubernatorial election, secured passage of a series of amendments to further toughen the bill. Most notably, Thompson introduced a school zone provision, which increased the maximum sentence by five years for cocaine distribution within a thousand feet of a school building. The provision's drafting file indicates that the concept had been borrowed—like so much else in Wisconsin drug law—from federal precedent; the Controlled Substances Penalties Amendments Act had also included a similar school zone enhancement. A large share of the Wisconsin Legislature's drug-control efforts over the next four years would be devoted to extending this protected-zone concept in various ways.

The assembly adopted the toughened cocaine bill by an overwhelming 94–4 margin, and, in an election-year special session, the senate had no stomach for a fight. Adelman's motion to strip the mandatory minimums from the bill failed, and the assembly's version became law in short order.

The 1986 cocaine law established the template for the way the legislature would fight the War on Drugs over the coming years. Despite the turn to increased harshness, Wisconsin law never returned to the indiscriminate toughness of pre-UCSA days. Rather, Wisconsin continued to distinguish sharply between distribution and simple possession, and between heroin and marijuana. If the UCSA's sentencing structure can be analogized to a house, several additions have been completed since 1972, but much of the original architectural scheme is still apparent. Still, the structure has become rather ungainly. As printed in the Wisconsin Code, the UCSA's sentencing provisions grew from a mere three pages in 1985 to seven by 1997.

In 1988, the legislature essentially normalized the 1986 cocaine sentencing system as the general system for all drugs of concern.[35] Leading the charge were assembly Democrat Peter Barca from Kenosha, which was always among the state leaders in number of drug arrests, and Republican attorney general Donald Hanaway, who had promised to focus on drugs after his election in 1986.[36] Their bill extended the weight-based approach from cocaine distribution to heroin, methamphetamine, LSD, and marijuana, with six-month and one-year mandatory minimums associated with higher-volume distribution. Additionally, the five-year school zone enhancement for cocaine distribution was extended to all controlled substances.[37] Even simple possession of marijuana saw a severity increase, with the maximum sentence raised to six months for a first offense and one year for a second. This reflected a national trend in the late 1980s to try to ensure greater accountability for all drug offenses no matter how minor,[38] shades of Harry Anslinger. At about the same time, Congress was adopting a five-year mandatory minimum for simple possession of crack.

By now, the tough-on-drug laws were coming fast and furious. In 1989, the legislature expanded the school zone law yet again.[39] First, the protected zones were extended to include parks, public pools, youth and community centers, and school buses. Then, a three-year mandatory minimum was added to the penalty for distributing heroin, cocaine, or marijuana in any of the protected zones (or just one year for a small quantity of marijuana). And, as if the prison terms were not enough, the legislature also mandated one hundred hours of community service and a loss of driver's license for protected-zone violations. Included in the biennial budget bill, these changes were able to avoid a potentially fatal referral to Lynn Adelman's Judiciary Committee.

But these amendments to the school zone law proved only a preliminary foray by the 1989–90 legislature into the drug arena. National polls were indicating that drugs had become the nation's number one public concern,[40] and individual legislators responded by introducing a multitude of new bills on the topic. Pressure for a major new reform package came particularly from two directions. Initially, three Democratic legislators began to press for Governor Thompson to call a special session of the legislature to adopt increased penalties for "drug kingpins."[41] As they put it in a letter to the governor, "While we properly spend a lot of money on drug education to prevent people from becoming abusers, it is clear that a tougher focus on the drug pusher is long overdue." With the expansion of the school zone law *less than three weeks old*, the letter may have slightly stretched the meaning of "long overdue," but it is fair to say that the proponents had in mind an extraordinary ratcheting up of penalties for the highest-volume traffickers; their minimums would be upped from one to ten years and their maximums from fifteen to thirty. The legislators' concerns specifically focused on cocaine, which was said to account for over half of the value of all illegal drugs sold in Wisconsin. But why a special session? Senator Joseph Andrea, one of the three proponents, publicly cited a desire to circumvent

Lynn Adelman's Judiciary Committee.[42] In any event, Governor Thompson, never one to allow the Democrats to outflank him to the right on crime issues, did call a special session in the fall of 1989.

A second key initiative was the Task Force for a Drug Free Milwaukee, which was established in September 1989 and co-chaired by a pair of Democrats, U.S. senator Herb Kohl and Milwaukee's fiery young mayor, John Norquist.[43] The Task Force focused on obtaining enhanced funding for drug education, treatment, and enforcement efforts but also called on the legislature to increase penalties. "Drug treatment is important and needed, but not enough," the task force opined. "If we are to be successful, we urgently need a combination of drug enforcement, prevention, education, and treatment programs."

The work of the task force proceeded parallel to the legislature's special session in the fall of 1989 and early winter of 1990. A Milwaukee prosecutor acted as a liaison between the two efforts and helped to ensure that the law finally passed in Madison in January would embody many of the task force's priorities, including longer sentences for drug traffickers.

Was all of this just a matter of crass politics? It was certainly disingenuous to suggest that the legislature had been ignoring penalties, and perhaps ill-advised to adopt a fifth wave of sentence increases in less than four years—much too soon for anyone to know the costs and benefits of the earlier get-tough efforts. There can be little doubt that political considerations must have figured prominently in many legislators' minds as they put together and enacted the special session drug law.

On the other hand, putting the superficial political posturing to one side, there were good reasons for Wisconsinites to view cocaine with increasing concern over the course of the 1980s. The 1986 Cocaine Task Force found that the drug had become much cheaper and more readily available in Wisconsin beginning in 1982, and documented corresponding sharp increases in cocaine-related overdose deaths and emergency room admissions by the mid-1980s.[44] Moreover, cocaine trafficking was becoming a significant quality-of-life issue in some Wisconsin communities in this time period. The Milwaukee Police Department set up a new "Community Against Pushers" hotline in October 1984, and within six months had received about 1,300 drug trafficking complaints, the vast majority of which related to cocaine dealing.[45] Janine Geske, who served at the time as an elected circuit court judge in Milwaukee, recalls hearing a great deal of frustration from community groups over drug-related crime.[46] These groups saw firsthand the adverse effects of drug houses, such as increased muggings in the neighborhood, and worked to draw police attention to the problem. Even when the police took action, however, group members were often disappointed to see the dealers out on bail shortly after arrest and ultimately receiving probationary sentences. Frustrated by such seeming impunity, many Wisconsinites demanded tougher penalties. When the legislature scheduled a public hearing on the special session bill, only one hour was initially set aside for public comment, but the length grew to nearly five hours due to the unexpectedly large number of people who turned out to voice their opinions, mostly in favor of stiffer sentences.[47]

In any event, whatever their actual necessity, the complexity and ambition of the special session reforms were beyond doubt. Among other things, they required schools to adopt disciplinary policies for drug violations by students, regulated the use of electronic communication devices on school premises, required juvenile courts to impose additional penalties in drug cases, made it easier for the government to seize the property of drug offenders, criminalized the use or possession of drug paraphernalia, criminalized the *attempted* possession of drugs, criminalized the use of a juvenile for drug distribution, established a drug court in Milwaukee County, authorized the adoption of ordinances by local government imposing civil penalties for marijuana possession, and facilitated the use of electronic surveillance against drug suspects.

In the sentencing area, the special session added new layers to the weight-based severity scheme, introducing enhanced penalty ranges for higher-volume distributors. These reforms were in line with the calls for tougher sentences for "drug kingpins," which had been the principal focus of the legislators who requested the special session. The special session also created a new sentence enhancement for the use of public transit as part of a drug distribution offense.

But the special session's most important sentencing reform was directed specifically to the perceived menace of crack. Previously, Wisconsin law had recognized no difference between the powder and crack forms of cocaine. Now, however—once again following the federal lead—Wisconsin adopted much tougher penalties for crack. If the 1986 law had moved cocaine from the severity level of marijuana to nearly that of heroin, the 1990 law then moved crack well beyond even heroin. Indeed, as indicated in table 7.3, for any given level of crack, a person might need twenty to forty times as much powder to trigger the same statutory minimum prison term.[48] Although this was not as sharp a disparity as the federal system's infamous 100:1 ratio, it nonetheless signaled dramatically different attitudes toward the two forms of cocaine. Also noteworthy was the absence of *any* triggering quantity for the one-year minimum—distributing any amount of crack, no matter how small, would bring at least one year behind bars.

Yet, amid all of this toughening, the 1990 drug sentencing law included one notable softening provision, as Senator Lynn Adelman continued his tenacious resistance to mandatory minimums. After the bill passed the assembly, a

Table 7.3. Triggering weight of drugs for statutory minimums, 1990 law

Drug	1 year	3 years	5 years	10 years
Crack cocaine	>0 g	>3 g	>10 g	>40 g
Powder cocaine	>25 g	>100 g	>400 g	>800 g
Heroin	>10 g	>50 g	>200 g	>400 g

conference committee was formed to make modifications necessary to secure approval in the senate. Adelman sat on the committee, as did his colleague Gary George, the powerful African American Democrat from Milwaukee who shared some of Adelman's reservations about tough-on-crime legislation. At Adelman's behest, George had a safety valve added to the bill:[49] "Any minimum sentence under this chapter is a presumptive minimum sentence. . . . [T]he court may impose a sentence that is less than the presumptive minimum sentence or may place the person on probation only if it finds that the best interests of the community will be served and the public will not be harmed and if it places its reasons on the record."[50] Thus modified, the bill passed the senate unanimously and the assembly 89–9. The presumptive minimum provision seemed to attract little attention, and it is unclear whether many of the legislators who voted for the 1990 law were even aware of this brief, last-minute addition to a long bill.

The 1990 law proved something of a high-water mark for the tough-on-drugs era in the Wisconsin Legislature. No more mandatory or presumptive minimums would be adopted for drug offenses, and the legislature would not add to the extensive menu of drug sentence enhancements. Still, operating within the basic framework that was in place at the decade's start, the legislature nonetheless managed to augment the system's severity through a series of laws adopted over the 1990s. In 1991, the legislature toughened penalties for marijuana distribution and required a suspension of driving privileges—previously only mandated for distribution in a protected zone—for *all* violations of the controlled substances law, including simple possession.[51] In 1996, in a statutory reorganization freighted with symbolism, the legislature moved the entire set of controlled substances laws, previously located with other public health measures, into the state's criminal code.[52] In 1998, as discussed in chapter 6, the legislature raised maximum penalties across the board by 50 percent for drug-distribution offenses as part of the more general increases included in the truth-in-sentencing (TIS) law.[53] Finally, as a coda to the tough-on-drugs era in 2000, the legislature

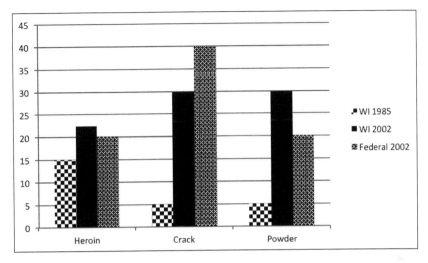

Figure 7.1. Maximum sentence for distribution, 30 grams (first offense), Wisconsin and federal systems, 1985 and 2002

raised the penalties for meth distribution, bringing the weight-based ranges into conformity with those used in heroin cases.[54]

During this era, only one aspect of the new drug sentencing laws seemed to engender major controversy. As in other jurisdictions that boosted crack penalties in the 1980s, the crack-powder disparity in Wisconsin was criticized on racial grounds. Given the close association of crack with urban blacks, tougher sentences for crack were believed to contribute to Wisconsin's racial disparities in imprisonment.[55] The legislature responded by eliminating the crack-powder disparity in 1993. Characteristically, though, this was accomplished not so much by reducing crack sentences as by increasing sentences for powder.[56] When all was said and done, the statutory penalties for powder, as for crack, had grown considerably tougher than even those for heroin.

By 2002, Wisconsin's drug sentencing regime was clearly much more severe than it had been in 1985. This was most especially the case with cocaine distribution offenses, but penalties had also been significantly raised for distribution of other drugs and even for simple possession. Figure 7.1, for instance, compares the maximum penalties for distribution of thirty grams of heroin, crack cocaine, and powder cocaine in the two years.[57] Even this figure understates the real scope of the change, for it does not indicate that a defendant possessing thirty grams in 2002 would have been subject to a presumptive minimum of either one year (heroin) or three years (crack and powder), and would have faced the possibility of many additional enhancers, such as the five-year increase for distribution in a protected zone. Figure 7.1 also indicates that the Wisconsin maximums were roughly in line with the federal maximums, although the federal system was still probably tougher as a whole based on its use of mandatory (not presumptive) minimums and its harsh presumptive sentencing guidelines.

Table 7.4 reveals Wisconsin's prolific addition of sentence-enhancing provisions during the war on cocaine era.[58] As has normally been the case with the state's drug laws, Wisconsin was more follower than leader. A 1999 study by the National Criminal Justice Association found replication of many of the same provisions in state after state.[59] For instance, all forty-nine other states had a school zone law, while twenty-seven others had an enhancement for use of a child to distribute drugs. Several of these enhancers had also worked their way into the oft-revised model Uniform Controlled Substances Act.

Despite all of the statutory changes in the 1980s and 1990s, Wisconsin preserved at least two key features of the UCSA as it had originally been enacted by the state in 1972. First, the judge's sentencing discretion continued to be emphasized. Minimums were presumptive, not mandatory; judges could circumvent them in the "best interests of the community." Enhancers, moreover, tended to increase maximums to a much greater extent than minimums; their net effect was to give judges considerably wider ranges within which to sentence and hence more power over punishment, not less. Additionally, Wisconsin never went in for some of the most draconian minimums adopted in the federal system, such as the five-year mandatory minimum for even simple possession of crack and mandatory life terms for three drug convictions. It is fair to wonder how deeply committed Wisconsin's policymakers really were to ensuring reliably longer prison terms for drug distribution. In any event, it is clear that such a policy aim did not lead to dramatic departures from the general preference for judicial discretion and individualized punishment that we have seen reflected in Wisconsin sentencing policy throughout the era of mass incarceration.

Second, Wisconsin law continued to make sharp distinctions between distributors and mere users and to provide treatment-based alternatives for the latter. To be sure, Wisconsin did not entirely avoid the national trend toward increased accountability for users in the late 1980s and early 1990s. If convicted of any drug offense, a user faced mandatory suspension of driving privileges. Moreover, if convicted of simple possession in certain protected zones, the user would also be required to perform a hundred hours of community service. Yet Wisconsin law never eliminated the option of conditional discharge for a first-time possession offense, as adopted in 1972. Wisconsin judges also retained the option of permitting even repeat possession offenders to undergo treatment in lieu of sentencing. Additionally, the authorization in 1990 of local ordinances

Table 7.4. Sentence enhancers for drug offenses, 1985 and 2002

1985	2002	UCSA
Second or subsequent offense	Second or subsequent offense	Yes
Distribution to minor	Distribution to minor	Yes
Distribution to prisoner	Distribution to prisoner	No
	Weight-based enhancements for distribution	Yes
	Use of a child for drug distribution or manufacturing	Yes
	Distribution in school zone	Yes
	Distribution in public housing zone	No
	Distribution in public pool zone	No
	Distribution in youth or community center zone	No
	Distribution in school bus zone	No
	Distribution in drug or alcohol treatment facility zone	No
	Use of public transit in distribution offense	No

providing civil penalties for certain drug offenses offered police an alternative to referring low-level offenders to the district attorney for criminal prosecution.

Thus far, we have considered the war-on-cocaine era as a legislative phenomenon. To what extent, though, did the extraordinary flurry of tough-on-drugs legislative activity in the 1980s and 1990s actually produce increased imprisonment?

Perhaps surprisingly, average sentences in drug cases did not change much. The first Wisconsin Sentencing Commission collected data on drug-distribution sentences in the early 1990s after the adoption of all of the new presumptive minimums.[60] Although organized a bit differently, the commission data make for an interesting comparison with the Shane-DuBow drug sentencing study of a decade earlier. Demographically, the earlier and later offender populations looked quite similar in education, employment, and many other respects, although the later group was markedly less white (down from 74 percent to 53 percent) and more likely to have a prior felony conviction (up to 26 percent from 7 percent). However, neither the offenders' greater criminal history nor all of the new tough-on-drugs laws caused imprisonment to become the sentencing norm; the great majority of drug-distribution convictions in the early 1990s—fully 60 percent—resulted in sentences of probation. Moreover, among those who were sentenced to prison, the average term had barely increased from 3.1 to 3.3 years.

It is easy enough to see why the presumptive minimums did not have more of an impact: only 17 percent of the convictions carried a minimum of at least one year, and only 4 percent carried a minimum of at least three years. These numbers, in turn, reflected the substances involved: nearly 90 percent of the convictions were for marijuana or powder cocaine distribution. Although powder was now being treated more severely than marijuana, the legislature had not yet raised powder to the same level as crack. The two substances with the stiffest minimums, heroin and crack, accounted for only 0.7 percent and 5.7 percent of the caseload, respectively. Moreover, the quantities charged tended to be modest: for nearly two-thirds of the charges, the value of the drugs involved was noted as $500 or less. Similarly, more than 86 percent of the charges involved individuals at the lowest end of the distribution chain—the "pusher/seller." So much for the legislature's goal of targeting the "kingpins." The higher-level dealers avoided apprehension or were prosecuted in federal court under federal law.[61]

Nor were the many new enhancers listed in table 7.4 used very often in practice; the commission data indicate that fewer than 13 percent of charges were enhanced based on protected-zone violations or other special statutory considerations.

Where minimums did kick in, judges not infrequently took advantage of their merely presumptive character. For instance, in 17 percent of the cases carrying a minimum of three years or more, the judge imposed a *probationary* sentence instead.

All of these tendencies softened the impact of the new minimums on average sentence length. Yet to focus only on overall drug sentencing averages is to miss very real changes that did occur with respect to *cocaine* sentencing. Consider this. From the perspective of, say, 1980, it would be very surprising to learn that average drug sentences were remaining about the same despite the *almost complete disappearance of heroin offenses* from the docket. In the older Shane-DuBow study, 19 percent of the charges had involved heroin,[62] and the presence of heroin had been found to be a leading driver of longer sentences. By the early 1990s, though, cocaine cases were far surpassing heroin in frequency and were accounting for more than half of the total distribution charges. Given this shift in the drug docket, one might have expected a marked *decrease* in overall severity if sentencing practices remained the same. The fact that average severity did not drop indicates that cocaine sentences had become much tougher. As the statutory changes contemplated, cocaine was now being treated by the judges much more like heroin than like marijuana. Average sentences remained fairly constant because the disappearance of heroin cases was offset by increased toughness in the cocaine cases.

Given the merely presumptive character of the new minimums, judges were not *required* to boost their cocaine sentences. Nonetheless, all of the new drug sentencing laws likely contributed to increased cocaine sentences in at least three ways. First, dramatically increased maximum sentences gave much more room for longer sentences in the most aggravated cases and also gave more opportunity for the true drug-warrior judges to go to their preferred extremes. Expanded sentencing headroom could thus push up the average cocaine penalty even without regard to the effect of the minimums. Some sense of the importance of the increased maximums comes from this rather startling fact: at the higher-volume levels, the *average* cocaine-distribution sentence in the early 1990s had grown longer than what the *maximum* had been a decade earlier.[63]

Second, even though the minimums were not binding, they proved a very influential benchmark in the cases to which they applied. For instance, for charges with a three-year minimum, the modal (most common) sentence was precisely three years. For charges with a ten-year minimum, the median and mode were both exactly ten years. Likewise, in powder cases subject to the five-year minimum, the median and modal sentences were both five years. For the most part, judges seem to have regarded these minimums as being at the high end of propriety and declined to go above them very often. Yet, in a strongly antidrug political context, in which the legislature had specifically endorsed these minimums, judges seemed about equally disinclined to go below them. To be sure, the minimums did not apply to a large percentage of drug cases, but the minimums were sufficiently common and sufficiently followed to help boost the overall cocaine averages.

Third, and finally, there is another mechanism by which the presumptive minimums may have effectively toughened drug sentencing in a way that would not show up in the Sentencing Commission data. Even though a case is not formally *sentenced* as a minimum case, the possibility of a minimum may nonetheless shape the terms of the *plea agreement*. The commission data indicate that drug-distribution defendants pleaded guilty or no contest to 92 percent of the charges against them in the early 1990s—a strong indication of pervasive plea bargaining, and somewhat higher than the 84 percent reported by Shane-DuBow a decade earlier. We cannot know precisely to what extent this increased bargaining was influenced by the overhanging shadow of a presumptive minimum, but it is very likely that many defendants pleaded guilty to more serious charges than they would have without the threat of a minimum, or accepted more aggressive sentencing recommendations from the prosecutor.

For instance, consider a defendant arrested while carrying a certain quantity of powder cocaine in a school zone. The prosecutor would like to secure a conviction for possession with intent to distribute, but the defendant maintains that the cocaine was for personal use, and he stands a decent chance of winning on this point at trial. However, the prosecutor can threaten the three-year presumptive minimum for a school zone violation. Recognizing this big downside risk to going to trial, the defendant might be willing to plead guilty to the distribution offense in return for the prosecutor dropping the school zone charge. Thus, as a result of the minimum, the defendant may be sentenced as a distributor rather than a simple possessor. In this way, the minimum is apt to drive up the defendant's sentence even though the minimum has not been formally applied by the judge.

The corrections data plainly reflect the impact of the war on cocaine. Recall that drug offenders accounted for only 4 percent of Wisconsin's prisoner population in 1973, and their portion remained a mere 4.5 percent in 1986 as Governor Earl was launching the war on cocaine. The drug portion nearly tripled over the next six years, which coincides with the period of greatest legislative activity in the drug area.[64] The number stabilized in the mid-1990s but then resumed its growth at the end of the decade, eventually reaching 14.6 percent in 2002. In July of that year, 3,204 Wisconsinites were imprisoned for drug crimes—nearly fourteen times the number from 1986. Cocaine (crack and powder) drove the surge, accounting for 59 percent of Wisconsin's drug prisoners by 2004.[65] Nearly two-thirds of these cases involved five grams or less, and about 90 percent of these low-level cocaine cases involved black defendants.

The surge in drug imprisonment resulted in part from the lengthening of cocaine sentences, which, in turn, resulted in part from the various increases in statutory minimums and maximums. These changes in drug sentencing law were amplified by at least two additional developments. First, drug-distribution arrests tripled between 1986 and 2001. Changing police priorities and tactics pushed more drug defendants into the system at the front end, making it practically inevitable that there would also be more at the back end (prison). Second, the phasing out of parole meant that the lengthening of judge-imposed sentences would have a greater impact on the imprisonment numbers.

Significantly, the biggest jump in drug prisoners in absolute terms occurred between 1996 and 2000. The only change in drug sentencing law coinciding with this burst in drug imprisonment was the equalization of penalties for crack and powder, which likely played a significant role.[66] The law effectively raised the presumptive minimums for powder, and we have already seen evidence from the early 1990s that judges tended to impose the minimum in powder cases. Perhaps even more important, though, was the tightening of discretionary parole that occurred even before truth in sentencing officially took effect. The earlier liberalization of parole helped to restrain the impact of increasingly tough drug sentences. Indeed, in the mid-1990s, when discretionary releases were at their height, the percentage of prisoners serving time for drug crimes actually fell a bit. After the de facto end of parole, the drug portion of the prison population grew even as the drug portion of prison *admissions* dropped. This indicates that the swelling numbers of drug inmates in that time period owed more to delayed releases and longer real prison terms than to the entry of new drug offenders into the system.

Whatever the relative importance of the various drivers of drug imprisonment—more aggressive policing and prosecuting, longer sentences, and the elimination of parole—it is important to bear in mind that the War on Drugs never had quite the impact in Wisconsin that it did elsewhere. In 2001, for instance, drug offenders accounted for more than 20 percent of prisoners nationally—nearly half again as much as in Wisconsin.[67] Moreover, in Wisconsin, the growth in drug imprisonment, impressive though it was, accounted for less than 18 percent of the total increase in imprisonment over the 1986–2001 time period. Indeed, even if Wisconsin had released all of its inmates imprisoned on drug charges in 2002, the state's prison population would still have been about nine times higher than it had been in the early 1970s. The War on Drugs did matter in the history of mass incarceration in Wisconsin, but much less so than many critics assume.

Rehabilitation's Revival, 2002–2016

Adopted in 2002, Wisconsin's truth-in-sentencing implementation legislation might be seen as the end of the war-on-cocaine era. As discussed in chapter 6, "TIS II" disappointed many who hoped for a more thorough rollback of the across-the-board, 50 percent increase in maximum sentences established by TIS I. Although the Criminal Penalties Study Committee—the source of the TIS II bill—chose to retain the enhanced maximums for many violent and sexual offenses, the committee did soften sentencing laws in some other areas, and drug crime may have been the single most important of these. Most significantly, TIS II eliminated all of the presumptive *minimum* sentences that had accumulated in the statutes, like barnacles on the bottom of a boat, since 1986. Additionally, TIS II decreased the *maximum* sentences for cocaine distribution at all volume levels. The net effect was more or less to bring cocaine back into line with heroin.

The basic TIS II drug sentencing regime has proven durable, remaining intact through the mid-2010s even as heroin has reemerged as a major public concern—resuming its long-running, back-and-forth competition with cocaine as Public Drug Enemy No. 1. Cynics suggest that the heroin story of the 2010s is

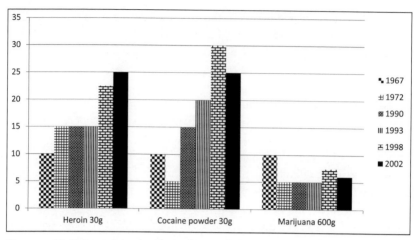

Figure 7.2. Maximum sentence for distribution (first offense), 1967–2002

playing out differently than the crack story of the 1980s because heroin is seen as a "white drug," while crack was thought to be a "black drug"; white legislators are perhaps less likely to pass tough new minimums when they can more easily identify with the offenders on whom the sentences will be imposed. (In retrospect, this tendency may help to explain why there were no sentence increases associated with the war on marijuana, which had been directed overwhelmingly against white juveniles.) In any event, figure 7.2 ties together the long-term trends in drug sentencing law, depicting the particular volatility of cocaine sentencing.[68]

Did the statutory softening under TIS II have an effect on actual sentencing practice? A study released by the second Wisconsin Sentencing Commission in 2007 suggested that not much changed in sentencing practice in the immediate wake of the massive sentencing reform.[69] Based on data from 2003–6, the commission found that 57 percent of drug-distribution defendants received probation—down just slightly from the 60 percent reported by the first commission in 1992—and the average prison term (initial confinement) was two years. At first blush, the latter number might seem a significant reduction from the 3.3-year average of 1992, but recall that none of these sentences from 2003–6 could be reduced through parole. In 1992, the very longest a prisoner would have served on a three-year term would have been two years, with a possibility of release in less than half that time. In other words, *real* sentences for drug distribution in 2003–6 were probably a bit longer than they had been in the early 1990s. As we will see, however, Wisconsin did stand by that time on the cusp of a sharp decline in drug imprisonment.

Notably, Wisconsin's abandonment of drug minimums in 2002 reflected broader national trends—a general turning away, it seemed, from the harsh deterrence-based approaches of the War on Drugs. In 1998, for instance, Michigan scaled back its "650-lifer" law, which was reputed to be the nation's toughest drug legislation for its use of mandatory life-without-parole sentences. Likewise, in 2004, New York softened the "Rockefeller Drug Laws," whose adoption in 1973 had inspired Michigan and other states to adopt their drug minimums. In 2010, even Congress backed off a little on the federal crack minimums. Consistent with such legislative trends, opinion surveys indicated that support for mandatory drug sentences dropped from 45 percent in 2001 to only 32 percent in 2014.[70]

Such shifts were likely related, in part, to a growing public sense that the War on Drugs had proven ineffectual at achieving its aims, corrupting to law enforcement, and oppressive to racial minorities—views reflected in many notable works of popular culture in the new millennium, such as the television series *The Wire* (2002–8) and the film *Traffic* (2000). In Wisconsin, the sense of futility was nicely captured in a passage from the report of Governor Thompson's Task Force on Sentencing and Corrections: "Task Force staff heard from police about one street corner in Milwaukee at which 94 drug arrests were made in a recent three-month period. Despite the removal of these offenders, the police (and the community) report that this location continued to be a center of drug trafficking, and to pose manifest risks to safety."[71]

The national policy shifts were also likely related to increased public confidence in treatment as a viable alternative to punishment for many drug offenders. In a 2014 poll, for instance, two-thirds of respondents said that government should focus more on treatment for cocaine and heroin users than on prosecution.[72] Nowhere, though, was the national rehabilitation revival more apparent than in the explosive growth in drug treatment courts (DTCs). First developed in Miami in 1989, DTCs spread over the ensuing two decades to hundreds of jurisdictions in all fifty states.[73] The federal government stimulated much of this growth through a grant program authorized by Congress in 1994.[74] DTCs might be thought of as an alternative sentencing mechanism for drug offenses, although many are formally structured as a pre-sentencing or even pre-conviction process. However fit into the conventional prosecution system, a DTC centers on court-supervised addiction treatment; regular court appearances help establish accountability for compliance with the treatment regimen. The judge publicly recognizes progress and sanctions backsliding, including through short jail terms.

Wisconsin participated in the national rehabilitation revival. Indeed, the state had never entirely abandoned rehabilitation. The Declaration of Intent incorporated into the state's version of the Uniform Controlled Substances Act in 1972 remains there, still specifying that rehabilitation is the overriding sentencing objective for drug users. A proposal was made in 1989 to the Legislative Council Special Committee to revise this aspect of the Declaration of Intent, but—even at the very height of the drug panic—the proposal went nowhere.[75] Likewise, Wisconsin law has retained the treatment option for sentencing judges that was first enacted, in somewhat different form, in 1935 as part of the original Uniform Narcotic Drug Act. Similarly, Wisconsin has retained the option for special probation and dismissal of charges for first-time drug offenders that was adopted in 1972. Indeed, even the 1989 special session, despite its primary focus on enforcement and punishment, provided additional funding for treatment and established a new "boot camp" program for young offenders with drug treatment needs.[76] Under the TIS II law in 2002, completion of this Challenge Incarceration Program or of another new drug-treatment option, the Earned Release Program, could lead to early release from incarceration.[77]

Still, Wisconsin's nominal preference for rehabilitation over punishment for many drug offenders had important limitations through the early years of the new millennium. At a philosophical level, there was the unresolved tension between the declared goal of rehabilitation for users but tough deterrence for dealers, given significant overlap between these offender populations.[78] Indeed, the tension may have grown more acute in the 1990s in Wisconsin's most important battleground in the War on Drugs. Researchers in Milwaukee found an important shift in the inner-city drug market, as entrepreneurs moved away from drug houses and other stationary sales venues to a more mobile system that was harder for police to disrupt.[79] The new system relied on "runners," who served as go-betweens for retail sales. Typically, the runners were addicts themselves and were paid in drugs, rather than cash. The system effectively insulated from arrest the sorts of purely mercenary dealers who were nominally targeted for tough deterrence, while exposing the hapless runners to law enforcement and all of the enhanced penalties associated with distribution.

Data from the Department of Corrections in 2004 highlighted the problem.[80] Among prisoners sentenced for drug offenses, the DOC determined that fully 83 percent had drug or alcohol treatment needs. Moreover, these needs were most pronounced among the prisoners whose charges had involved the smallest amounts—five grams or less of cocaine. Such addicted, low-level offenders challenged the UCSA's seemingly neat user-dealer distinction. Despite the stated objective of rehabilitation for addicts, it was clear that many thousands were being sent to Wisconsin's prisons.

But the state's rehabilitative agenda may have been even more severely limited by money problems. In 2000, the Governor's Task Force to Enhance

Probation found significant underfunding of drug and alcohol treatment for probationers.[81] This contributed to the judiciary's general lack of confidence in the efficacy of probation sentences and discouraged the use of alternatives to incarceration. In many cases, rehabilitation might have seemed preferable to deterrence, but treatment was simply not available.

As the governor's task force recognized, the problem was especially acute in Milwaukee. Thus, for instance, the Sentencing Commission's data from 2003–6 found that probation was used less frequently in drug-distribution cases in Milwaukee than in any of the other five major regions of the state. Even holding offense severity constant, Milwaukee was consistently at or very near the bottom of the state in probation utilization.[82] This contributed to Milwaukee's high incarceration rate: more than triple that of the rest of the state in 2004 for all offenses, and more than six times that of the rest of the state for drug offenses.[83]

To be sure, as astute readers might recall, the state funded a Milwaukee drug court in the 1990 special session legislation. However, this drug court was not a drug *treatment* court; its exclusive purpose was to expedite the processing of drug cases. Milwaukee would prove remarkably slow to set up a true DTC.

The elimination of presumptive drug minimums in 2002 and the general de-escalation of drug war rhetoric in the new millennium gave sentencing judges more space in which to pursue rehabilitative alternatives to incarceration, but it did nothing to address the funding gap. The state finally made a modest start in 2005, when the legislature established the Treatment Alternatives Diversion (TAD) program.[84] The TAD legislation authorized "grants to counties to enable them to establish and operate programs, including suspended and deferred prosecution programs and programs based on principles of restorative justice, that provide alternatives to prosecution and incarceration for criminal offenders who abuse alcohol or other drugs." TAD was said to be the very first program to provide *state* money to Milwaukee and other counties for treatment-based alternatives to conventional prosecution.[85] Traditionally in Wisconsin, public mental health services have been funded at the county level, not the state.

TAD resulted, in part, from the tenacious advocacy of WISDOM, a statewide coalition of left-leaning, faith-based community organizations. Indeed, of all of the reforms discussed in this book, TAD is unique for the prominent role played by grassroots activists. WISDOM had its origin in the Milwaukee Inner-city Congregations Allied for Hope (MICAH), which was formed in the late 1980s by a group of mostly Baptist and Lutheran congregations in Milwaukee's predominantly black inner city.[86] Neighborhood safety was a particular focus of MICAH, and the group claimed to have shut down at least three hundred drug houses. After a few years, though, members realized that new drug houses seemed to be springing up as quickly as the old ones were shut down, and the group began turning to treatment-oriented responses as a more promising strategy. In 2000, members noted with great interest the adoption of Proposition 36 in California, which mandated treatment for drug offenders. The following year, MICAH launched its Treatment Instead of Prison (TIP) initiative, which sought state funding for local diversion programs. By then, MICAH had sister organizations in Racine and Kenosha, and WISDOM had been formed to provide statewide coordination as new groups continued to emerge.[87] Even beyond the drug issue, WISDOM and its local affiliates developed a more general interest in reducing incarceration; county-level political battles over jail construction proved a major stimulus to the creation and growth of new affiliates across the state.[88]

Unlike many other liberal reformers, the WISDOM activists have framed mass incarceration primarily in ethical, rather than fiscal, terms. "Fundamental issues of injustice frame and feed the scandal of mass incarceration in Wisconsin," they say. "Basic racial and economic justice issues are intertwined with mass incarceration." Yet they are also quick to point out that "treatment and diversion programs are less costly [than prison] and more effective in reducing recidivism and lowering crime rates."[89] According to David Liners, WISDOM's executive director, people get involved in the organization's incarceration work for one of three reasons: (1) they see a religious dimension to the issue, particularly in relation to the ideal of redemption; (2) they have personal experience with incarceration, either their own or that of a family member; or (3) they "look at the numbers [the fiscal costs of incarceration, the black incarceration rate, the comparison of Minnesota's incarceration rate with Wisconsin's] and are outraged."[90] Joe Ellwanger, a retired Lutheran pastor who has long played a prominent role in WISDOM's criminal justice initiatives, explains the appeal of this work by citing Matthew 25 ("I was . . . in prison and you visited me") and observing simply, "God calls us to do justice."[91]

With the GOP still in control of the legislature, WISDOM needed a Republican champion in order to get state support for the Treatment Instead of Prison initiative. Milwaukee Democrat Gwen Moore, the first African American woman to serve in the Wisconsin State Senate, helped WISDOM connect with Senator Carol Roessler, a moderate Republican from Oshkosh who agreed to serve as lead sponsor of what became the TAD legislation.[92] This was not a passive role for Roessler. Liners says that she was "cautious" about the treatment initiative, insisting, for instance, that the program be able to pay for itself. The legislative proposal evolved over time through input from Roessler, the Department of Corrections, and others. WISDOM, which does not normally involve itself in the nitty-gritty of legislative drafting, helped secure the assistance of the Drug Policy Alliance, a national organization that had played a lead role in the development of California's Proposition 36.

Roessler eventually became convinced that treatment would be a more cost-effective strategy than incarceration for dealing with many addicted offenders.[93] Over the long run, it seemed that treatment might indeed pay for itself through reduced corrections costs. A study supported by the Drug Policy Alliance found that 2,900 Wisconsin prisoners might qualify for diversion under the emerging proposal, with imprisonment savings of as much as $83 million annually.[94] Tantalizing though they may have been, these projected savings presented a catch-22 for Roessler and other sympathetic legislators: there was no money for treatment until corrections costs came down, but corrections costs would not come down until offenders were being successfully diverted into treatment. The ultimate solution was to get the start-up funding from offenders themselves, with an increased "drug abuse improvement program" surcharge for drug violations and a new $10 surcharge for property convictions. WISDOM was not happy with this arrangement, nor with the inflexible exclusion built into the bill for addicted offenders who had prior convictions for violent crime.[95] Nonetheless, the organization threw its support behind Roessler's proposal.

TAD cleared the senate with ease in 2004 but stalled without a vote in the assembly. In the next legislative session, though, supporters managed to get TAD in the mammoth state budget bill, which normally eases passage. WISDOM made TAD the major focus of its biennial "Madison Action Day," which attracts hundreds of WISDOM supporters to the Capitol for a public event and individual meetings with legislators. This time, the assembly raised no roadblock, and TAD became law.

Although TAD marked a symbolically notable recommitment by Wisconsin to its purported rehabilitative aims, the program could hardly be interpreted as a veiled form of decriminalization (which had been one of the charges lobbed against Proposition 36 in California). Rather, consistent with the national DTC model, TAD expressly contemplated a system of graduated sanctions to enforce the offender's compliance with the prescribed treatment regimen.[96] This could, and sometimes did, mean that the offender would face short spells of incarceration as a consequence of falling off the wagon. The TAD legislation underscored the central role of criminal justice agencies in the program's vision by requiring that county grant proposals be developed with input from local judges, prosecutors, and law enforcement officials, and that these same officials be given a formal oversight role in the implementation of the grant-funded initiatives.[97]

Even to the extent that TAD represented a genuine paradigm shift from the War on Drugs, its modest size meant that not many offenders would benefit from the new program. In its first five years of operation, TAD only funded diversion initiatives in seven of Wisconsin's seventy-two counties. Moreover, the million-dollar annual funding level paled by comparison to the state's billion-dollar corrections budget, a very sizable share of which continued to be devoted to the imprisonment of drug-dependent offenders. When the University of Wisconsin Population Health Institute undertook a systematic review of the costs and benefits of TAD through 2013, researchers calculated that the program had averted 231,533 days of incarceration (jail and prison).[98] Although this was undoubtedly a significant accomplishment, some perspective is needed: over the same time period, close to five thousand drug offenders entered Wisconsin prisons; even assuming that each served only the minimum one year for a prison term, that would translate into more than 1.8 million days of imprisonment. And many more days would have been served by those sentenced to *jail* for drug offenses.

On the other hand, although TAD generated only modest reductions in imprisonment through 2013, the University of Wisconsin researchers found that, in light of the program's relatively low fiscal burden, TAD's benefits far outweighed its costs. Every dollar invested in TAD was said to yield $1.96 in benefits through reduced incarceration and crime.

Meanwhile, WISDOM launched its "11×15" campaign in early 2012, aiming to cut Wisconsin's prison population in half—that is, to eleven thousand inmates—in three years. As part of the initiative, WISDOM sought an expansion of TAD funding to seventy-five million dollars. Although an increase of this size was likely a political nonstarter, the organization had success in drawing press attention to the positive results TAD was getting, and politicians on both sides of the aisle responded favorably to the idea of *some* increase—this despite Roessler's departure from the legislature and the absence of any substitute champion for TAD. In 2014, WISDOM again turned out its members en masse at budget hearings to agitate for more TAD support. Ultimately, lawmakers settled on an annual budget of four million dollars, quadrupling the funding level of the program's first decade.[99]

Complementing the state's TAD program, various local initiatives also supported the rehabilitation revival. Perhaps most notably, Milwaukee finally jumped on the bandwagon for a drug treatment court in 2008.[100] Supported by federal grants, the Milwaukee DTC developed capacity for 80 offenders. As of late 2013, the DTC had successfully graduated 76 "clients," but nearly twice as many (143) had been terminated and returned to the regular criminal justice system.[101] The average recommended prison sentence in the event of termination was two years.[102] And even among the minority of clients who successfully completed the program, more than one in three faced new criminal charges within one year of graduation.[103] Though discouraging, the numbers were not

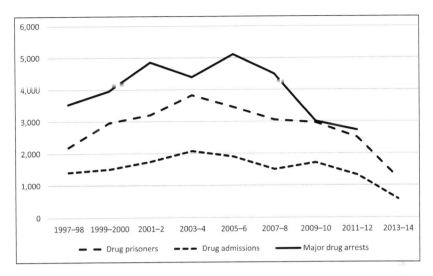

Figure 7.3. Drug prisoners, drug prison admissions, and major drug distribution arrests, 1997–2014

out of line with the experience of other jurisdictions[104] and highlighted the inherent challenges of accomplishing personal transformation through a system of coercive state control.

The Milwaukee DTC numbers also pointed to the revival of heroin as a leading drug of concern: nearly half of the clients identified heroin as their major problem, as compared to less than a quarter for cocaine.[105] Indeed, heroin overdose deaths in Milwaukee County increased from 20 in 2005 to 119 in 2014, overshadowing both homicides and motor vehicle fatalities that year.[106]

Despite many signs of growing public concern over heroin in the past decade, Wisconsin has not duplicated the punitive turn taken in the 1980s when cocaine emerged as a major issue. To the contrary, as indicated in figure 7.3, the numbers of drug prisoners and new prison admissions on drug charges have fallen sharply and consistently since the drug minimums were eliminated in 2002.[107]

The imprisonment trends depicted in figure 7.3 resulted, in part, from a dramatic decline in heroin and cocaine distribution arrests, which peaked in 2006 and then fell by more than 50 percent over the next five years. However, the drop in prison admissions on drug charges from the peak has been much larger at about 75 percent, which suggests that arrest trends alone may not account for the imprisonment trends. Moreover, the drop in arrests did not begin until 2007, which is after the drop in imprisonment began. Finally, the drop in imprisonment continued to accelerate after arrests rebounded slightly in 2012. All of this would support a conclusion that changes in sentencing law and the

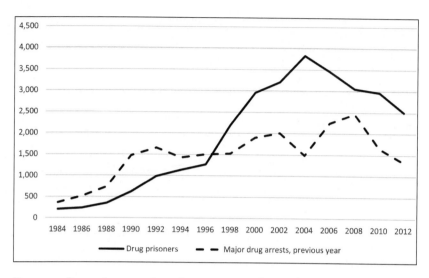

Figure 7.4. Drug prisoners and previous-year arrests for cocaine or heroin distribution, 1984–2012

implementation of new rehabilitative alternatives have played a significant, if secondary, role in amplifying the effect of declining arrest rates.

Figure 7.4 provides a longer-term view of the arrest–imprisonment relationship. Between the mid-1980s and the mid-1990s, arrests for cocaine and heroin distribution rose closely in sync with the number of drug prisoners, which suggests that arrestees were on average being treated with roughly consistent severity over that time period.[108] Over the next decade, from the mid-1990s to 2004, the number of prisoners increased far more sharply and consistently than the number of arrestees, which indicates that the system grew more severe. (Recall that this is the time period in which parole was effectively phased out.) Finally, between 2005 and 2012, drug imprisonment dropped off about as sharply and consistently as it had previously risen, even as arrests first spiked up and then spiked down. Over time, it seems clear that changes in policing can affect drug imprisonment, but that the rest of the system also operates in dynamic ways that can accentuate, soften, or even entirely offset changes in arrest rates.

In any event, as a result of the recently shrinking number of new drug admissions, drug offenders have accounted for a declining share of the overall state prison population (figure 7.5).[109] By 2014, the proportion had fallen to under 6 percent, reaching a level not seen since about the time Governor Earl launched the war on cocaine in 1986. Indeed, as the state's overall prison population slowly receded from its 2004 peak, it was reductions in drug imprisonment

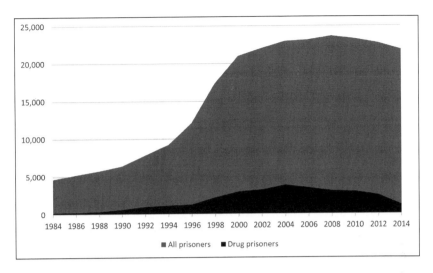

Figure 7.5. Drug prisoners' share of total prison population, 1984–2014

that led the way. Between 2008 and 2014, declining drug imprisonment accounted for the *entirety* of the state's reduced imprisonment and then some. Put differently, if drug imprisonment had simply held steady over that time period, Wisconsin's imprisonment would not have shrunk but would have continued to grow to a new record peak.

Following long-standing trends, Wisconsin continued to hold a smaller percentage of its prisoners on drug charges than did the nation as a whole. In 2014, the most recent year for which data are available, drug prisoners accounted for nearly 16 percent of state prisoners in the United States,[110] but fewer than 9 percent of Wisconsin's inmates. The national figures, too, had dropped markedly from the early 2000s, supporting the view that the drug imprisonment declines in Wisconsin were related to broader trends that also affected many other states. For instance, as in Wisconsin, national reductions in drug imprisonment were associated with reductions in arrests for drug distribution. Between 2001 and 2012, national arrests for distribution dropped almost 15 percent.[111] Despite national reductions in drug arrests, though, Wisconsin continued to devote a lower share of its total arrests to drugs than did the nation as a whole. As throughout the time period covered by this chapter, the drug war remained less intense in Wisconsin than in many other states.

In sum, since 2002, Wisconsin has achieved a notable decrease in its rate of drug imprisonment. This reduction has been associated with declining confidence in the efficacy of deterrence as a response to the drug problem and a growing enthusiasm for treatment as a more cost-effective strategy. What has not changed in any discernible way is the perception that drug use and distribution are a *social* problem that merits a coercive societal response; it is simply that incarceration is being replaced by mandatory court- or prosecutor-supervised treatment as the preferred coercive response. Notably lacking has been any serious effort to reframe drug use as a matter of personal choice. As a handful of other jurisdictions legalized recreational marijuana after 2012, Wisconsin continued to resist even the legalization of *medical* marijuana—a reform adopted in twenty-three other states as of this writing.

Conclusion

Drug sentencing law in Wisconsin has moved cyclically between the poles of rehabilitation and deterrence, shifting in conjunction with national trends and changes in federal law. Neither libertarian nor nakedly moralistic perspectives have been much in evidence. Rather, drug use and distribution have been seen primarily as matters of public health and safety—and as matters of sufficient social concern to warrant robust criminal justice responses, whether with a rehabilitation or deterrence orientation.

Although Wisconsin policymakers often seem to take their cues in this area from the federal government, Uniform Law Commission, and trends in other states, Wisconsin's drug imprisonment rate has remained well below national norms. While Wisconsin's *overall* imprisonment rate has also consistently been lower than the national average, the gap in drug imprisonment has been far larger. To some extent, this gap reflects below-average drug arrest rates; with fewer drug offenders entering the court system at the front end, we should naturally expect fewer drug prisoners exiting at the back end. To some extent, the gap also reflects the unusually wide discretion exercised by Wisconsin's sentencing judges; although they have imposed plenty of long drug sentences over the years, the system's flexibility and individualization ideal have probably helped, on the whole, keep drug imprisonment below national norms, especially in recent years as political and financial support have increased for rehabilitative alternatives to incarceration.

Wisconsin's above-average rate of imprisonment growth suggests that the state has not been well served overall by its embrace of almost limitless judicial sentencing discretion, but the drug story suggests at least two lessons about discretion that are more positive. First, a system with a strong tradition of discretion may have some helpful insulation against the long-term adverse effects of crime panics on sentencing and corrections. To be sure, elected judges and prosecutors will be subject to the same get-tough pressures and inclinations as legislators during a time of panic—it is not realistic to think that discretion will be exercised by legal actors without regard to their social context—but the decisions of local judges and prosecutors do not get codified in statutory minimums that may remain on the books long after the panic is over. Wisconsin's discretion tradition likely contributed to the fact that its minimums were less draconian than those adopted in many other jurisdictions (e.g., they were presumptive rather than mandatory) and were repealed en masse in relatively short order.

Second, Wisconsin's TAD experience indicates that judges and prosecutors may embrace alternatives to incarceration if they are provided with the resources to establish effective, locally controlled treatment options. Local discretion seems most pernicious when the only alternative to incarceration is a community supervision system run by a state bureaucracy that the local actors do not control or trust. As we have seen, that was precisely Milwaukee's situation in the 1990s. TAD, as well as the federal DTC grant, has allowed local officials in Milwaukee to establish a plethora of new supervision options that they do control and trust. The result has been a sizeable decrease in the use of incarceration. Local sentencing discretion may work best when it is accompanied by local control over corrections, assuming adequate financial support and accountability for results.

The TAD story may be the most hopeful one in this book, but some cautionary notes must be sounded. For one thing, the sobering numbers from Milwaukee's DTC remind us that rehabilitation is far from an exact science. Locally administered corrections alternatives will experience plenty of failures, and one cannot help but wonder whether local officials will be able to maintain their commitment over the long run when the whole messy enterprise can always be dumped back into the lap of the state Department of Corrections at any time. Perhaps more fundamental structural changes are needed in state–local relations, such as adoption of a community corrections act model, as discussed in chapter 4.

Additionally, the TAD approach seems to lock Wisconsin further into its long-standing position that drug use and distribution are fundamentally issues for coercive state control. Expanding TAD has been a primary focus of liberal criminal justice reform advocates like WISDOM for the past decade. Perhaps their energy would have been better spent on advocating for more radical reforms. For instance, as other states legalize recreational marijuana use, it is striking how little this option is part of the public conversation in Wisconsin. At present, liberals seem quite satisfied to see the agencies of criminal justice pursue a rehabilitative agenda. However, the history suggests that disenchantment with rehabilitation will eventually set in, a drug panic will eventually occur, and public demand will grow for tough deterrence. At that time, some may regret a missed opportunity to achieve a true paradigm shift.

8

Lessons

Wisconsin's era of explosive imprisonment growth seems over, but the state remains saddled with a prison population nine times higher than its historic norm. This is essentially the same situation facing the United States as a whole. The national prison population peaked in 2009 but has only dropped slightly since then. Just one state, California, accounted for nearly all of the nation's modest post-2009 imprisonment reduction. And that state adopted a radical restructuring of its corrections system only because it was forced to do so by court order. Acting without such compulsion, most other states have adopted a variety of other reforms intended to reduce imprisonment, but, with just a few exceptions, these reforms have proven a disappointment.[1] It is time for Wisconsin, and the nation as a whole, to take stock.

The Wisconsin experience suggests a number of lessons that might inform future reform efforts. I highlight ten such lessons in this chapter. To be sure, every state is unique. Not all of the Wisconsin lessons will apply to every other state. Still, as a medium-sized state with an imprisonment rate near the national average, and as a "purple" state with a Republican–Democrat divide that closely mirrors the national political split, Wisconsin's lessons may have broader relevance than those of many other states. Close attention to the experiences of states like Wisconsin may point the way to more effective reform efforts in the future.

Lesson 1:
Penal Populism Remains a Potent Force

We have seen penal populism grow as an influence on policymaking in Wisconsin since the 1970s, reaching a high point with the adoption of truth in sentencing in 1998. Since then, various developments indicate that populism has lost some of its influence, while managerialism has gained. The 2002 truth-in-sentencing law (TIS II) law abolished most existing minimums and reversed some of the increase in maximums; few new minimums have been created since then; the Treatment Alternatives Diversion grant program has become a durable part of the criminal justice landscape; and new diversion programs have flowered in Milwaukee and many other counties. Yet populism remains influential, as demonstrated most vividly by the repeal of the short-lived earned-release reforms in 2011. The rhetoric surrounding this repeal recalled much of what we saw in the 1990s: an exaggerated and indiscriminate fear of criminals, a pronounced mistrust of corrections officials, a cavalier dismissal of data and cost-benefit analysis, and a belief that more imprisonment is almost always better for society.

More subtly, the influence of populism can also probably be seen in a number of other places in the post-2000 story: the failure of TIS II to deal more fully with the severity increases that were implicit in the original truth-in-sentencing law; the belated, inconsistent effort by judges to adjust their nominal sentences downward to offset the impact of TIS; the high revocation rates for probationers and parolees; the chronic inability of hundreds of low-risk "old law" prisoners (that is, those sentenced for pre-TIS crimes) to secure the parole release for which they are still theoretically eligible; the failure of the second Sentencing Commission to make any progress on Governor Doyle's managerial agenda; the timidity of the Earned Release Review Commission during its short lifespan; the modest size of the Treatment Alternatives Diversion program; and, at the most general level, the inability of Wisconsin to achieve sizeable reductions in its prison population since 2004. Although populism has not been the only causal factor, there can be little doubt that many policymakers and criminal justice officials have been influenced by populist beliefs and by the knowledge that critics can play effectively on populist sensibilities in attacking the use of alternatives to imprisonment.

Polling results confirm that populist beliefs remain widespread. Since 2012, I have worked with colleagues at Marquette University on a series of annual telephone surveys of a representative sample of Wisconsin voters on criminal justice issues.[2] Our results included the following:

- 62 percent of respondents believe that the courts are too lenient with criminals.
- 84 percent support tougher sentences for repeat offenders.
- Only 34 percent say that the justice system is doing a good job of ensuring that people who commit crimes receive the punishment they deserve.
- Only 27 percent agree that many of the people locked up in prison do not deserve to be there.
- Only 37 percent agree that many prisoners could be safely released.[3]

To be sure, national research demonstrates that survey results like these often reflect a misunderstanding of actual sentencing practices.[4] The point remains, however, that politicians wishing to score easy points against opponents can draw on a deep well of suspicion of criminals and criminal justice officials.

Yet, while populism has been strong enough to stifle bold managerial reforms at the state level, there has not been a steady stream of new tough-on-crime legislation since 2000, as there had been in the 1990s. Indeed, even in the 1990s, much of the tough-on-crime legislation was largely symbolic. It seems clear that many purveyors of populist rhetoric have not actually wanted to shift state policy in a sharply populist direction. In some cases, this may be simply a matter of political opportunism: populist positions have been taken to secure partisan advantage, but without any real commitment to making the system tougher. Perhaps more commonly, the reality has been that competing policy objectives have been given greater weight, especially the desire to keep some kind of constraint on the corrections budget. This, for instance, is how Governor Tommy Thompson accounts for the narrow reach of the Wisconsin mandatory minimums adopted in the 1990s; when asked why Wisconsin did not go for even tougher minimums, he replied, "Look at who the Governor was. . . . I was concerned about building too many prisons."[5] To be sure, *some* prison building was clearly acceptable in the Thompson era, but that was in the context of sustained economic growth and large, long-term increases in the overall state budget, which grew by 128 percent between 1988 and 2001. By contrast, over the next decade, the budget only increased by 33 percent.[6] Indeed, as we have seen, recurring fiscal crises since 2001 have made the containment of corrections costs a much more pressing priority.

In Wisconsin, as in many other states, the lingering effects of the 2007 recession, coupled with an increasingly prominent strain of low-tax, antigovernment conservatism, have created a fiscal and political environment in which a new wave of prison construction is unlikely. Although this environment discourages the adoption of new tough-on-crime legislation, populist sentiment may still be strong enough to threaten the viability of large-scale imprisonment-reducing reforms.

Lesson 2:
Reforms Should Be Grounded in Ethical, Egalitarian Arguments, Not Just Economics

While cost concerns may operate in the background to deter or soften populist legislation, they have not provided decisive, durable support for reforms intended

to reduce the size of the state prison population. The 2009 earned-release reforms provide a clear example. Sold primarily as a cost-reducing measure, the
reforms proved a political lightning rod and lasted only two years.

There are two fundamental problems with trying to save money by reducing the prison population, both of which are illustrated by Wisconsin's earned-
release experience. First, it is hard to convince people that imprisonment really
can be reduced without endangering public safety. Recall the poll numbers
discussed above: only 37 percent agree, and 48 percent disagree, with the
proposition that "many of the people who are locked up in prison could be
safely released." Republican opponents of earned release were thus able to play
on voters' fear of crime. Moreover, when people think of crime, they tend to
think of the worst-case scenarios that dominate the local news. In reality, most
offenses committed by released prisoners are nonviolent. Indeed, less than 1 percent of ex-cons are arrested for homicide, and less than 2 percent for rape, as
opposed to nearly 27 percent for simple drug possession—the single most
common cause for the arrest of former prisoners.[7] Yet the thought of early
release is more likely to summon images of harrowing violent and sexual crimes
than of a homeless man shooting up in an alley. If Willie Horton lurks in the
shadows, it is hard to say that any amount of cost savings would justify reduced
imprisonment. There is little wonder, then, that Wisconsin voters seem ambivalent or uncertain about reducing the costs of imprisonment; in our survey research, for instance, we found that only 49 percent agree that "Wisconsin spends
too much on prisons," while an unusually high 21 percent say they are unsure
about this question.[8]

Second, it is very difficult to achieve projected savings, especially in the
short run. Again, consider earned release, which actually saved only a small
fraction of the $30 million projected for the program's first two years. It can
take time to readjust institutional processes, including reentry planning and
programming, in light of new release opportunities. Additionally, in a populist-
influenced political environment, many criminal justice officials will feel com-
pelled to err on the side of caution in implementing reforms. Moreover, there is
little to be saved by reducing the prison population unless a tipping point is
reached that permits the closure of an entire facility; given the low marginal costs
of feeding and caring for most prisoners, there is little budgetary impact from
reducing each institution's count by a few dozen. And even if the tipping point
is achieved in a numerical sense, there might still be considerable political resistance to facility closures, given the economic role that many facilities are thought
to play in their host communities. All of these considerations seem to make it
almost inevitable that imprisonment-reduction reforms will prove disappointing
if evaluated only from a fiscal standpoint. And, as we saw in the earned-release
story, critics can be expected to seize on such fiscal underperformance. Indeed,

there seems almost something of a catch-22 for reformers: go fast, and you will be skewered for endangering public safety; go slow, and your efforts will be written off as a failure.

If cost concerns can put a damper on some imprisonment-*increasing* measures, it may seem odd that such concerns cannot equally well support imprisonment-*reducing* reforms. Upon reflection, though, this asymmetry should not be surprising. Inertia is a powerful force. Inertia must be overcome to build new prisons, but once they are in place, inertia helps to ensure that they remain. Merely keeping an existing prison open does not normally require any new taxes or a reallocation of money from other government programs. Closing a prison, however, may generate political opposition from the host community, require the unpleasantness of layoffs, and give rise to conflict over who will capture the fiscal benefits (taxpayers? other prisons? other agencies?). As behavioral economists have demonstrated, people tend to value holding onto what they already have more highly than acquiring something of seemingly equivalent value.[9] These loss-aversion dynamics may help to explain why there seems much more interest in avoiding additional prison building than in achieving prison closures.

It is not entirely clear whether or how the combination of institutional inertia and penal populism can be overcome, but doing so would likely require, among other things, a strong ethical case for imprisonment reduction to complement the economic. On the national stage, law professor Michael Tonry has articulated this point most forcefully, and his observations merit quoting at length:

> For the past 40 years, most advocates for humane criminal justice policies have made the fundamental mistake of arguing disingenuously. Instead of arguing that unduly harsh policies are unjust, and should be repealed or modified for that reason, they much more often argued that policies—which they believed to be unjust—should be changed because they are ineffective or too costly. Proposed alternatives . . . are generally supported by arguments about reduced cost or improved recidivism reduction. This is a mistake. . . .
>
> [T]he strategy of disingenuous argument has failed because it does not recognize that the supporters of harsh contemporary punishment policies do not much care about cost savings or program effectiveness. . . . [Punitive sentencing laws] were adopted—usually openly—because their supporters believed they were morally justifiable, that "we" deserve to be protected from the dangerous "them" and that "they" have forfeited any claim to have their interests or human rights taken into account. . . . The ultimately moral arguments about

disproportionate punishments, ruined lives, and social injustice need to
be made explicitly if the argument is ever to change minds.[10]

What is needed, if Tonry is correct, would be something like a revival of the
egalitarian ideology and rhetoric that we saw in Wisconsin in the early 1970s, in
the work of Governor Pat Lucey's Council on Criminal Justice and Committee
on Offender Rehabilitation. Penal egalitarianism sees crime not as the exclusive
preserve of a depraved "other" but as a common and inevitable consequence
of modern social arrangements, insists that offenders retain their membership
in the political community, and imposes an obligation on the community to
support their rehabilitation and return to full citizenship status. More recently, these views have been echoed in the work of WISDOM, the faith-based
community-organizing group that has called for Wisconsin's prison population
to be cut in half. Interestingly, as discussed in chapter 7, WISDOM initially
operated in the economic vein that Tonry criticizes, pressing the claim that
treatment would be a more cost-effective way to deal with drug offenders than
incarceration, but the group has since become more overtly moral in its rhetoric.
Doing so has not impaired WISDOM's (admittedly modest thus far) influence
in any obvious way.

The economic argument against mass incarceration avoids the central ethical question raised by penal populism: that is, whether the person who commits
a serious or repeat offense thereby forfeits any legitimate claim on the care or
compassion of other members of the community. Indeed, the economic arguments may subtly reinforce the exclusionary populist position. By framing
the offender as a risk to be managed—albeit in the most cost-effective way—
economic arguments sometimes seem to buy into the "othering" of the offender.
Social-scientific research confirms the common-sense expectation that we tend
to treat offenders more harshly when we see them as outsiders who do not
belong to our own social group.[11]

Can excluded individuals really be brought back within the circle of social
concern? Can enhanced feelings of kinship and compassion really lead to fundamental institutional change? We may find some hope in an earlier story that
offers striking parallels to mass incarceration. Between 1880 and 1955, the
number of individuals held in psychiatric facilities in the United States increased thirteenfold—more than four times the rate of growth of the population
as a whole.[12] National rates of institutionalization rose to about three times the
incarceration rate. After 1955, however, the institutionalized mental health
population began to fall sharply. By 1980, the figure had dropped an astonishing
75 percent. By then, the nation's burgeoning incarceration rate far exceeded
the institutionalization rate. Now, the question is how to achieve reductions in

incarceration on the same scale as our earlier reductions in institutionalization for mental illness (and, of course, without the surge in homelessness and other social ills that accompanied deinstitutionalization).

Political scientist and law professor Bernard Harcourt highlights three leading causes of deinstitutionalization, one of which was changing social attitudes regarding the mentally ill. (The other two are noted later in this chapter.) A variety of developments helped to evoke more compassion toward this historically stigmatized group. For instance, many soldiers returning home from World War II—a population seen in highly sympathetic terms—suffered from mental illness. Additionally, widely circulated journalistic accounts of degrading conditions in mental hospitals sparked public outrage. Meanwhile, society's declining confidence in the ability of institutions to cure the mentally ill dovetailed with a rising confidence in the potential of community-based treatment. The mentally ill were not hopelessly "other," it seemed, but could be successfully reintegrated into the community. Indeed, some authors went so far as to suggest that mental illness was simply an artificial social construct used to control deviancy. Notably, much of the critique of institutionalization resonated with the egalitarian critique of imprisonment that emerged at about the same time.

Of course, as a historical matter, we know that the critique of institutionalization succeeded, while the critique of imprisonment failed. Would an egalitarian push against mass incarceration in the 2010s fare any better than, say, the efforts of the Committee on Offender Rehabilitation to shut down Wisconsin's prison system in the early 1970s? We cannot know for certain until a more concerted attempt is made, but some circumstances do suggest a more fertile ground for egalitarianism today. Perhaps most importantly, when the Committee on Offender Rehabilitation was in operation, Wisconsin and the nation as a whole were already a decade into a dramatic, long-term increase in crime rates. The resulting atmosphere of fear and anger was hardly conducive to the development of more inclusionary sentencing policies. However, crime rates have been mostly stable or down in Wisconsin and nationally for the past two decades. Additionally, in the 1970s and 1980s, Wisconsin and other nearby states were absorbing the brunt of regional deindustrialization. If David Garland and other sociologists are correct, the feelings of instability and anxiety bred by this wrenching economic reorganization contributed to the public punitiveness of the time period.[13] By contrast, the advent of a more stable post-industrial economy may lessen the social and political impetus to scapegoat criminals. Yet another hopeful sign may be the resurgence of public interest in rehabilitation; recall that the 1970s and 1980s were the heyday of "nothing works" cynicism about treatment. Some measure of public confidence in rehabilitation may be a prerequisite for penal egalitarian arguments to succeed; the potential for rehabilitation makes it possible to think of offenders as "us," not "them." The rehabilitation revival is considered in more detail below.

At the same time, we must recognize an important barrier to the development of more egalitarian attitudes toward prisoners: race. In some respects this barrier may be even more imposing in Wisconsin than in the United States as a whole. In the state with the nation's highest black male incarceration rate, imprisonment is an even more racialized phenomenon than it is elsewhere. Egalitarian arguments to end mass incarceration are not likely to succeed unless white voters and political leaders are able to feel a sense of connectedness and kinship with African Americans. Unfortunately, Wisconsin's hypersegregation, including the concentration of three-quarters of the state's black population in the intensely disadvantaged neighborhoods sprawling to the north and west of downtown Milwaukee, impedes the development of the sort of constructive personal relationships across racial lines that might soften feelings of racial resentment.

Lesson 3:
Rehabilitation Has Regained Legitimacy
as an Important Function
of the Criminal Justice System

As discussed in chapters 6 and 7, rehabilitation has staged a comeback in Wisconsin (and nationally) since the nothing-works era. The growing availability and use of treatment options has both practical and symbolic significance in relation to mass incarceration. On a practical level, if treatment is seen as something that can make some otherwise-threatening offenders safe, then those offenders are more likely to be diverted from prison or released early. On a symbolic level, rehabilitative programming signals hope for offenders and may lessen some of the "othering" tendencies that seem so pronounced in public conversations on crime. Similarly, going back to the deinstitutionalization story, Bernard Harcourt identifies the development of psychiatric medication in the 1950s as one of the key causes for the movement of the mentally ill back into the community; new drugs both provided a seemingly effective way to manage symptoms on an outpatient basis and helped change public perceptions of mental illness. "Tangible medicalization, in the form of a pill, promoted the mentally ill 'to the status of patients in the eyes of many members of the public.'"[14]

Wisconsin's Treatment Alternatives Diversion grant program, recently quadrupled in size, points to the emergence of durable support among state policymakers for rehabilitative responses to crime. Our polling research, moreover, confirms that Wisconsin voters would like the criminal justice system to do more to promote rehabilitation. Nearly *three-quarters* of respondents say that it is very important or absolutely essential for the system to rehabilitate offenders, but only 22 percent think that the system is doing a good job of this.[15] Similarly, 70 percent agree that "if the prison system did more to foster rehabilitation, Wisconsin would be a safer place," and two-thirds say that "Wisconsin should recognize prisoners' rehabilitative accomplishments by awarding credits toward early release."[16] Large majorities also say that completion of educational programming and addiction treatment in prison should be taken into account in deciding when a prisoner should be released.[17]

Such strong support for rehabilitation may seem surprising, given what we saw earlier about equally strong support for various punitive attitudes. Closer analysis of the survey results reveals the existence of a substantial group of "swing voters," who express support for both tough-on-crime policies and rehabilitation-oriented policies.[18] This group comprises about 30 percent of the electorate. The internal tensions in the views of this group suggest a certain malleability to public opinion and point to the importance of the framing of criminal justice policy proposals. For instance, given the public ambivalence we have seen when it comes to cutting corrections costs, imprisonment-reducing proposals might be better framed as rehabilitation-promoting rather than merely cost-saving measures. The 2009 earned-release reforms were presented as advancing both goals, but cost savings were emphasized more. Perhaps if the emphasis had been reversed, there would have been stronger support for the legislation.

At the same time, reformers must be careful about the risk of overpromising what rehabilitative programming will achieve, just as they must be wary about exaggerated cost-savings claims. We have indeed advanced beyond "nothing works," but human beings are not automatons whose mental circuitry can be easily rewired, and no program can guarantee 100 percent success. Recall, for instance, the data from the Milwaukee Drug Treatment Court. Although this was a thoughtfully constructed intervention based on well-established best practices, failures have outnumbered successes by a two-to-one margin. Such experiences do not mean that programming is a waste of time. A distinguished committee of the National Research Council recently concluded, "The available research indicates that, when carried out properly, certain forms of cognitive-behavioral therapy, drug treatment, academic programs, and vocational training appear to reduce recidivism."[19] But, even in a good program, the magnitude of reduction is apt to be ten percentage points or less. Public expectations must be kept in line with this reality; otherwise, another disillusioned backlash against rehabilitation seems inevitable. As Michael Tonry suggests, major reductions in imprisonment will likely require the articulation of strong, clear ethical arguments against mass incarceration, not just the instrumental arguments about cost savings and recidivism reduction.

Lesson 4:
Reformers Cannot Just Focus
on the Nonviolent Offenders

Beyond its direct effect of diverting some offenders from prison, Wisconsin's Treatment Alternatives Diversion program may also have a broader symbolic significance, indicating some movement away from populist beliefs about the inherent depravity of criminals. More hopeful, inclusionary attitudes toward offenders seem a prerequisite to achieving real reductions in the prison population. Yet the current support for rehabilitation and second chances may be limited in ways that largely negate its potential value as a basis for imprisonment reduction. TAD itself highlights the problem: the legislature prohibited participation in the locally administered diversion programs by "violent" offenders, which includes offenders with *any* prior violent conviction, no matter how old.[20] It seems that violent offenders may continue to bear the stigma of irredeemable depravity, even as drug offenders have to some extent been welcomed back into the circle of social concern.

Such a drug-violence distinction may matter a great deal in Wisconsin because violent offenders comprise a much larger share of the state's prison population than drug offenders, as indicated in figure 8.1.[21] Sexual offenders likely carry a similar stigma as the violent offenders, and these two groups together account for fully two-thirds of the prison population. Indeed, assuming it remains politically difficult to move violent and sexual offenders out of prison, the picture may be even bleaker than figure 8.1 indicates. The data only reflect the current offenses for which the inmates are now serving time, but many classified as "drug" or "property" offenders for these purposes probably have *prior* violent or sexual convictions. In many cases, such a prior record would help to explain why they ended up in prison for a drug or property conviction. In any event, to judge by the lines drawn in the TAD law, there may not be that many inmates who qualify for hopeful, inclusionary treatment.

In Wisconsin and nationally, reformers like to promote the idea that prisons are full of nonviolent drug offenders. As discussed in chapter 7, this claim may be somewhat truer in the nation as a whole than in Wisconsin. Even at the national level, though, the War on Drugs and mass incarceration are distinct

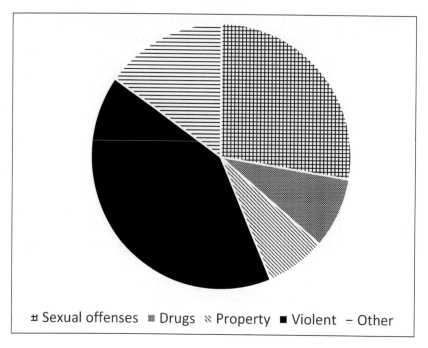

Figure 8.1. Wisconsin prison population by offense category, 2014

phenomena, and ending the former would by no means result in an end to the latter. Drug offenders account for less than 16 percent of all U.S. prisoners in state institutions.[22]

Reformers must thus face up to the hard truth that most prisoners have been convicted of crimes that provoke considerable public fear and anger. Indeed, if the end goal is to return imprisonment rates to their historic norms, it may be counterproductive to continue to focus on moving "nonviolent" offenders out of prison; the rhetoric merely reinforces the perception that violent offenders are a uniquely and inherently dangerous group.

Rather than trying to distinguish among offenders based on current offense of conviction, reformers might do better to focus on what the data say about actual risk and on the extraordinary length of some sentences. As a whole, the prisoners convicted of violent and sexual offenses do not necessarily present significantly different risks than the drug and property offenders. Indeed, the violent offenders have a *lower* recidivism rate than the drug and property offenders, and the sexual assault offenders have a recidivism rate that is lower still.[23] Nor do violent offenders particularly specialize in violent crime; among those who do recidivate, the new offense is violent only about one-third of the time.[24] Indeed, the property offenders are only a little less likely to recidivate violently than the "violent" offenders.

Even more important may be developing the ethical and pragmatic case against the very long sentences that are often imposed on violent and sexual offenders. About a quarter of Wisconsin's prison population is serving a sentence longer than ten years, including the life-sentenced inmates.[25] Regardless of the underlying crime, ten years is a very long time in anyone's life, and whatever sort of risk an offender presents upon entry to prison, the picture may look quite different ten or more years later. The social need for continued imprisonment is especially dubious for the older inmates; in general, crime is a young person's game. The Wisconsin Legislature has implicitly recognized these realities through the compassionate release program discussed in chapter 6, although the program has not been utilized much in practice. Life sentences raise particularly sharp ethical problems, which even the United States Supreme Court has recognized in recent cases.[26] As the court has suggested, a due regard for basic human dignity may preclude sentences that rob the offender of all hope and deny opportunities and incentives for rehabilitation.

None of this is to suggest that reformers will have an easy time convincing policymakers or the public to see violent offenders through an egalitarian-rehabilitative lens, but squarely confronting the challenge is probably necessary if really meaningful reductions in the prison population are to be achieved.

Lesson 5:
Increasing Judicial Discretion
Will Not Draw Down Prison Populations

Mass incarceration is often attributed to mandatory minimums and presumptive sentencing guidelines.[27] However, as we have seen, Wisconsin has never had presumptive guidelines, while the state's statutory minimums have had little direct effect on the state's imprisonment rate. Although the state adopted numerous statutory minimums between the mid-1980s and mid-1990s, they were narrowly focused, merely presumptive, or otherwise modest in severity. Moreover, most were repealed by the TIS II legislation in 2002. Wisconsin thus preserved its judicial sentencing discretion to a much greater extent than many other jurisdictions but still experienced an above-average increase in imprisonment during the era of mass incarceration. The lesson is clear: judges do not need legislative mandates in order to send an ever-greater number of offenders to prison for ever-longer periods of time.

This should not be surprising. It is commonly recognized that legislators face electoral pressures to appear tough on crime. Yet in Wisconsin and most other states, judges are also elected. It would be naïve to think that the political dynamics that drive legislators to support more severe sentences would not also put pressure on elected judges to impose tougher sentences, whether or not such sentences are mandated by law. Moreover, in at least one respect, the dynamics may actually have a stronger impact on judges: legislators have budgetary responsibilities that, at least in theory, should cause them to think twice about adopting new sentencing laws that will require additional corrections spending, while judges have little incentive to contemplate the fiscal consequences of their actions. At present, in Wisconsin and many other states, there is no meaningful economic check on whatever tendencies a judge might have to indulge or accommodate populist sensibilities.

If judges are to be given wide discretion over sentences, then stronger incentives should be put into place for local officials to develop and utilize cost-effective alternatives to imprisonment. Wisconsin's experience with the Intensive Sanctions Program demonstrates that it is not enough for state officials to develop new alternatives; if local prosecutors and judges do not trust the state program, then they will not use it. By contrast, Milwaukee's positive recent experience with new diversionary programs points to the potential value of local "ownership" of the alternatives. This point is developed more fully in Lesson 8 below.

Lesson 6:
Guidelines Should Be Presumptive and Designed to Curtail Over-imprisonment

The Wisconsin experience suggests that sentencing reformers should not bother with advisory guidelines. Wisconsin has tried and abandoned advisory guidelines twice. With perhaps just a couple of exceptions, other states have had similarly disappointing experiences with advisory guidelines.[28] Judges have proven fiercely protective of their discretion and resentful of even very modest efforts to nudge them into greater uniformity. To be sure, we can identify various missteps that were made as Wisconsin's guidelines were designed and implemented. However, given the judiciary's palpable disdain for the guidelines concept in Wisconsin, it is hard to believe that there is anything that might have been done differently to generate substantially higher levels of compliance. Indeed, the basic political realities facing locally elected judges seem to push strongly against their adherence to any state-developed sentencing norms.

It is not worth the trouble to develop and implement a comprehensive guidelines system without an unequivocal indication from the political system that the guidelines should be followed in most cases. In other words, the guidelines should be *presumptive*. In theory, such guidelines activate the appellate courts of a state as enforcers of statewide sentencing standards. Although appellate judges may be subject to just as much political pressure as the lower-court judges, their accountability is not so intensely localized, which means that they are more likely to take into account state-level policy considerations. Of course, presumptive guidelines have never been tried in Wisconsin, but they do have a positive track record in a few other states. Assessing the evidence, the National Research Council's incarceration committee has observed, "Minnesota's [presumptive] guidelines took effect in 1980. Oregon, Pennsylvania, and Washington created similar systems in the 1980s. Evaluations showed that well-designed and -implemented presumptive guidelines made sentencing more predictable, reduced racial and other unwarranted disparities, facilitated systems planning, and controlled correctional spending. Kansas, North Carolina, and Ohio created similar systems. . . . Presumptive sentencing guidelines developed by a sentencing commission are the most promising means available to jurisdictions that want to reduce or avoid unwarranted sentencing disparities, improve budgetary and policy planning, or both."[29] The prestigious American Law Institute, currently revising its model sentencing law, has also endorsed presumptive guidelines.[30]

Despite positive experiences in a handful of places, reformers in other states should think carefully before initiating a push for presumptive guidelines. It has proven difficult to sustain the political will necessary to establish and preserve a coherent, effective guidelines system. A promising effort to create a guidelines system in New York foundered, notwithstanding broad support for the guidelines concept at the outset.[31] Ohio, Oregon, and Pennsylvania have retreated in varying ways from their presumptive systems.[32] The federal presumptive guidelines were subjected to intense criticism for many years and eventually converted to advisory.[33] More generally, it may be telling that no states have implemented new presumptive systems for two decades. In Wisconsin, in particular, the absence of any serious presumptive guidelines proposal in the legislature since 1980 hardly bodes well for the prospects of such a proposal today. Presumptive guidelines are not a new innovation. Their potential benefits have been well documented and recognized nationally for decades. Yet, states have not been flocking to the concept. This likely reflects, at least in part, an implicit weighing of the benefits of guidelines relative to the expected magnitude of judicial resistance and the difficulty of crafting a specific set of guidelines that are acceptable to prosecutors, defense lawyers, corrections officials, and other stakeholders.

The calculus will not change unless the benefits of presumptive guidelines appear more compelling. Guidelines may be hampered by their historic association with the goal of reducing disparities, which was the primary purpose of the guidelines in Minnesota and other early-adopting states.[34] Yet, in Wisconsin anyway, we have seen little evidence of any real commitment to statewide uniformity in sentencing as an end in itself. This indifference does not seem unjustified. As the Wisconsin Supreme Court observed when it rebuffed the first guidelines, "Neither the interests of the individual being sentenced nor those of the community in which that individual lives are susceptible of accurate assessment in terms of statistical data gathered from other sentencing courts in the state. While each convicted felon is an individual deserving of individual treatment at sentencing, the interests of the public, too, will vary according to the particular community in which the crime was committed, the capacity of the community to rehabilitate the criminal, and the needs of that community for protection from that type of criminal activity."[35]

Many voters seem to share this perspective. In our polling research, we asked whether respondents agreed that "it is important for Wisconsin to have uniform, statewide sentencing policies, even if that means that judges have less freedom to take into account local needs and values in determining sentences." Only 41 percent agreed, while 48 percent disagreed.[36]

Guidelines proposals are unlikely to gain political traction unless they are seen as an effective mechanism to achieve a more important goal than greater statewide uniformity. In this regard, North Carolina offers an intriguing contrast to Minnesota. North Carolina implemented guidelines in 1994 that were primarily intended to constrain growth in the size of the state's prison population.[37] The results were rapid and remarkable. In just a few years, North Carolina went from having one of the nation's highest imprisonment rates to having a rate lower than the national average. This was accomplished by rigorously holding the line on imprisonment at a time when most other states, including Wisconsin, were experiencing dramatic increases.

Since the 1970s and early 1980s, when the first guidelines systems were put into place, mass incarceration has become a much more pressing policy problem than disparity per se (although, of course, concerns about mass incarceration are driven, in part, by its disproportionate impact on people of color). There might be more enthusiasm for new guidelines proposals if guidelines were seen as an effective response to the mass-incarceration problem. The North Carolina experience provides a basis for this framing. To be sure, the real challenge in Wisconsin and many other states is now to *reduce* imprisonment, and not merely, as in North Carolina in the 1990s, to *stabilize* imprisonment. As discussed earlier in the chapter, the political dynamics surrounding reduction seem rather more complicated than those surrounding stabilization. However, if a state were willing and able to make a strong commitment to reduction, there is reason to think that presumptive guidelines might help to achieve that goal.

Lesson 7:
Parole Does Not Provide Much Protection against Over-imprisonment

As states across the nation have worked in recent years to reduce their prison populations, many have attempted to give greater discretion to corrections officials to release prisoners early.[38] However, the Wisconsin experience demonstrates that such discretion—whether denominated "parole," "earned release," or something else—hardly guarantees restraint in imprisonment. Truth in sentencing, which was intended to eliminate discretionary parole, did not really take effect in Wisconsin until well into our story, only applying to crimes committed on or after December 31, 1999. As of that date, Wisconsin already had 20,390 prisoners—more than nine times its total at the start of the era of mass incarceration. Nearly all of the total imprisonment growth that Wisconsin would experience had already occurred *with parole still fully in place*. Moreover, TIS did not actually start to have a direct impact on the size of the prison population for several more years; it would take time for the first TIS offenders to be apprehended, prosecuted, convicted, and sentenced, and then to serve the amount of time that they would have served if parole had been available to them. As a result, TIS likely had little net effect on the prison population until about 2004, when the population was already essentially at its peak. In short, TIS helped keep Wisconsin's prison population high but contributed very little to its growth. In principle, parole was available to most prisoners throughout the growth period, but parole discretion was not exercised in a way that came anywhere close to keeping the number of prisoners in line with the state's prison capacity. Parole discretion, no less than judicial sentencing discretion, failed to prevent a massive run-up in Wisconsin's prison population.

The Wisconsin experience is in line with what has happened in many other states. For instance, one national study found that eight of the ten states with the highest imprisonment rates retained parole discretion.[39] Conversely, most states that abolished parole during the era of mass incarceration experienced below-average imprisonment growth.[40] This is not to say that TIS necessarily restrains imprisonment, but it is to say that parole can be—and often is—administered with far less lenience than the public often assumes.

The underlying dynamics echo the dynamics of judicial sentencing discretion. Corrections officials must operate in the same general political environment as legislators and judges. Although the officials are not elected themselves, they are ultimately answerable to a governor who is elected, and they understand perfectly well that a controversial release decision can be a career killer. To be sure, there is an important countervailing pressure: corrections officials must also be mindful of prison overcrowding. In Wisconsin in the early and mid-1990s, capacity concerns did indeed contribute to a liberalization of parole. However, in retrospect, this period of time seems the exception that proves the rule. Liberalization provoked a political backlash, and Parole Chair John Husz—publicly branded "the most dangerous man in Wisconsin" by one DA—was forced out of office. Parole was then restricted even before TIS went into effect. To this day, more than two thousand "old law" inmates remain in Wisconsin prisons, theoretically eligible for parole but unable to secure release.[41] These include about four hundred housed in minimum-security institutions.[42] Even with these low-risk inmates, the Parole Commission has been unwilling to take a chance with early release.

Overcrowding concerns are most powerful during times of rapid growth in imprisonment, like the 1990s. At other times, such as the present, corrections officials may actually perceive their economic interests to run counter to generous parole, which might cause the prison population to dip low enough that layoffs, institutional closures, and budget cuts will be expected. Even during times of growth in imprisonment, reining in that growth may not be perceived as an especially high priority. In the short term, the costs of overcrowding are borne by the inmates, who are essentially powerless, and by the guards and other correctional employees based in the institutions, who may be several layers of bureaucracy removed from the officials who make release decisions. Eventually, of course, new institutions will have to be built if parole does not offset increased prison admissions and longer nominal sentences, but there is no reason to assume that corrections officials will face intolerable political heat for new building needs—certainly nothing compared to the heat John Husz faced for his relatively aggressive approach to parole.

For these reasons, for any state wishing to reduce imprisonment, it may be less helpful to enhance release discretion than to establish or strengthen no- or low-discretion release mechanisms. Perhaps the most promising reform for Wisconsin and many other states would be in the area of "good time"—credits toward early release that are earned through good behavior. As we have seen, Wisconsin eliminated good time in 1984 when it seemed that parole provided adequate incentives for good behavior. Whether or not that was actually so, good time should have been reinstituted when parole was abolished. Research in other states indicates that good conduct time can reduce incarceration, reduce rates of disciplinary infractions in prison, reduce recidivism rates after release, and ultimately save money for state taxpayers.[43] Best of all, good-time release is not dependent on the discretion of politically sensitive corrections officials. Rhode Island provides an example of a state that has achieved some meaningful reductions in its prison population (a 20 percent decrease between 2006 and 2011), largely due to the expansion of good-time credits.[44]

Alternatively, or in combination with good time, a state might adopt parole guidelines that rely mostly or wholly on objective considerations and establish presumptive release dates. Parole guidelines are not a new idea; early experiments were conducted in the 1970s at about the same time that the first sentencing guidelines were being developed.[45] Researchers found that parole guidelines were able to reduce unwarranted disparities in release dates, but the parole guidelines movement was soon eclipsed by the sentencing guidelines movement and the first wave of parole-abolition statutes. More recently, law professor and Pennsylvania Sentencing Commission chair Steve Chanenson has argued that parole guidelines can and should be developed in a coordinated way with sentencing guidelines.[46] Although Chanenson's model has yet to be tested, New Jersey offers some reason to believe that parole reform can be a major driver of imprisonment reduction. New Jersey reduced its prison population by 26 percent between 1999 and 2012, tied with New York for best in the nation over that time period.[47] Much of the reduction is attributed to a dramatic increase in parole approval rates, which went from 30 percent to 51 percent after the parole board adopted various procedural reforms in response to litigation.

Lesson 8:
Local Officials Should Be Given More Ownership over Corrections

Throughout the era of mass incarceration, we have seen repeated expressions of concern that Wisconsin's judges and prosecutors are not making adequate use of alternatives to incarceration. However, the state's effort to establish a new, more appealing alternative, the Intensive Sanctions Program, failed. Milwaukee's more recent experience with new diversion programs provides more hope. What differentiates the Milwaukee programs of the early 2000s from the ISP of the 1990s? In part, Milwaukee's success is likely due to a broader shift in attitudes toward rehabilitation and a modest weakening of populist sentiment. However, some of the success is also likely due to the local "ownership" of the Milwaukee programs. Run by the distrusted Department of Corrections, the ISP made little headway with judges and prosecutors. However, with primary leadership provided by Milwaukee's DA and chief judge, the local initiatives have been much better positioned to gain the support of line prosecutors and judges. Moreover, if the initiatives failed, there was a shared understanding of dire *local* consequences—with Jail and House of Correction populations in chronic violation of a court order, an expensive new facility might be the only alternative. Local officials thus owned both the administration of the diversion programs and the fiscal consequences if they failed.

The Milwaukee experience highlights the importance of Wisconsin's decision not to adopt a community corrections act similar to Minnesota's. As discussed in chapter 4, such a possibility was considered and rejected by a Legislative Council special committee in the early 1980s, even though Wisconsin had already adopted (and still maintains) local responsibility for *juvenile* corrections. In the early 1980s debate, even some who were sympathetic to the idea of local responsibility felt the time was not right. Circumstances now may be more favorable. The "nothing works" mentality, which may have peaked in the 1980s, has faded, and local officials now have a plethora of proven models for supervising and treating offenders in the community. Moreover, crime rates, which had been on the rise for two decades when the Minnesota system was first debated, have long since stabilized, giving local officials more breathing room for the development of new programs.

Local ownership of community corrections, as in the Minnesota system, seems capable of generating higher levels of confidence among judges and prosecutors in the reliability of alternatives to incarceration; promoting the development of more innovative programming; and facilitating the tailoring of community supervision to local needs, values, and resources. Importantly, local ownership also involves economic incentives for responsible decision-making. There may be fiscal carrots, fiscal sticks, or both to support greater use of alternatives to incarceration. This should at least partially counter a fundamental flaw in our decentralized sentencing systems in the United States. As the late law professor William Stuntz observed, "States pay for . . . penitentiaries, but local officials—chiefly prosecutors and trial judges—make the decisions that fill them. To the local voters who elect those officials, and hence to the officials they elect, prison sentences are nearly a free good."[48] As with any free good, we can expect overconsumption of imprisonment. Local ownership, though, can make imprisonment somewhat more costly at the local level. There should normally be some local economic consequence resulting from a prison sentence, whether that be in the form of a foregone state subsidy for community supervision or a direct charge-back for the utilization of state correctional resources. Such economic consequences would lead to less overconsumption of imprisonment.

Local ownership, of course, is not an either-or proposition but a question of degree. Thus, for instance, the recent Milwaukee innovations only reflect a

limited degree of local ownership because the basic form of community supervision, probation, remains within state control. The Milwaukee initiatives have
been in the area of pretrial diversion, as well as a few programs connected to
the locally administered House of Correction, which supervises short sentences
of incarceration. Structural reforms to state law would be required for Milwaukee and other interested communities to be able to create a more seamless,
coherent system of locally administered community corrections, incorporating
not only pretrial diversions but also probation, postprison supervision, and
alternatives to revocation. More robust local ownership might produce an even
more significant flowering of local innovation.

Like presumptive guidelines, local ownership has a positive track record in
Minnesota and a few other states going back several decades. (The Minnesota
experience also demonstrates that local ownership can work in a coordinated
fashion with presumptive guidelines; these are not alternative but potentially
complementary reforms.) Notably, state grants for locally administered alternatives to incarceration were also part of North Carolina's imprisonment-
stabilization story in the 1990s.[49] More recently, there has been a new wave of
experimentation with various approaches to local ownership. Most importantly,
California turned to local ownership in a dramatic way in 2011 as a way to
achieve court-ordered reductions in prison overcrowding.[50] The state's "realignment" policy included these components: (1) offenders with nonviolent,
non-sex-related, nonserious ("non-non-non" in the new lingo) current and
prior convictions are no longer incarcerated in state prisons; (2) returning non-
non-non prisoners are no longer supervised in the community by the state parole
agency but by local officials; and (3) probationers and parolees are no longer
sent to prison for technical violations of the conditions of release. In effect, the
state decreed that if incarceration was going to be used for certain categories of
offenders, it would thenceforth have to be in the locally financed jails, not the
state-financed prisons. The policy change contributed to a remarkably sharp
drop in imprisonment. Since realignment, the state has shed nearly twenty-five
thousand prisoners, or about 15 percent of its total.[51] To be sure, the state's jail
population rose by about eleven thousand over the same time period. Still, that
left a net reduction of incarceration of nearly fourteen thousand. On the whole,
local officials seemed more restrained in their use of incarceration when it was
local facilities that were being used. Notably, there has been little or no impact
on crime rates as a result of realignment and decarceration in California.[52]

A few other states have also recently enhanced local ownership, albeit on a
much smaller scale. In 2008, for instance, the Arizona Legislature created new
financial incentives for probation departments (which are county agencies in
the state) to reduce the flow of probationers into prison; counties are permitted

to keep 40 percent of the cost savings when they reduce revocation and re-offense rates.[53] Over the following two years, revocations to prison fell by 28 percent, while the number of probationers convicted of a new felony dropped by 31 percent.[54] Overall savings were estimated to be $36 million. Kansas adopted a similar law at about the same time and experienced a similar drop in revocations.[55] Pennsylvania is now also using "performance incentive funding" to encourage fewer commitments of low-level offenders to state prisons.[56]

Although the Wisconsin experience, particularly the recent experience in Milwaukee, draws particular attention to the importance of economic incentives at the local level, new financial arrangements may also be helpful in other contexts. To hearken back to the extraordinary deinstitutionalization of the mentally ill in the 1960s, another important cause was the creation of the federal Medicaid and Medicare programs in 1965.[57] The new arrangements pushed states to move patients out of the mental hospitals, which were state funded, and into other treatment venues, where federal reimbursement was possible. The experience indicates that state agencies, not just local, may be responsive to economic incentives. A more recent and directly pertinent illustration comes from an experiment by the California Department of Corrections in the early 1990s.[58] In the hope of reducing revocations, the CDC allocated each of its parole units a certain number of prison beds for technical violations; if the number was exceeded, then the unit's budget was reduced, but if the unit used fewer beds than were allocated, it would be given additional support services for its parolees. Parole agents were also given additional training on alternatives to revocation. The experiment was ultimately credited with reducing revocation by ten thousand in 1992. To the extent that important penal decisions, like revocation, remain in state agency hands, new incentive structures like those used in California may complement enhanced local ownership over other aspects of the correctional system.

Lesson 9:
Do Not Forget the Police

Discussions about how to reverse mass incarceration normally focus on sentencing and corrections policies. Policing, however, should not be neglected. Consider the recent Wisconsin experience recounted in chapter 7. Serious drug trafficking arrests fell by more than 50 percent between 2006 and 2011, which contributed to an even more dramatic decline in new prison admissions for drug offenses. There is no reason to think that the drop in drug arrests resulted from some sudden, sharp drop in drug usage; to the contrary, as we have seen, public-health records indicate that heroin use became an increasingly important problem over the time period. Rather, the drop in drug arrests resulted from changes in policing strategy, particularly in Milwaukee. Policing policy thus deserves about as much credit, if not more, than sentencing or corrections policy for Wisconsin's modest drop in imprisonment after 2006.

The Wisconsin experience echoes that of New York. Along with New Jersey and California, New York is one of the three significant decarceration success stories in the United States, with a 26 percent decline in its prison population between 1999 and 2012.[59] Much of that drop has been attributed to a 50 percent reduction in felony drug arrests in New York City over the same time period. Like the Milwaukee Police Department, the NYPD shifted its enforcement priorities away from the War on Drugs approach of the 1990s, with important collateral effects on state imprisonment rates.

To be sure, drug enforcement may be unique insofar as it is an area of wide police discretion that is capable of making a significant direct contribution to imprisonment rates. As a practical matter, police have little real discretion when it comes to investigating the serious violent and sexual offenses that play such an important role in mass incarceration. Assuming the incidence of homicide and rape remain constant, the public would not likely tolerate a 50 percent reduction in homicide or rape arrests. Arrest discretion matters the most with respect to offenses whose severity is either low or (in the case of drugs) uncertain and socially contested. For these types of offenses, there are real choices for the police to make about whether and how to enforce the law. In general, however, arrests for these offenses do not directly contribute to imprisonment to the same extent as drug arrests. The police could turn the enforcement intensity up or down for, say, streetwalking, retail theft, reckless driving, vandalism, or vagrancy without having much direct effect on the prison population; however many are arrested in these categories, very few will be sent to prison.

Still, even beyond drug enforcement, policing strategy may merit attention as an *indirect* driver of mass incarceration. Although low-level arrests tend to produce probationary sentences, there is always a risk that probation will be revoked. Low-level arrests may also lead to revocations on earlier sentences or generate criminal history that may cause the offender's next sentence to be more severe. Moreover, low-level arrests reduce employability and generate fines and fees, which poor offenders will struggle to pay. The economic effects of low-level convictions may exacerbate the psychological and financial pressures that can contribute to more serious criminality. None of this is to say that police should necessarily abandon the enforcement of quality-of-life and other lesser criminal laws, but it is to suggest that there are a variety of subtle, and potentially collectively significant, ways that such enforcement may contribute to mass incarceration.[60] These mechanisms warrant additional research and possibly the adoption of less aggressive enforcement strategies.

Lesson 10:
Firm Commitments to Specific Decarceration Goals May Be Necessary

Once the infrastructure for mass incarceration is in place, the forces of institutional inertia help ensure that imprisonment rates remain high. In order to overcome that inertia, it may be necessary to make a firm commitment to specific decarceration goals. If it is clear that the status quo is no longer an option, the system is likely to prove surprisingly creative and effective in adjusting to new realities. Certainly, that was the experience in moving *to* historically high imprisonment rates. As the prison population boomed in Wisconsin, the system adjusted: single-person cells became double-person cells; common spaces were reconfigured as dormitory housing; the construction of new institutions was facilitated by the adoption of new site-selection processes; the Intensive Sanctions Program was developed to relieve some of the overcrowding pressure; and when the ISP failed, prisoners were transported en masse to out-of-state facilities. There seems no reason why the system could not similarly adjust to pressures to *decarcerate*.

California provides a powerful example. Chronic overcrowding led to a court order for the state to reduce its prison population by at least thirty-eight thousand.[61] The state responded by adopting its bold plan for local ownership. Some predicted a public safety disaster, but the required reductions were achieved with little or no measurable impact on crime rates.

In Wisconsin, the grassroots activists of WISDOM may have had the right idea by calling for a similarly clear numerical target to be reached: a halving of the state's prison population in three years. That particular target was unrealistically aggressive, but law professor Michael Tonry's call for halving national incarceration rates in *six* years might be within the realm of feasibility, or at least close enough to be a conversation starter, instead of a conversation stopper.[62] Thinking about reform objectives in this way helps keep the focus on the ethical mandate to reduce imprisonment per se, thus avoiding the complications that are raised when the primary focus is on cutting costs or reducing recidivism.

Litigation may be necessary to make goals of this nature stick. It is striking how prominent a role litigation has played in the various success stories discussed in this chapter. California provides only the most prominent example. New Jersey, too, adopted its important parole reforms in response to litigation.

North Carolina's imprisonment-constraining guidelines system also resulted, in part, from litigation.[63] Even in Wisconsin, Milwaukee's recent reforms were spurred, at least initially, by the threat of litigation over jail overcrowding. In truth, lawsuits and court orders may have little ability to overcome determined resistance by government officials; a well-known example comes from the Deep South's successful resistance to school desegregation in the decade following *Brown v. Board of Education*.[64] However, when key officials independently have some interest in politically controversial reform, litigation can provide important cover.

Wisconsin's prison population exploded because serious violent crime exploded and because an increasingly populist environment made it politically desirable, perhaps even necessary, for judges and prosecutors to get tougher, while also discouraging the development and use of community-based alternatives to imprisonment. The great cocaine panic that began in the mid-1980s complemented these trends by fueling a surge of drug defendants into a court system that was shifting its emphasis from rehabilitation to deterrence. The combination of more convicted offenders and tougher sentences forced corrections officials to liberalize parole in order to prevent the prisons from being overwhelmed. The liberalization of parole, in turn, provoked a populist backlash that led to the restriction and then elimination of parole. The system was saved from disaster by a fortuitous decline in crime rates and by the mass shipment of prisoners to for-profit facilities in other states pending the construction of new prisons in Wisconsin. As the new prisons finally came on line and the out-of-state prisoners returned home, the state prison population reached a stable equilibrium of about twenty-two thousand to twenty-three thousand—nine times higher than its historical norms.

The criminal justice system has adapted itself to the world of mass incarceration. A vast new penal infrastructure has established itself, and important institutional interests now have a stake in maintaining incarceration at present levels. Inertia has set in, aided and abetted by the continued vitality of populist attitudes. While politicians do not compete as aggressively to be the toughest on crime as they did in the 1990s, no one wants to be tagged with the label of soft on crime. Thus, in Wisconsin and across the United States, policymakers have moved cautiously into the area of sentencing reform. There seems little real motivation to achieve dramatic cuts in imprisonment—to return imprisonment to where it was twenty years ago, say, let alone to where it was forty years ago. Legislators and governors do not want to be called upon to build new prisons, but they seem relatively indifferent when it comes to closing existing prisons.

There is some hope in the striking resurgence of interest in rehabilitation. Some reforms that support rehabilitation, such as awarding good-time credits to prisoners based on their participation in programming, may make a significant dent in imprisonment rates as an ancillary benefit. Still, major reductions seem unlikely unless decarceration is accepted as an express goal in its own right, as deinstitutionalization of the mentally ill was in the 1960s. As with deinstitutionalization, the decarceration goal should be framed in egalitarian terms, not solely economic.

To the extent that policymakers adopt meaningful decarceration goals, a variety of promising policy options are available, including presumptive sentencing guidelines, good-time credits and similar early-release mechanisms, and enhanced local control and financial responsibility in the corrections area. If there is a will to decarcerate, there are ways that it can be done without large public safety costs. The harder part is the ethical challenge: that is, convincing larger numbers of citizens to see in criminal offenders a shared humanity and a real potential for good—to recognize them as a part of *us*, and not simply a frightening *them*.

Notes

Introduction

1. NAT'L CRIM. JUST. INFORMATION & STATISTICS SVC., U.S. DEP'T OF JUST., CENSUS OF PRISONERS IN STATE CORRECTIONAL FACILITIES 1973 (1976).

2. PATRICK A. LANGAN ET AL., U.S. DEP'T OF JUST., HISTORICAL STATISTICS ON PRISONERS IN STATE AND FEDERAL INSTITUTIONS, YEAREND 1925–86 (1988), *available at* https://www.ncjrs.gov/pdffiles1/digitization/111098ncjrs.pdf.

3. These trends are based on year-end jurisdiction totals, which are collected and reported on an annual basis for each state by the United States Department of Justice's Bureau of Justice Statistics. The data are available in convenient form through an online tool: http://www.bjs.gov/index.cfm?ty=nps.

4. These figures include only those held in *state* institutions. If federal prisons were also included, there would be about 200,000 additional inmates in 2013.

5. NAT'L CRIM. JUST. INFORMATION & STATISTICS SVC., *supra* note 1; E. ANN CARSON, U.S. DEP'T OF JUST., PRISONERS IN 2013 (2014).

6. DAVID GARLAND, THE CULTURE OF CONTROL: CRIME AND SOCIAL ORDER IN CONTEMPORARY SOCIETY (2001).

7. JAMES Q. WHITMAN, HARSH JUSTICE: CRIMINAL PUNISHMENT AND THE WIDENING DIVIDE BETWEEN AMERICA AND EUROPE (2003).

8. MICHELLE ALEXANDER, THE NEW JIM CROW: MASS INCARCERATION IN THE AGE OF COLORBLINDNESS (2010).

9. Other valuable studies include MARIE GOTTSCHALK, THE PRISON AND THE GALLOWS: THE POLITICS OF MASS INCARCERATION IN AMERICA (2006); MARC MAUER, RACE TO INCARCERATE (2006); JULIAN V. ROBERTS ET AL., PENAL POPULISM AND PUBLIC OPINION: LESSONS FROM FIVE COUNTRIES (2003); JONATHAN SIMON, GOVERNING THROUGH CRIME: HOW THE WAR ON CRIME TRANSFORMED AMERICAN DEMOCRACY AND CREATED A CULTURE OF FEAR (2007); MICHAEL TONRY, THINKING ABOUT CRIME: SENSE AND SENSIBILITY IN AMERICAN PENAL CULTURE (2004); BRUCE WESTERN, PUNISHMENT AND INEQUALITY IN AMERICA (2006).

10. William Spelman, *Crime, Cash, and Limited Options: Explaining the Prison Boom*, 8 CRIMINOLOGY & PUB. POL'Y 29, 57 (2009).

11. Thomas D. Stucky et al., *Partisan Politics, Electoral Competition and Imprisonment: An Analysis of States over Time*, 43 CRIMINOLOGY 211, 232 (2005).

12. Richard S. Frase, *Sentencing Guidelines in Minnesota, 1978–2003*, 32 CRIME & JUST. 131 (2005); Ronald F. Wright, *Counting the Costs of Sentencing in North Carolina, 1980–2000*, 29 CRIME & JUST. 39 (2005). For a similarly valuable work on yet another state's experience with guidelines, see David Boerner & Roxanne Lieb, *Sentencing Reform in the Other Washington*, 28 CRIME & JUST. 71 (2001).

13. Other notable state-specific studies include JOHN H. KRAMER & JEFFREY T. ULMER, SENTENCING GUIDELINES: LESSONS FROM PENNSYLVANIA (2009); PAMALA L. GRISET, DETERMINATE SENTENCING: THE PROMISE AND THE REALITY OF RETRIBUTIVE JUSTICE (1991) (New York); DALE G. PARENT, STRUCTURING CRIMINAL SENTENCES: THE EVOLUTION OF MINNESOTA'S SENTENCING GUIDELINES (Daniel J. Freed ed., 1988). Additionally, California has been the subject of several outstanding studies. *See infra* note 15. A number of scholars have also ably explored the development of the federal sentencing system. *See, e.g.*, KATE STITH & JOSÉ A. CABRANES, FEAR OF JUDGING: SENTENCING GUIDELINES IN THE FEDERAL COURTS (1996); Marc L. Miller & Ronald F. Wright, *Your Cheatin' Heart(land): The Long Search for Administrative Sentencing Justice*, 2 BUFF. CRIM. L. REV. 723 (1999).

14. MONA LYNCH, SUNBELT JUSTICE: ARIZONA AND THE TRANSFORMATION OF AMERICAN PUNISHMENT (2010).

15. *See, e.g.*, VANESSA BARKER, THE POLITICS OF IMPRISONMENT: HOW THE DEMOCRATIC PROCESS SHAPES THE WAY AMERICA PUNISHES OFFENDERS (2009); JOSHUA PAGE, THE TOUGHEST BEAT: POLITICS, PUNISHMENT, AND THE PRISON OFFICERS UNION IN CALIFORNIA (2011); FRANKLIN E. ZIMRING ET AL., PUNISHMENT AND DEMOCRACY: THREE STRIKES AND YOU'RE OUT IN CALIFORNIA (2001).

16. David Mills & Michael Romano, *The Passage and Implementation of the Three Strikes Reform Act of 2012 (Proposition 36)*, 25 FED. SENT'ING RPTR. 265 (2013).

17. Matt Taibbi, *Cruel and Unusual Punishment: The Shame of Three Strikes Laws*, ROLLING STONE, Mar. 27, 2013, *available at* http://www.rollingstone.com/politics/news/cruel-and-unusual-punishment-the-shame-of-three-strikes-laws-20130327.

18. I borrow the term "managerialism" from Vanessa Barker's analysis of the New York experience, although my usage may differ a bit from hers. *See* Barker, *supra* note 15, at 45–46.

19. Other scholars have used the term "penal populism" in a variety of different ways. Again, I roughly follow Barker's usage. *Id.* at 43.

20. Prisoner numbers here reflect year-end jurisdiction totals from the online prison data tool of the U.S. Bureau of Justice Statistics (http://www.bjs.gov/index.cfm?ty=nps). Major violent arrest numbers are adult arrests for the violent "index" crimes (nonnegligent homicide, rape, robbery, and aggravated assault). Data come from the annual statewide arrest reports prepared by the Wisconsin Office of Justice Assistance and its predecessor agencies.

21. Michael M. O'Hear, *Mass Incarceration in Three Midwestern States: Origins and Trends*, 47 VAL. U. L. REV. 709, 724 (2013).

22. Michael M. O'Hear & Darren Wheelock, *Imprisonment Inertia and Public Support for Truth in Sentencing*, 2015 BYU L. REV. 257.

Chapter 1. Setting the Stage, Meeting the Players

1. The view of sentencing and plea bargaining presented here synthesizes the dozens of interviews that I conducted for this book, many informal conversations I have had over the years with Wisconsin judges and lawyers, and much of the relevant socio-legal literature. Some of the literature that I have found especially helpful includes MARVIN E. FRANKEL, CRIMINAL SENTENCES: LAW WITHOUT ORDER (1973); MILTON HEUMANN, PLEA BARGAINING: THE EXPERIENCES OF PROSECUTORS, JUDGES, AND DEFENSE ATTORNEYS (1978); MALCOLM M. FEELEY, THE PROCESS IS THE PUNISHMENT: HANDLING CASES IN A LOWER CRIMINAL COURT (1979); JOHN H. KRAMER & JEFFREY T. ULMER, SENTENCING GUIDELINES: LESSONS FROM PENNSYLVANIA (2009); WILLIAM J. STUNTZ, THE COLLAPSE OF AMERICAN CRIMINAL JUSTICE (2011); PROSECUTORS AND POLITICS: A COMPARATIVE PERSPECTIVE (Michael Tonry ed., 2012); Albert W. Alschuler, *The Defense Attorney's Role in Plea Bargaining*, 84 YALE L.J. 1179 (1975); Daniel J. Freed, *Federal Sentencing in the Wake of the Guidelines: Unacceptable Limits on the Discretion of Sentencers*, 101 YALE L.J. 1681 (1992); Kate Stith & José A. Cabranes, *Judging Under the Federal Sentencing Guidelines*, 91 Nw. U. L. REV. 1247 (1997); Stephen J. Schulhofer & Ilene H. Nagel, *Plea Negotiations Under the Federal Sentencing Guidelines: Guideline Circumvention and Its Dynamics in the Post-Mistretta Period*, 91 Nw. U. L. REV. 1284 (1997); Stephanos Bibas, *Plea Bargaining Outside the Shadow of Trial*, 117 HARV. L. REV. 2463 (2004); Chris M. Guthrie et al., *Blinking on the Bench: How Judges Decide Cases*, 93 CORNELL L. REV. 1 (2007); Chad M. Oldfather, *Writing, Cognition, and the Nature of the Judicial Function*, 96 GEO. L.J. 1283 (2008).

2. WIS. LEG. FISCAL BUREAU, INFORMATIONAL PAPER 59: STATE CRIMINAL JUSTICE FUNCTIONS 47 (2015).

3. WIS. STATISTICAL ANALYSIS CTR., DEPT. OF JUSTICE, ARRESTS IN WISCONSIN, 2012 (2013).

4. WIS. LEG. FISCAL BUREAU, *supra* note 2, at 53.

5. State ex rel. Kalal v. Circuit Court for Dane County, 2004 WI 58, ¶ 31.

6. A respected Wisconsin judge, the late Ralph Adam Fine, attracted considerable attention with a 1986 book attacking plea bargaining. The title left no doubt about his basic position—*Escape of the Guilty*. Despite his success in sparking conversation and debate, there is no indication that Fine changed the basic dynamics of plea bargaining in a fundamental, widespread way.

7. SANDRA SHANE-DUBOW, WISCONSIN CENTER FOR PUBLIC POLICY, FELONY SENTENCING IN WISCONSIN 193 (1979).

8. DAVID C. ANDERSON, CRIME AND THE POLITICS OF HYSTERIA: HOW THE WILLIE HORTON STORY CHANGED AMERICA (1995).

9. Patrick Marley et al., *Brad Schimel Defeats Susan Happ for Wisconsin Attorney General*, Milw. J. Sentinel, Nov. 4, 2014, *available at* http://www.jsonline.com/news/statepolitics /brad-schimel-defeats-susan-happ-for-wisconsin-attorney-general-b99382153z1- 281551151.html.

10. Interview with Lee Wells, Milwaukee County Circuit Court Judge, 1981–2004, in Milwaukee, Wis. (Nov. 18, 2013).

11. Interview with James E. Doyle, District Attorney, Dane County, 1977–83, Wisconsin Attorney General, 1991–2003, Wisconsin Governor, 2003–11, Of Counsel, Foley and Lardner, 2011 to present, in Milwaukee, Wis. (Sept. 30, 2014).

12. Wis. Leg. Fiscal Bureau, *supra* note 2, at 63.

13. *Kalal*, 2004 WI 58, ¶ 28.

14. Wis. Leg. Fiscal Bureau, Informational Paper 58: Wisconsin Court System (2015).

15. Wis. Leg. Ref. Bureau, 2013–2014 Wisconsin Blue Book 877 (2013).

16. Wells, *supra* note 10.

17. Patrick Marley et al., *TV Ad by Gableman Comes Out Swinging: Spot Accuses Butler of Helping Child Sex Offender*, Milw. J. Sentinel, March 15, 2008, *available at* http://www .jsonline.com/news/statepolitics/29486784.html.

18. Milwaukee County is an exception in relation to the court of appeals; Wisconsin's largest county constitutes an entire court of appeals district unto itself.

19. Michael M. O'Hear, *Appellate Review of Sentences: Reconsidering Deference*, 51 Wm. & Mary L. Rev. 2123 (2010); Michael M. O'Hear, *Appellate Review of Sentence Explanations: Learning from the Wisconsin and Federal Experiences*, 93 Marq. L. Rev. 751 (2009).

20. I base this burglary example on an observation provided to me by veteran defense lawyer Stephen Hurley, who has practiced widely both within and outside Wisconsin.

21. Jason J. Czarnezki, *Voting and Electoral Politics in the Wisconsin Supreme Court*, 87 Marq. L. Rev. 323, 345 (2003).

22. Carlos Berdejo & Noam Yuchtman, *Crime, Punishment, and Politics: An Analysis of Political Cycles in Criminal Sentencing*, 95 Rev. Econ. & Statistics 741 (2013).

23. Michael M. O'Hear, *Rethinking Drug Courts: Restorative Justice as a Response to Racial Injustice*, 20 Stan. L. & Pol'y Rev. 463, 468–72 (2009).

24. 2004 WI 42, ¶ 40.

25. Wis. Leg. Fiscal Bureau, Informational Paper 55: Adult Corrections Program (2015).

26. Bureau of Justice Statistics, U.S. Dep't of Justice, Sourcebook of Criminal Justice Statistics—2003, at 13 (2003), *available at* http://www.albany.edu /sourcebook/pdf/t110.pdf.

27. Wis. Leg. Fiscal Bureau, *supra* note 25, at 2.

28. Arthur L. Srb, *Legislation Might Have Prevented Killing Spree*, St. Paul Pioneer Press, Aug. 18, 1991.

29. *See, e.g.*, Wisconsin Sent'ing Comm'n, Sentencing in Wisconsin: Drug Trafficking 3 (2007).

30. Governor's Task Force to Enhance Probation, Final Report 20 (2000).

31. *Id.* at 11.

32. Interview with Diane Sykes, Milwaukee County Circuit Court Judge, 1992–99, Wisconsin Supreme Court Justice, 1999–2004, U.S. Seventh Circuit Court of Appeals Judge, 2004–present, in Milwaukee, Wis. (Dec. 18, 2013).

33. Jim Stingl, *Suspect Triggered 158 Alerts in 7 Months, Log Shows*, Milw. J. Sentinel, Aug. 28, 1997, at 1A.

34. Wis. Leg. Ref. Bureau, *supra* note 15, at 920.

35. Craig Gilbert, *The Red & the Blue: Political Polarization Through the Prism of Metropolitan Milwaukee*, Marquette Lawyer, Fall 2014, at 9, 10.

36. *Id.* at 11.

37. *Id.* at 10.

38. *Id.* at 22.

39. Doris P. Slesinger et al., African Americans in Wisconsin: A Statistical Overview 6 (2d ed.), http://www.apl.wisc.edu/publications/African_American_Chartbook.pdf.

40. U.S. Census Bureau, State & County QuickFacts: Wisconsin, http://quickfacts.census.gov/qfd/states/55000.html.

41. John Gurda, The Making of Milwaukee 361 (2008); Slesinger et al., *supra* note 39, at 16.

42. Jason DeParle, American Dream: Three Women, Ten Kids, and the Nation's Drive to End Welfare 59 (2004).

43. Gurda, *supra* note 41, at 374.

44. *Id.* at 371–74.

45. Doris P. Slesinger et al., *supra* note 39, at xv–xvi.

46. Kevin Crowe & Robert Gebelhoff, *Hispanics Now Make Up Wisconsin's Largest Minority Group*, Milw. J. Sentinel, June 25, 2014, *available at* http://www.jsonline.com/news/wisconsin/hispanics-now-make-up-wisconsins-largest-minority-group-b99299305z1-264687531.html.

47. DeParle, *supra* note 42, at 62.

48. Wis. Leg. Ref. Bureau, Blue Book, 1995–1996, at 662 (1995); Wis. Leg. Ref. Bureau, Blue Book, 2009–2010, at 685 (2009).

49. Barry T. Hirsh et al., Union Density Estimates by State, 1964–2014, http://unionstats.gsu.edu/MonthlyLaborReviewArticle.htm; Jason Stein, *Union Membership in Wisconsin Plummets in Wake of GOP Measures*, Milw. J. Sentinel, Jan. 28, 2016.

50. Gilbert, *supra* note 35, at 18.

51. *Id.* at 21.

52. *Id.* at 18.

53. Wis. Leg. Ref. Bureau, *supra* note 15, at 258, 705.

54. Interview with Tommy Thompson, Wisconsin Governor, 1987–2001, in Madison, Wis. (April 1, 2014).

55. Wis. Leg. Ref. Bureau, *supra* note 15, at 258.

56. Gilbert, *supra* note 35, at 22.

57. *See, e.g.*, Interview with Joanne Huelsman, Wisconsin State Representative, 1983–91, Wisconsin State Senator, 1991–2003, in Waukesha, Wis. (Jan. 15, 2014).

58. Interview with Chuck Chvala, Wisconsin State Representative, 1983–85, Wisconsin State Senator, 1985–2005, in Madison, Wis. (Dec. 3, 2013).

59. Interview with Thomas Barland, State Court Judge, Eau Claire County, 1967–2000, in Madison, Wis. (Oct. 21, 2013).

60. Telephone Interview with Sheryl Gervasi, Legislative Liaison, Wisconsin State Court System, 1972–2003, Deputy Director, Court Operations, Wisconsin State Court System, 2003–11 (Oct. 7, 2013).

61. Huelsman, *supra* note 57.

62. Interview with Robert Jambois, District Attorney, Kenosha County, 1989–2005, in Middleton, Wis. (Jan. 15, 2014).

63. Interview with Adam Plotkin, Legislative Liaison, Wisconsin State Public Defender, 2011–present, in Madison, Wis. (Oct. 21, 2013).

64. Marc Mauer, Race to Incarcerate 188 (2d ed. 2006).

65. Vanessa Barker, The Politics of Imprisonment: How the Democratic Process Shapes the Way America Punishes Offenders 91 (2009).

66. *Id.*

67. O'Hear, *supra* note 23, at 470–71.

Chapter 2. The Seventies Synthesis

1. Thomas G. Blomberg & Karol Lucken, American Penology: A History of Control 74–77 (2d ed. 2010).

2. Bastian v. State, 54 Wis. 2d 240, 247–48 (1972) (adopting Am. Bar Ass'n, Standards Relating to Probation Std. 1.3 [1970]).

3. Wis. Leg. Council Staff, Staff Brief 80–2: The Adult Correctional System in Wisconsin 19 (1980).

4. *Id.* at 11, 25.

5. *Id.* at 19.

6. Bastian, 54 Wis. 2d at 248 n.1.

7. For a complete list of the parole criteria in force in 1980, see Wis. Leg. Council Staff, *supra* note 3, at 39.

8. Wis. Council on Crim. J., Wisconsin Criminal Justice Improvement Plan 65 (1972).

9. *Id.* at 224.

10. Ted Gest, Crime & Politics: Big Government's Erratic Campaign for Law and Order 19–21, 31 (2001).

11. Patrick J. Riopelle, Wis. Council on Crim. J., The "Safe Streets Act" and the Wisconsin Council on Criminal Justice: Intent, Implementation, and Impact, 1969–1978, at 12–13 (1980).

12. Gest, *supra* note 10, at 22.

13. Jan Uebelherr, *From Governor to Ambassador, Patrick Lucey Served State, Nation*, Milw. J. Sentinel, May 11, 2014, *available at* http://www.jsonline.com/news/obituaries /from-governor-to-ambassador-lucey-guided-wisconsin-national-politics-b99255307 21-250022761.html.

14. *Warren Expects Shift of Council on Justice*, Milw. J., Jan. 9, 1971.

15. Thomas G. Lubenow, *Justice Council Halts Funding of Riot Control Gear*, Milw. J., Sept. 17, 1971.

16. Wis. Council on Crim. J., *supra* note 8, at 515–24.

17. *Id.* at 224–25.

18. Citizens Study Committee on Offender Rehabilitation, Final Report to the Governor i (1972).

19. *Id.* at 1, 3.

20. *Id.* at 2, 4.

21. *Id.* at 1.

22. *Id.* at 2.

23. *Id.*

24. *Id.* at 19.

25. *Id.*

26. *Id.* at 13.

27. *Stop Building Prisons, Panel Says*, Milw. J., Oct. 15, 1973, at 8; Gest, *supra* note 10, at 29–30.

28. Charles E. Friederich, *Shutting of Prisons by '75 Opposed by Guards' Union*, Milw. J., July 21, 1972, at 7.

29. *Study It More*, Milw. Sentinel, Apr. 27, 1973, at 22.

30. Quincy Dadisman, *Prison as Punishment Is "Last Resort,"* Milw. Sentinel, Apr. 30, 1975, at 5, 20.

31. *Id.*

32. *Felon Agency's Funds Cut Off*, Milw. Sentinel, July 4, 1974, at 5.

33. Gest, *supra* note 10, at 29–30.

34. Special Comm. on Crim. J. Stds. & Goals, Wis. Council on Crim. J., Final Report 3 (1977).

35. For a complete list of the members, see *id.* at iii–v.

36. *Id.* at 3–4.

37. Robert Martinson, *What Works: Questions and Answers About Prison Reform*, 35 Pub. Int. 22, 25 (1974), *quoted in* Rick Sarre, Beyond "What Works?": A 25 Year Jubilee Retrospective of Robert Martinson 2 (1999), http://www.aic.gov.au/media_library /conferences/hcpp/sarre.pdf.

38. Special Comm. on Crim. J. Stds. & Goals, *supra* note 34, at 117.

39. *Id.* at 104 (emphasis added).

40. *Id.*

41. *Id.* at 102.

42. *Id.* at 116 (emphasis added).

43. *Id.* at 116–34.

44. RIOPELLE, *supra* note 11, at 23.

45. GEST, *supra* note 10, at 22.

46. *Id.* at 24, 37.

47. *Id.* at 34–35.

48. *Id.* at 38.

49. WIS. LEG. AUDIT BUREAU, A MANAGEMENT AUDIT OF THE WISCONSIN COUNCIL ON CRIMINAL JUSTICE 6 (1985).

50. The violent crime rate is the number of homicides, rapes, robberies, and aggravated assaults reported to the police per 100,000 state residents. The data are summarized in Michael M. O'Hear, *Mass Incarceration in Three Midwestern States: Origins and Trends*, 47 VAL. U. L. REV. 709, 719 (2013).

51. SAMUEL WALKER, SENSE AND NON-SENSE ABOUT CRIME, DRUGS, AND COMMUNITIES 7 (7th ed. 2007).

52. These possibilities are discussed, for example, in JAMES Q. WILSON, THINKING ABOUT CRIME 4, 43 (1977).

53. *See* WIS. DIV. OF CORR., FISCAL YEAR SUMMARY REPORT OF POPULATION MOVEMENT, Stat. Bull. C-60A (1974); WIS. DIV. OF CORR., FISCAL YEAR SUMMARY REPORT OF POPULATION MOVEMENT, Stat. Bull. C-60A (1984).

54. WIS. COUNCIL ON CRIM. J., *supra* note 8, at 88.

55. *Id.* at 221.

56. WIS. FELONY SENT'ING GUIDELINES ADV. COMM., REPORT 9–10 (1983).

57. MICHELLE ALEXANDER, THE NEW JIM CROW: MASS INCARCERATION IN THE AGE OF COLORBLINDNESS 11 (rev. ed. 2012).

58. *See* Heather Ann Thompson, *Why Mass Incarceration Matters: Rethinking Crisis, Decline, and Transformation in Postwar American History*, 97 J. AM. HIST. 703, 707 (2010).

59. For a discussion of the underlying social-scientific theorizing and empirical research, see Shaun A. Thomas et al., *The Contingent Effect of Race in Juvenile Court Detention Decisions: The Role of Racial and Symbolic Threat*, 3 RACE & J. 239 (2013).

60. MICHAEL TONRY, THINKING ABOUT CRIME: SENSE AND SENSIBILITY IN AMERICAN PENAL CULTURE 39 (2004).

61. JULIAN V. ROBERTS ET AL., PENAL POPULISM AND PUBLIC OPINION: LESSONS FROM FIVE COUNTRIES 62–63 (2003).

62. TONRY, *supra* note 60, at 51.

63. DAVID GARLAND, THE CULTURE OF CONTROL: CRIME AND SOCIAL ORDER IN CONTEMPORARY SOCIETY 81 (2001).

64. TONRY, *supra* note 60, at 51–52.

65. ROBERTS ET AL., *supra* note 61, at 69.

66. *Id.*

67. For a discussion of the link between mistrust in government and the "three strikes" mandatory minimum law in California, see FRANKLIN E. ZIMRING ET AL., PUNISHMENT AND DEMOCRACY: THREE STRIKES AND YOU'RE OUT IN CALIFORNIA 173–75 (2001).

68. ROBERTS ET AL., *supra* note 61, at 74.

69. *Id.* at 68.

70. TONRY, *supra* note 60, at 5.

71. *Id.* at 7.

72. Interview with Fred Risser, Wisconsin State Representative, 1957–62, Wisconsin State Senator, 1962–present, in Madison, Wis. (Oct. 14, 2013); ORLAN L. PRESTEGARD, WISCONSIN LEGISLATIVE COUNCIL, REPORT NO. 2 TO THE 1975 LEGISLATURE ON LEGISLATION RELATING TO CRIMINAL PENALTIES (1975).

73. Ina Jaffe, *At 85, "Old-School" Politician Shows No Signs Of Quitting*, National Public Radio, Feb. 27, 2013, *available at* http://www.npr.org/2013/02/27/172431659/at-85-old-school-politician-shows-no-signs-of-quitting.

74. Interview with Tommy G. Thompson, Wisconsin State Representative, 1967–87, Wisconsin Governor, 1987–2001, in Madison, Wis. (April 1, 2014).

75. 1997 A.B. 831.

76. O'Hear, *supra* note 50, at 722.

77. Richard S. Frase, *Sentencing Guidelines in Minnesota, 1978–2003*, 32 CRIME & J. 131, 137 (2005).

78. William Spelman, *Crime, Cash, and Limited Options: Explaining the Prison Boom*, 8 CRIMINOLOGY & PUB. POL'Y 29, 57 (2009).

79. WIS. LEG. COUNCIL, REPORT NO. 30 TO THE 1979 LEGISLATURE: LEGISLATION RELATING TO CRIMINAL SENTENCING (1980).

80. JOE FONTAINE, WIS. SENT'ING COMM'N, SENTENCING POLICY IN WISCONSIN: 1975–2005, at 6–7 (2005).

81. Frase, *supra* note 77, at 143–47.

82. FELONY SENT'ING GUIDELINES ADV. COMM., *supra* note 56, at 10–11.

83. LEG. COUNCIL, *supra* note 79, at 5–6.

84. *Id.* at 6–7.

85. *Id.* at 8.

86. Thompson, *supra* note 74.

87. 1979 Wis. A.B. 1190.

Chapter 3. The Equivocal Assault on Discretion, 1980–1995

1. Interview with Jon Wilcox, Wisconsin State Representative, 1969–75, Judge, Waushara County Circuit Court, 1979–92, Chair, Wisconsin Sentencing Commission, 1987–92, Justice, Wisconsin Supreme Court, 1992–2007, in Wautoma, Wis. (Nov. 5, 2013).

2. JOE FONTAINE, WIS. SENT'ING COMM'N, SENTENCING POLICY IN WISCONSIN: 1975–2005, at 9 (2005).

3. The full set of guidelines, as they existed in 1983, is available as Appendix G in WIS. FELONY SENT'ING COMM'N, REPORT (1983).

4. *Id.* at 24.

5. *Id.* at ii.

6. *Id.* at 35.

7. In the Matter of Implementation of Felony Sentencing Guidelines, 335 N.W.2d 868 (Wis. 1983).

8. 1983 Wis. Act 371, § 10.

9. Interview with Tommy G. Thompson, Wisconsin State Representative, 1967–87, Wisconsin Governor, 1987–2001, in Madison, Wis. (April 1, 2014).

10. In the Matter of Judicial Administration Felony Sentencing Guidelines, 353 N.W.2d 793 (Wis. 1984).

11. Sandra Shane-DuBow, *The Demise of the Wisconsin Sentencing Commission: Lessons for Future Reformers*, 8 FED. SENT'ING RPTR. 99, 100 (1995).

12. WIS. SENT'ING COMM'N, ANNUAL REPORT 13 (1990) [hereafter 1990 ANNUAL REPORT].

13. WIS. SENT'ING COMM'N, ANNUAL REPORT 7 (1994).

14. 1990 ANNUAL REPORT, *supra* note 12, at 17, 23.

15. Wilcox, *supra* note 1.

16. Interview with Robert Donohoo, Assistant District Attorney, Milwaukee County, 1973–88, Deputy District Attorney, 1988–99, Chief Deputy District Attorney, 2000–2006, in Milwaukee, Wis. (Sept. 30, 2013).

17. Eldon Knoche, *Judge Cites Attila the Hun to Make Point*, MILW. SENTINEL, Jan. 22, 1988, at 1.

18. Telephone Interview with David Deininger, Wisconsin State Representative, 1987–94, Judge, Green County Circuit Court, 1994–96, Judge, Wisconsin Court of Appeals, 1996–2007 (Sept. 16, 2013).

19. Interview with Lee Wells, Judge, Milwaukee County Circuit Court, 1981–2004, in Milwaukee, Wis. (Nov. 18, 2013).

20. *Id.*

21. Interview with Thomas Barland, Wisconsin State Representative, 1961–67, Judge, Eau Claire County Circuit Court, 1967–2000, Chair, Criminal Penalties Study Committee, 1998–99, in Madison, Wis. (Oct. 21, 2013).

22. Wilcox, *supra* note 1.

23. FONTAINE, *supra* note 2, at 15.

24. Barland, *supra* note 21.

25. Telephone Interview with Sheryl Gervasi, Legislative Liaison, Wisconsin State Court System, 1972–2003, Deputy Director, Court Operations, Wisconsin State Court System, 2003–11 (Oct. 7, 2013).

26. Interview with Stephen Hurley, Shareholder, Hurley, Burish and Stanton, S.C., in Madison, Wis. (Dec. 3, 2013).

27. *See, e.g.*, Interview with Patrick J. Fiedler, Secretary, Wisconsin Department of Corrections, 1991–93, Judge, Dane County Circuit Court, 1993–2011, Partner, Hurley, Burish & Stanton, S.C., in Madison, Wis. (Sept. 10, 2013); Wells, *supra* note 19.

28. FONTAINE, *supra* note 2, at 18; Pat Schneider, *Sentencing Panel Takes Budget Hit, Budget Would Abolish Funds*, CAP. TIMES, April 26, 1995, at 6A.

29. Interview with David Prosser, Wisconsin State Representative, 1979–97, Wisconsin Supreme Court Justice, 1998–2016, in Madison, Wis. (Sept. 10, 2013).

30. WIS. LEG. REF. BUREAU, BLUE BOOK 256 (2011).

31. Deininger, *supra* note 18.

32. Interview with Chuck Chvala, Wisconsin State Representative, 1983–85, Wisconsin State Senator, 1985–2005, in Madison, Wis. (Dec. 3, 2013).

33. FONTAINE, *supra* note 2, at 15–16.

34. Prosser, *supra* note 29.

35. FONTAINE, *supra* note 2, at 14–15.

36. WIS. FELONY SENT'ING COMM'N, REPORT, *supra* note 3, at ii.

37. WIS. SENT'ING COMM'N, WISCONSIN SENTENCING GUIDELINES MANUAL ii (1994).

38. Michael M. O'Hear, *Mass Incarceration in Three Midwestern States: Origins and Trends*, 47 VAL. U. L. REV. 709, 722 (2013).

39. *Id.*

40. Michael M. O'Hear, *Sentencing Commissions, in* ENCYCLOPEDIA OF CRIMINOLOGY AND CRIMINAL JUSTICE (Gerben Bruinsma and David Weisburd eds. 2013).

41. Shane-DuBow, *supra* note 11, at 100.

42. Deininger, *supra* note 18.

43. Interview with Sandra Shane-DuBow, Executive Director, Wisconsin Sentencing Commission, 1985–95, in Milwaukee, Wis. (Oct. 4, 2013).

44. *See, e.g.,* Prosser, *supra* note 29.

45. Mike Flaherty, *Budget Panel Axes Sentencing Commission*, WIS. ST. J., April 29, 1995, at 3B.

46. 1987 Wis. Act 412.

47. Robert Margolies, Wis. Dept. Health & Soc. Svcs., Fiscal Estimate Relating to Parole and Probation for Persons Convicted of Crimes Punishable by Life Imprisonment (1988), *available in* Legislative Drafting File for Nov. 1987 Special Sess. A.B. 8.

48. FRANKLIN E. ZIMRING ET AL., PUNISHMENT AND DEMOCRACY: THREE STRIKES AND YOU ARE OUT IN CALIFORNIA 4 (2001).

49. Daniel W. Stiller, *Initiative 593: Washington's Voters Go Down Swinging*, 30 GONZ. L. REV. 433, 434 (1995).

50. *Wisconsin Adopts "Three Strikes" Law*, WASH. TIMES, April 15, 1994, at A13.

51. Craig Gilbert, *Crime the Key Issue, Voters Telling Rosenzweig*, MILW. J., March 15, 1993; Craig Gilbert, *West Allis Could Be Key for Cullen*, MILW. J., March 19, 1993.

52. Craig Gilbert, *Cullen, Rosenzweig Each Question the Other's True Position on Issues*, MILW. J., Apr. 1, 1993.

53. Craig Gilbert, *Rosenzweig Overcomes Attack-Style Ads*, MILW. J., April 7, 1993.

54. Steven Walters, *Senate Turns Down Capital Punishment*, MILW. J., Oct. 20, 1993.

55. Interview with Peggy Rosenzweig, Wisconsin State Representative, 1983–93, Wisconsin State Senator, 1993–2003, in Milwaukee, Wis. (April 23, 2014).

56. Telephone Interview with John Gard, Wisconsin State Representative, 1987–2007 (May 13, 2014).

57. *Id.*

58. Peggy Rosenzweig, *Polly's Murder Points to Need for "Three Strikes and Out" Law*, MILW. SENTINEL, Jan. 15, 1994.

59. *Id.*

60. *Id.*

61. *Capitol Report*, WIS. ST. J., Jan. 5, 1994, at 3D.

62. *Three-Strikes Law May Carry Big Price Tag*, ST. PAUL PIONEER PRESS, Jan. 31, 1994, at 5E.

63. Richard P. Jones, *Thompson Message: Fight Crime*, MILW. J., Jan. 28, 1994.

64. Karl J. Karlson, *3 Felonies Add Up to Life Term in Wisconsin Bills*, ST. PAUL PIONEER PRESS, Jan. 26, 1994, at 1A.

65. Steve Schultze, *Crime Far Outweighs Other Worries in State Survey*, MILW. J., Feb. 8, 1994.

66. *Three-Strikes Law May Carry Big Price Tag*, *supra* note 62.

67. Richard P. Jones, *GOP Revives "Three Strikes" Measure*, MILW. J., March 15, 1994.

68. 1993 Wis. A.B. 1173.

69. Scott Russell, *State Poll Finds Taxes, Crime Atop List of Residents' Concerns*, CAP. TIMES, March 8, 1994, at 3A.

70. Tim Kelley, *Lawmakers Dig Their Teeth into Crime Bills This Week*, WIS. ST. J., March 13, 1994, at 1A.

71. Scott Russell, *3 Strikes Bill Clears Assembly, GOP Changes Ok'd*, CAP. TIMES, March 16, 1994, at 1A.

72. Jones, *supra* note 67.

73. Rosenzweig, *supra* note 55.

74. Daniel Bice, *Sexual Predator Bill Dies; Aim Was to Keep Offenders Locked Up*, MILW. SENTINEL, March 17, 1994.

75. Jones, *supra* note 67.

76. Richard P. Jones, *Conferees Must Unsnarl 3-Strikes Bill*, MILW. J., March 24, 1994.

77. Amy Rinard & Steven Walters, *3-Strikes Bill Passes Legislature; Anti-Crime Plan Includes New Prison for Teens*, MILW. SENTINEL, March 25, 1994.

78. Richard P. Jones, *Anti-Crime Measures Proceed to Governor*, MILW. J., March 25, 1994.

79. Richard P. Jones, *Thompson Signs 3 Strikes Bill Despite Criticism About Costs*, MILW. J., April 13, 1994.

80. Rinard & Walters, *supra* note 77.

81. ZIMRING ET AL., *supra* note 48, at 4.

82. WALTER DICKEY & PAM STIEBS HOLLENHORST, THREE STRIKES LAWS: FIVE YEARS LATER 6, 9 (1998).

83. ZIMRING ET AL., *supra* note 48, at 4–6.

84. Russell, *supra* note 69.

85. Steve Schultze, *Longshot Places Bet on Governor's Job*, MILW. J. April 25, 1994.

86. Thompson, *supra* note 9.

87. 1993 Wis. Act 97, §§ 14–15.

88. 1993 Wis. Act 98, § 137m.

89. *Id.*

90. 1993 Wis. Act 98.

91. *Id.*

92. 1993 Wis. Act 224.

93. 1993 Wis. Act 194.

Chapter 4. The Quest for Improved Community Corrections, 1980–1997

1. 1979 Laws Ch. 221, § 2033(2)(a).

2. Keith Johnson & Pam Shannon, Wis. Leg. Council, Research Bulletin 82-1: Wisconsin Prison Programs and Inmate Classification 8 (1982).

3. Keith Johnson, Wis. Leg. Council, Programs and Issues in Community Corrections: An Overview 9–10 (1980).

4. Wis. Leg. Fiscal Bureau, Information Paper 56: Juvenile Justice and Youth Aids Program 28 (2015).

5. Special Comm. on Community Corrections Progs., Wis. Leg. Council, Summary of Proceedings, Oct. 30, 1980, at 10. McClendon had earlier suggested that CCJ funds might be made available for this purpose. Special Comm. on Community Corrections Progs., Wis. Leg. Council, Summary of Proceedings, Sept. 25, 1980, at 9.

6. Special Comm. on Community Corrections Progs., Wis. Leg. Council, Summary of Proceedings, Nov. 21, 1980, at 2–5.

7. Special Comm. on Community Corrections Progs., Wis. Leg. Council, Summary of Proceedings, Dec. 18, 1980, at 9.

8. Telephone Interview with Walter Dickey, Professor of Law Emeritus, University of Wisconsin (July 17, 2015).

9. Special Comm. on Community Corrections Progs., *supra* note 7, at 10.

10. *Id.*

11. Special Comm. on Community Corrections Progs., Wis. Leg. Council, Summary of Proceedings, Jan. 14, 1982, at 4–5.

12. *Id.* at 5.

13. Johnson, *supra* note 3, at 14.

14. Special Comm. on Community Corrections Progs., Wis. Leg. Council, Summary of Proceedings, Sept. 25, 1980, at 4–5.

15. Johnson, *supra* note 3, at 17.

16. Michael M. O'Hear, *Mass Incarceration in Three Midwestern States: Origins and Trends*, 47 Val. U. L. Rev. 709, 719, 722 (2013).

17. Wis. Dep't of Corrections, Fiscal Year Summary Report of Population Movement, Stat. Bull. C-60A (1992).

18. Bureau of Justice Statistics, Sourcebook of Criminal Justice Statistics 8 (1988); Bureau of Justice Statistics, Sourcebook of Criminal Justice Statistics 10 (1994).

19. Wis. Correctional System Rev. Panel, Final Report 6 (1991).

20. Tommy G. Thompson, Power to the People: An American State at Work 181 (1996).

21. Wis. Correctional System Rev. Panel, *supra* note 19, at 3.

22. Interview with Walter Dickey, Professor of Law Emeritus, University of Wisconsin, in Madison, Wis. (Sept. 10, 2013).

23. Correctional System Rev. Panel, *supra* note 19, at 6.

24. *Id.* at 21.

25. Patrick J. Fiedler, *The Wisconsin Department of Corrections: An Expensive Proposition*, 76 Marq. L. Rev. 501, 504 (1993).

26. Thompson, *supra* note 20, at 184, 186.

27. Jason De Parle, American Dream: Three Women, Ten Kids, and a Nation's Drive to End Welfare (2004).

28. Thompson, *supra* note 20, at 186.

29. Arthur L. Srb, *Legislation Might Have Prevented Killing Spree*, St. Paul Pioneer Press, Aug. 18, 1991.

30. Fiedler, *supra* note 25, at 505.

31. Intensive Sanctions Rev. Panel, Final Report 3 (1998).

32. 1991 Wis. Act 39, § 3640r.

33. 1991 Wis. Act 39, § 3128hv.

34. *Id.*

35. Wis. Correctional System Rev. Panel, *supra* note 19, at App. 1, p. 8.

36. Interview with Patrick J. Fiedler, Secretary, Wisconsin Department of Corrections, 1991–93, Judge, Dane County Circuit Court, 1993–2011, Partner, Hurley, Burish & Stanton, S.C., in Madison, Wis. (Sept. 10, 2013).

37. Wis. Leg. Fiscal Bureau, Informational Paper #53: Adult Corrections Program 14–16 (1993).

38. Intensive Sanctions Rev. Panel, *supra* note 31, at 8.

39. Thompson, *supra* note 20, at 184–85.

40. Wis. Leg. Fiscal Bureau, Informational Paper #53: Adult Corrections Program 37 (1997).

41. Intensive Sanctions Rev. Panel, *supra* note 31, at 6.

42. *Id.* at 7.

43. *Id.* at 6.

44. *Id.* at 5.

45. Wis. Correctional System Rev. Panel, *supra* note 19, at 13–14, 21–22.

46. Phil Brinkman, *Said and Said Again, Advice Has Been Consistent: More Treatment, Better Supervision, Complex Solutions Urged; Political Expediency Won Out*, Wis. St. J., Jan. 22, 2005.

47. Dickey, *supra* note 22.

48. Interview with Janine Geske, Judge, Milwaukee County Circuit Court, 1981–93, Justice, Wisconsin Supreme Court, 1993–98, in Milwaukee, Wis. (Aug. 26, 2013).

49. Interview with Stephen Hurley, Shareholder, Hurley, Burish and Stanton, S.C., in Madison, Wis. (Dec. 3, 2013).

50. Jeff Mayers, *Protection or Public Peril? Electronic Monitoring of Prisoners Criticized After Recent Incidents*, Wis. St. J., Sept. 14, 1997.

51. David Callender & Tim McLaughlin, *3 Slayings in State Cut the Odds for Program to Survive*, Capital Times, Oct. 25, 1997.

52. Intensive Sanctions Rev. Panel, *supra* note 31.

53. Interview with Elsa Lamelas, Judge, Milwaukee County Circuit Court, 1993–2011, in Milwaukee, Wis. (Jan. 3, 2014).

54. Sharon Theimer, *Electronic Monitoring of Inmates Suspended*, St. Paul Pioneer Press, Sept. 4, 1997.

55. Jim Stingl, *Suspect Triggered 158 Alerts in 7 Months, Log Shows*, Milw. J. Sentinel, Aug. 28, 1997, at 1A, 15A.

56. Callender & McLaughlin, *supra* note 51.

57. Stingl, *supra* note 55; Mayers, *supra* note 50.

58. Theimer, *supra* note 54.

59. Wis. Leg. Fiscal Bureau, Informational Paper #56: Adult Corrections Program 37 (1999).

60. Intensive Sanctions Rev. Panel, *supra* note 31, at 19.

61. Interview with Michael J. Sullivan, Secretary, Wisconsin Department of Corrections, 1993–99, in Milwaukee, Wis. (Oct. 16, 2013).

62. Theimer, *supra* note 54.

63. Intensive Sanctions Rev. Panel, *supra* note 31, at 14.

64. Jeff Mayers, *Prisoner Release Becomes Top Issue*, Wis. St. J., March 22, 1998, *available at* 1998 WLNR 5463443.

65. These activities are described in more detail in Gov.'s Task Force on Sent'ing & Corrections, Final Report App. I (1996).

66. Under the task force's proposal, judges would have only four sentencing options in felony cases: imprisonment, CCC, fine, or conditional supervision. *Id.* at 6. Conditional supervision was intended to provide very limited supervision in order to achieve certain specific objectives, such as the payment of restitution. The task force contemplated that the conditional supervision numbers would be very low—a small fraction of the numbers of CCC. *Id.* at 14.

67. Brinkman, *supra* note 46.

68. Joe Fontaine, Wis. Sent'ing Comm'n, Sentencing Policy in Wisconsin: 1975–2005, at 26 (2005).

69. Interview with Walter Dickey, Professor of Law Emeritus, University of Wisconsin, in Madison, Wis. (Oct. 21, 2013).

70. Jason Horowirz, *Scott Walker's Dismal Finish Is a Fitting Result, Old Foes Say*, N.Y. Times, Sept. 22, 2015.

71. Brinkman, *supra* note 46.

72. Dickey, *supra* note 69.

73. Mitchell's dissent was published in Appendix III of the Commission's *Final Report*.

74. Brinkman, *supra* note 46.

75. *Id.*

76. *See* Brinkman, *supra* note 46 (quoting Thomas Hammer).

77. *Id.*

Chapter 5. The Demise of Parole,
1994–2002

1. 1983 Wis. Act 64.

2. Wis. Div. of Corrections, Fiscal Estimate for 1983 A.B. 206 (1983).

3. 1983 Wis. Act 528.

4. Number of prisoners reflects year-end data compiled by the U.S. Bureau of Justice Statistics. Major violent arrests are adult arrests for the violent "index" crimes (murder, rape, aggravated assault, and robbery), as compiled in annual statewide arrest reports prepared by the Wisconsin Office of Justice Assistance and its predecessor agencies. Arrests from the two years preceding each prisoner total are counted.

5. WIS. DEP'T OF CORRECTIONS, DIVISION OF ADULT INSTITUTIONS SUMMARY REPORT, 1987–2001, at 2 (2002). This excludes 530 beds for segregation units and the 1,048 beds at the Milwaukee Secure Detention Facility, which was intended to hold probationers and parolees facing revocation. The cited report is contained in the Tommy G. Thompson Collection at Marquette University.

6. WIS. LEG. FISCAL BUREAU, INFORMATIONAL PAPER #56: ADULT CORRECTIONS PROGRAM 11 (1999).

7. Interview with John Husz, Chair, Wis. Parole Comm'n, 1991–98, in Milwaukee, Wis. (Sept. 24, 2013).

8. Interview with Michael J. Sullivan, Sec'ty, Wis. Dep't of Corrections, 1993–99, in Milwaukee, Wis. (Oct. 16, 2013).

9. Husz, *supra* note 7.

10. Patrick J. Fiedler, *The Wisconsin Department of Corrections: An Expensive Proposition*, 76 MARQ. L. REV. 501, 505 (1993).

11. WIS. LEG. FISCAL BUREAU, INFORMATIONAL PAPER #53: ADULT CORRECTIONS PROGRAM 6 (1993).

12. WIS. LEG. FISCAL BUREAU, INFORMATIONAL PAPER #53: ADULT CORRECTIONS PROGRAM 11 (1997).

13. Mike Flaherty, *Truth in Sentencing: End of Parole Could Jam Prisons, Boost Budget*, WIS. ST. J., Apr. 12, 1998, at 1A.

14. JOE FONTAINE, WIS. SENT'ING COMM'N, SENTENCING POLICY IN WISCONSIN: 1975–2005, at 24 (2005).

15. Interview with Tommy Thompson, Wisconsin Governor, 1987–2001, in Madison, Wis. (April 1, 2014).

16. Husz, *supra* note 7.

17. Interview with James E. Doyle, Wis. Att'y Gen., 1991–2003, Wisconsin Governor, 2003–11, in Milwaukee, Wis. (Sept. 30, 2014).

18. Lynn Adelman, *The Adverse Impact of Truth-in-Sentencing on Wisconsin's Efforts to Deal With Low-Level Drug Offenders*, 47 VAL. U. L. REV. 688, 693 (2013).

19. Thompson, *supra* note 15.

20. COMM. ON CAUSES AND CONSEQUENCES OF HIGH RATES OF INCARCERATION, NATIONAL RESEARCH COUNCIL OF THE NATIONAL ACADEMIES, THE GROWTH OF

Incarceration in the United States: Exploring Causes and Consequences 79 (2014).

21. Telephone Interview with Stewart Simonson, Legal Counsel, Wisconsin Governor Tommy Thompson, 1995–99, Legal Advisor, The CRUDEM Foundation/ Hôpital Sacré-Coeur, 2013–present (Jan. 8, 2014).

22. Fontaine, *supra* note 14, at 25.

23. Thompson, *supra* note 15.

24. Fontaine, *supra* note 14, at 25; Adelman, *supra* note 18, at 693–94.

25. James E. Doyle, *Wisconsin Needs "Truth in Sentencing,"* 20 Wis. B. Crim. L. News 17, 18 (1997).

26. Doyle, *supra* note 17.

27. *Id.*

28. *Doyle Urges Halt to Earlier Releases; Report Shows Felons Are Serving Shorter Sentences Than Six Years Ago,* Wis. St. J., Oct. 15, 1996.

29. Sullivan, *supra* note 8.

30. 1997 Wis. A.B. 351.

31. Simonson, *supra* note 21.

32. Daniel Bice et al., *Federal Judges Lynn Adelman, Rudolph Randa Are Polar Opposites,* Milw. J. Sentinel, May 10, 2014, *available at* http://www.jsonline.com/news/statepolitics /federal-judges-lynn-adelman-rudolph-randa-are-polar-opposites-b99266693 z1-258783561.html.

33. Matt Pommer, *Governor, Doyle Announce Crime Code Overhaul,* Cap. Times, Jun. 6, 1997, at 2A.

34. Matt Pommer, *Truth-in-Sentencing Action to Wait on Special Election,* Cap. Times, Feb. 13, 1998, at 8A.

35. E-mail from Brian Burke, Wisconsin State Senator, 1988–2003, to author (Nov. 14, 2013).

36. Matt Pommer, *Truth Proposal Irks GOP,* Cap. Times, Nov. 10, 1997, at 2A.

37. Bice et al., *supra* note 32.

38. John Welsh, *Longer Sentences, Shorter Terms; Average Prison Stay in Wisconsin Has Been Decreasing, State Journal Analysis Finds,* Wis. St. J., Mar. 15, 1998, at 1A.

39. Jeff Mayers, *Prisoner Release Becomes Top Issue,* Wis. St. J., March 22, 1998, at 1C, *available at* 1998 WLNR 5463443.

40. Sullivan, *supra* note 8.

41. Husz, *supra* note 7.

42. Wis. Leg. Fiscal Bureau, Informational Paper #56: Adult Corrections Program 6 (2001); Wis. Leg. Fiscal Bureau, *supra* note 6, at 7.

43. 1997 Wis. Act 283.

44. Mike Flaherty, *The Republicans Are Confident; The Democrats Are Mocking Them,* Wis. St. J., May 22, 1998, at 4A.

45. *Id.*

46. Mike Flaherty, *Thompson Gets Bill Abolishing Parole; Other Anti-Crime Legislation Also Headed His Way,* Wis. St. J., May 6, 1998, at 1A.

47. FONTAINE, *supra* note 14, at 34.

48. Mike Flaherty, *One of State's Costliest Programs? Warning Issued as Senate OKs Sentencing Bill*, WIS. ST. J., May 2, 1998, at 1A.

49. Amy Rinard, *Parole, Feticide, "Cocaine Mom" Bills Pass Assembly with Thompson's OK, Measures Will End Parole, Act on Behalf of Fetuses*, MILW. J. SENTINEL, May 6, 1998, at 1.

50. Pommer, *supra* note 34.

51. Mike Flaherty, *Truth in Sentencing Measure Gets Cost-Effective Designation; A Study from the Governor Says Money Would Be Saved over Time in Crime Prevention*, WIS. ST. J., June 4, 1997, at 5C.

52. Michael M. O'Hear, *Good Conduct Time for Prisoners: Why (and How) Wisconsin Should Provide Credits Toward Early Release*, 98 MARQ. L. REV. 487, 490 (2014).

53. WILLIAM J. SABOL ET AL., URBAN INSTITUTE, THE INFLUENCES OF TRUTH-IN-SENTENCING REFORMS ON CHANGES IN STATES' SENTENCING PRACTICES AND PRISON POPULATIONS (2002).

54. *Id.* at iv.

55. *Id.* at 28.

56. Adelman, *supra* note 18, at 696.

57. *Id.*

58. Talking Points Memo, Meet ALEC's (Hoped For) Man in Washington: Scott Walker, Aug. 10, 2015, http://talkingpointsmemo.com/cafe/meet-alec-s-hoped-for-man-in-washington-scott-walker.

59. Dave Umhoefer, *Judges Want More Prisons, Alternatives*, MILW. J. SENTINEL, June 8, 1997.

60. Interview with Diane Sykes, Judge, Milwaukee County Circuit Court, 1992–99, Justice, Wisconsin Supreme Court, 1999–2004, Judge, U.S. Seventh Circuit Court of Appeals, 2004–present, in Milwaukee, Wis. (Dec. 18, 2013); Interview with Elsa Lamelas, Judge, Milwaukee County Circuit Court, 1993–2011, in Milwaukee, Wis. (Jan. 3, 2014). Detailed minutes of most of the CPSC's full committee meetings are included in the legislative drafting file of 1999 Assembly Bill 465.

61. Interview with Stephen Hurley, Shareholder, Hurley, Burish and Stanton, S.C., in Madison, Wis. (Dec. 3, 2013).

62. Lamelas, *supra* note 60.

63. FONTAINE, *supra* note 14, at 35.

64. The CPSC's reclassification work is described at length in CRIM. PENALTIES STUDY COMM., FINAL REPORT Pt. II (1999).

65. Michael B. Brennan et al., *Fully Implementing Truth-in-Sentencing*, WIS. LAWYER, Nov. 2002, at 46.

66. Walter J. Dickey, Dissenting Statement, *in* CRIM. PENALTIES STUDY COMMITTEE, FINAL REPORT 3 (1999).

67. CRIM. PENALTIES STUDY COMMITTEE, *supra* note 64, at Part II.

68. *Id.* at 23.

69. *Id.* at 150.

70. Governor's Task Force to Enhance Probation, Final Report (2000); Fontaine, *supra* note 14.

71. 1999 S.B. 357, § 934.

72. David Callender, *Makeover for McCallum?*, Cap. Times, Apr. 10, 2002, at 4A.

73. Sarah Wyatt, *Lawmakers at Odds over Prison Time; Budget Bills Differ on Truth in Sentencing*, Milw. J. Sentinel, Apr. 7, 2002, at 2.

74. Richard P. Jones, *Legislators Remain Divided on Changes for Criminal Code; They Praise Thompson's Plan but Differ over Modifying Prison Terms*, Milw. J. Sentinel, Jan. 28, 2000, at 1.

75. Sarah Wyatt, *Longer Prison Terms to Cost $40.9 Million; Truth-in-Sentencing Keeps Inmates Locked Up*, Milw. J. Sentinel, Feb. 27, 2002, at 2.

76. Sarah Wyatt, *Costs Push Sentencing Law Toward a Moment of Truth; Long Terms Mean Huge Price Tag*, Cap. Times, Mar. 11, 2002, at 2A.

77. Dickey, *supra* note 66.

78. Interview with Chuck Chvala, Wisconsin State Senator, 1985–2005, in Madison, Wis. (Dec. 3, 2013).

79. David Callender, *"Truth" Law Could Break the Bank*, Cap. Times, Apr. 20, 2002, at 1A.

80. Scott Milfred, *"Truth-in-Sentencing" on Agenda; McCallum Wants Action on the Revisions*, Wis. St. J., Jan. 13, 2002, at C1.

81. Fontaine, *supra* note 14, at 55.

82. Brennan et al., *supra* note 65, at 54–55.

83. Jesse J. Norris, *The Earned Release Revolution: Early Assessments and State-Level Strategies*, 95 Marq. L. Rev. 1551, 1583 (2012).

84. David Callender, *Doyle's Budget Surprises: "Truth in Sentencing" Takes a Hit*, Cap. Times, March 7, 2007, at A1.

85. David Callender, *Doyle Rips Gov as Soft on Truth in Sentencing*, Cap. Times, July 30, 2002, at 2A.

86. Interview with Walter Dickey, Professor of Law Emeritus, University of Wisconsin, in Madison, Wis. (Sept. 10, 2013).

87. Justice Strategies, Treatment Instead of Prisons: A Roadmap for Sentencing and Correctional Policy Reform in Wisconsin 1 (2005); Council of State Governments Justice Center, Justice Reinvestment in Wisconsin: Analyses & Policy Options to Reduce Spending on Corrections and Increase Public Safety 5 (2009).

88. Council of State Governments Justice Center, *supra* note 87, at 5.

89. The data come from the biennial reports on adult corrections produced by the Wisconsin Legislative Fiscal Bureau.

90. The figure is based on a 2012 data run provided by the Wisconsin Department of Corrections of average sentences of prison inmates at six-month intervals, June 30, 1990, through June 30, 2008.

Chapter 6. Managerialism's Modest Comeback, the Early 2000s

1. WIS. LEG. FISCAL BUREAU, INFORMATION PAPER NO. 56: ADULT CORRECTIONS PROGRAM 10 (1999) [hereinafter LFB 1999].

2. Sharon Theimer, *Thompson Wants Convicts Sent South; Shipping Inmates to Texas Could Ease Crowded Prisons*, DULUTH NEWS TRIB., Jan. 31, 1996, *available at* 1996 WLNR 1748794.

3. Richard P. Jones, *Legislator Backs Private Prisons for Wisconsin; Walker Will Propose Bill Because He Wants Jobs, Taxes to Stay in State*, MILW. J. SENTINEL, Dec. 8, 1998, *available at* 1998 WLNR 3051315.

4. WIS. LEG. FISCAL BUREAU, INFORMATION PAPER NO. 54: CIVIL COMMITMENT OF SEXUALLY VIOLENT PERSONS 15–16 (2013).

5. E-mail from Brian Burke, Wisconsin State Senator, 1988–2003, to author (Nov. 14, 2013).

6. 1997 Wis. Act 283 § 454(1)(e)(5).

7. MICHAEL E. SMITH & WALTER DICKEY, REFORMING SENTENCING AND CORRECTIONS FOR JUST PUNISHMENT AND PUBLIC SAFETY (1999).

8. WIS. CRIM. PENALTIES STUDY COMMITTEE, FINAL REPORT 110 (1999).

9. *Id.* at 110–11.

10. Only two members of the committee voted in favor of a proposal that would have essentially revived the far more objective first Wisconsin sentencing guidelines. CPSC Minutes of March 19, 1999.

11. *Id.* at 111.

12. *Id.* at 108.

13. Interview with Thomas Barland, Judge, Eau Claire County Circuit Court, 1967–2000, Chair, Criminal Penalties Study Committee, 1998–99, in Madison, Wis. (Oct. 21, 2013).

14. CRIM. PENALTIES STUDY COMMITTEE, *supra* note 8, at 111–13.

15. *Id.* at 115.

16. *Id.*

17. *Id.*

18. *Id.*

19. This guideline and other portions of the second Wisconsin guidelines are reprinted at 15 FED. SENT. REP. 19–31 (2002).

20. Barland, *supra* note 13.

21. CRIM. PENALTIES STUDY COMMITTEE, *supra* note 8, at 117, 118.

22. *Id.* at 119.

23. Scott McCallum, Partial Veto Message for Budget Repair Bill 21 (2002).

24. Michael B. Brennan et al., *Fully Implementing Truth-in-Sentencing*, WIS. LAWYER, Nov. 2002, at 55.

25. Interview with Ron Sklansky, Wisconsin Legislative Council, 1975–2010, in Madison, Wis. (Jan. 21, 2014).

26. Interview with James E. Doyle, District Attorney, Dane County, 1977–83, Wisconsin Attorney General, 1991–2003, Wisconsin Governor, 2003–11, Of Counsel, Foley and Lardner, 2011–present, in Milwaukee, Wis. (Sept. 30, 2014).

27. ANDREW WISEMAN & MICHAEL CONNELLI, JUDICIAL SENTENCING DISCRETION & SENTENCING OUTCOMES: INCORPORATING DATA FROM THE COURTROOM 89 (2008).

28. HY MATZ, SENTENCE DEPARTURES IN WISCONSIN: A STATISTICAL ANALYSIS OF FREQUENCIES AND CAUSES v (2007).

29. 2004 WI 42, 678 N.W.2d 197.

30. To some extent, the court was effectively reviving Walter Dickey and Michael Smith's "rule-of-law" sentencing proposal, which they had pushed in the Criminal Penalties Study Committee. Indeed, Dickey and Smith joined a special brief to the Supreme Court in *Gallion* urging this approach.

31. 2004 WI 42, ¶ 47.

32. Michael M. O'Hear, *Appellate Review of Sentence Explanations: Learning from the Wisconsin and Federal Experiences*, 93 MARQ. L. REV. 751, 769–72 (2009).

33. WIS. SENT'ING COMM'N, ANNUAL REPORT 2006, at 6–7 (2007).

34. Telephone Interview with Michael Connelly, Executive Director, Wisconsin Sentencing Commission, 2004–6 (Feb. 5, 2014).

35. Doyle, *supra* note 26. The judicialists seemed to gain further support in 2004 and 2005 from the United States Supreme Court, which erected new constitutional hurdles for presumptive sentencing guidelines through its decisions in *Blakely v. Washington* and *United States v. Booker*. Interview with Susan Steingass, Chair, Wisconsin Sentencing Commission, 2003–7, in Madison, Wis. (Apr. 22, 2014). These decisions raised questions about whether a workable guidelines system could ever be implemented.

36. Telephone Interview with Kristi Waits, Executive Director, Wisconsin Sentencing Commission, 2006–7 (Feb. 27, 2014).

37. Connelly, *supra* note 34.

38. *Id.*

39. WIS. SENT'ING COMM'N, ANNUAL REPORT 2004, at 13 (2005).

40. WIS. SENT'ING COMM'N, ANNUAL REPORT 2005, at 10 (2006).

41. WIS. SENT'ING COMM'N, RACE & SENTENCING: SENTENCE AND OFFENDER CHARACTERISTICS ACROSS FIVE CRIMINAL OFFENSE AREAS (2007).

42. Interview with Frederick Kessler, Wisconsin State Representative, 1960–72, 2004–present, in Milwaukee, Wis. (Sept. 13, 2013).

43. Barland, *supra* note 13.

44. Connelly, *supra* note 34.

45. Interview with Patrick J. Fiedler, Secretary, Wisconsin Department of Corrections, 1991–93, Judge, Dane County Circuit Court, 1993–2011, Partner, Hurley, Burish & Stanton, S.C., in Madison, Wis. (Sept. 10, 2013).

46. Interview with Robert Donohoo, Assistant District Attorney, Milwaukee County, 1973–88, Deputy District Attorney, 1988–99, Chief Deputy District Attorney, 2000–2006, in Milwaukee, Wis. (Sept. 30, 2013).

47. Telephone Interview with Sheryl Gervasi, Legislative Liaison, Wisconsin State Court System, 1972–2003, Deputy Director, Court Operations, Wisconsin State Court System, 2003–11 (Oct. 7, 2013).

48. John Gurda, The Making of Milwaukee 94 (3d ed. 2008).

49. Nor, by contemporary standards, was Wisconsin exactly a bastion of racial enlightenment in the Joshua Glover era, either, when blacks were denied the right to vote. *Id.* at 67.

50. Bureau of Research, Wis. Dept. of Pub. Welfare, Adult Offenders in Division of Corrections Adult Institutions (1966); Doris P. Slesinger et al., African Americans in Wisconsin: A Statistical Overview 6 (2d ed.), http://www.apl.wisc.edu/publications/African_American_Chartbook.pdf.

51. Bureau of Planning, Development & Research, Wis. Div. of Corrections, Offenders Resident in Wisconsin Adult Correctional Institutions on December 31, 1970, with Five-Year Trends for 1966–1977, tbl. 4 (1971).

52. Office of Info. Mgmnt., Wis. Div. of Corrections, Residents in Wisconsin Adult Correctional Institutions and Community Correctional Residential Centers on December 31, 1980, with Five-Year Trends for 1976–1980, tbl. 4 (1981).

53. Dave Haskin, *Swan Delights in Challenges of State Senate*, Milw. J., July 5, 1977, at 1.

54. Monroe Swan, Statement of Senator Monroe Swan Releasing Final Report 2 (1979), *reprinted in* Report of the Joint Senate-Assembly Subcommittee on Problems in Wisconsin's Adult Correctional Institutions (1979).

55. Eugene Kane, *Did Swan Trumpet George's Fall?*, Milw. J. Sentinel, Aug. 12, 2004, at B1.

56. Interview with Chuck Chvala, Wisconsin State Senator, 1985–2005, in Madison, Wis. (Dec. 3, 2013).

57. Governor's Task Force on Racial Profiling, Report 5 (2000).

58. This was included in Section 765 of the CPSC's proposed legislation.

59. Wis. Sent'ing Comm'n, *supra* note 41.

60. Patrick Marley, *At King Day Celebration, Doyle Proposes Commission; State Panel Would Study Issue of Black Male Incarceration*, Milw. J. Sentinel, Jan. 16, 2007, at B2.

61. Comm'n on Reducing Disparities in the Wis. Justice System, Final Report (2008).

62. Human Rights Watch, Targeting Blacks: Drug Law Enforcement and Race in the United States 23 (2008), *available at* https://www.hrw.org/report/2008/05/04/targeting-blacks/drug-law-enforcement-and-race-united-states.

63. Ryan S. King, The Sentencing Project, Disparity by Geography: The War on Drugs in America's Cities 15 (2008).

64. Michael M. O'Hear, *Rethinking Drug Courts: Restorative Justice as a Response to Racial Injustice*, 20 Stan. L. & Pol'y Rev. 463, 465 (2009).

65. Jack Zemlicka, *Bill Puts Racial Profiling Data at Risk*, Wis. L.J., March 4, 2011.

66. Racial Disparity Oversight Commission, Report to the Governor (2010).

67. COMM'N ON REDUCING DISPARITIES IN THE WIS. JUSTICE SYSTEM, *supra* note 61, at 3.

68. JOHN PAWASARAT & LOIS M. QUINN, WISCONSIN'S MASS INCARCERATION OF AFRICAN AMERICAN MALES: WORKFORCE CHALLENGE (2013),

69. Doyle, *supra* note 26.

70. The imprisonment data come from the biennial reports on adult corrections by the Wisconsin Legislative Fiscal Bureau. The crime data come from the FBI's uniform crime reporting system.

71. WIS. LEG. FISCAL BUREAU, INFORMATIONAL PAPER #56: ADULT CORRECTIONS PROGRAM 6 (2001) [hereafter LFB 2001]; WIS. LEG. FISCAL BUREAU, INFORMATIONAL PAPER #57: ADULT CORRECTIONS PROGRAM 12 (2011) [hereafter LFB 2011].

72. LFB 2001, *supra* note 71, at 12, 15, 40.

73. LFB 1999, *supra* note 1; LFB 2011, *supra* note 71.

74. COUNCIL OF STATE GOVERNMENTS JUSTICE CENTER, JUSTICE REINVESTMENT IN WISCONSIN: ANALYSES & POLICY OPTIONS TO REDUCE SPENDING ON CORRECTIONS AND INCREASE PUBLIC SAFETY 3 (2009).

75. JUSTICE STRATEGIES, TREATMENT INSTEAD OF PRISONS: A ROADMAP FOR SENTENCING AND CORRECTIONAL POLICY REFORM IN WISCONSIN 3 (2005).

76. COUNCIL OF STATE GOVERNMENTS JUSTICE CENTER, *supra* note 74, at 5.

77. Karen Rivedal, *Doyle Faces a $2 Million Question; If He Doesn't Seek Reelection, How Will the Governor Spend His Unused Campaign Cash?*, WIS. ST. J., Aug. 17, 2009, at A1.

78. 2009 Wis. A.B. 75.

79. Mark Pitsch, *Prisoner Proposal Defended; Critics Say Plan Guts Sentence Law*, WIS. ST. J., Feb. 19, 2009, at A1.

80. COUNCIL OF STATE GOVERNMENTS JUSTICE CENTER, VALIDATION OF THE WISCONSIN DEPARTMENT OF CORRECTIONS RISK ASSESSMENT INSTRUMENT (2009).

81. COUNCIL OF STATE GOVERNMENTS JUSTICE CENTER, *supra* note 74.

82. WISCONSIN LEGISLATIVE COUNCIL, REPORT TO THE LEGISLATURE: SPECIAL COMMITTEE ON JUSTICE REINVESTMENT INITIATIVE OVERSIGHT (2010).

83. Pitsch, *supra* note 79.

84. Steven Elbow, *Doyle Vetoes Rankle Friends and Foes; Both Sides of Aisle Irked as Governor Strips Budget of Key Prison Release Terms*, CAP. TIMES, July 8, 2009, at 17.

85. James Doyle, Partial Veto Message for 2009 Wisconsin Act 28, xvii (2009). For a helpful description of the key provisions of the earned release law as enacted, see Jesse J. Norris, *The Earned Release Revolution: Early Assessments and State Level Strategies*, 95 MARQ. L. REV. 1551 (2012).

86. Doyle, *supra* note 85, at xvii.

87. *Id.* at 4.

88. Pitsch, *supra* note 79.

89. Ben Poston, *Sentencing Reform Results Fall Short*, MILW. J. SENTINEL, July 11, 2010, at 1.

90. Telephone Interview with Al Graham, Wisconsin Parole Chair, 2006-9, Wisconsin Earned Release Review Commission Chair, 2009-11 (May 19, 2014).

91. Liam Marlaire, *Walker Signs Bill Ending Early Release Program*, Eau Claire Leader-Telegram, July 20, 2011.

92. Norris, *supra* note 85, at 1608.

93. Poston, *supra* note 89.

94. Dee Hall, *State's Big Prison Population Drop Called "Historic,"* Wis. St. J., Jan. 12, 2011.

95. Paul Fanlund, *Prison Policy a Bonanza for GOP Demagogues*, Cap. Times, July 27, 2011, at 5.

96. Nicole M. Murphy, *Dying to Be Free: An Analysis of Wisconsin's Restructured Compassionate Release Statute*, 95 Marq. L. Rev. 1679, 1708 (2012).

97. *Id.* at 1717.

98. Margaret E. Noonan & Scott Ginder, U.S. Dep't of Justice, Mortality in Local Jails and State Prisons, 2000–2011—Statistical Tables 24 (2013).

99. LFB 2011, *supra* note 71, at 12.

100. Fanlund, *supra* note 95.

101. Murphy, *supra* note 96, at 1718.

102. *Id.* at 1706. Suder presumably intended to put the apostrophe before the "Em."

103. Norris, *supra* note 85, at 1567.

104. James B. Kelleher, *Up to 100,000 Protest Wisconsin Law Curbing Unions*, Reuters .com (Mar. 12, 2011), http://www.reuters.com/article/2011/03/13/usa-wisconsin-idUSN 1227540420110313.

105. Tom Tolan & Patrick Marley, *Republicans Take 4 of 6 in Recall Elections, Hold Senate*, Milw. J. Sentinel, Aug. 10, 2011.

106. 2011 Wis. Act 38.

107. Marlaire, *supra* note 91.

108. Milwaukee County Office of the Comptroller Audit Services Division, Electronic Monitoring Can Achieve Substantive Savings for Milwaukee County, but Only If Pursued on a Large Scale with Satisfactory Compliance 28 (2013).

109. *Id.* at 31.

110. *Id.* at 33.

111. Peggy McGarry, Technical Assistance Report: Wisconsin First Judicial District (2009).

112. Milwaukee County Community Justice Council, CJC Executive Committee, *available at* http://milwaukee.gov/cjc/CJCExecutiveCommittee.htm.

113. Milwaukee County Office of the Comptroller Audit Services Division, *supra* note 108, at 11–15.

114. *Id.* at 33.

115. Rob Henken & Vanessa Allen, *Milwaukee County Detainee Populations at Historic Lows: Why Is It Happening and What Does It Mean?*, 99 Pub. Pol'y F. Res. Brief 1 (2011).

116. Milwaukee County Office of the Comptroller Audit Services Division, *supra* note 108, at 20.

117. David A. Clarke Jr., *Let's Treat Criminals Like . . . Criminals*, MILW. J. SENTINEL, Feb. 19, 2011.

118. MILWAUKEE COUNTY OFFICE OF THE COMPTROLLER AUDIT SERVICES DIVISION, *supra* note 108, at 20.

119. *Id.* at 21.

120. John Chisholm et al., *Rely on the Facts to Fight Crime*, MILW. J. SENTINEL, Feb. 26, 2011.

121. Number of prisoners reflects year-end data compiled by the U.S. Bureau of Justice Statistics. Major violent arrests are adult arrests for the violent "index" crimes (murder, rape, aggravated assault, and robbery), as compiled in annual statewide arrests reports prepared by the Wisconsin Office of Justice Assistance and its predecessor agencies. Arrests from the two preceding years are counted.

122. COMM. ON CAUSES AND CONSEQUENCES OF HIGH RATES OF INCARCERATION, NAT'L RESEARCH COUNCIL OF THE NAT'L ACADEMIES, THE GROWTH OF INCARCERATION IN THE UNITED STATES: EXPLORING CAUSES AND CONSEQUENCES (2014).

123. *Id.* at 221–27, 247.

124. *Id.* at 279.

125. The data in figure 6.4 reflect year-end jurisdiction numbers compiled by the U.S. Bureau of Justice Statistics. The "all states" figure does not include prisoners in the federal system. The data in figure 6.5 reflect violent "index" crimes, as compiled and reported annually for each state by the Federal Bureau of Investigation. The data up to 2012 are now available through a convenient online tool (http://www.ucrdatatool.gov/index.cfm). Data from 2013 and 2014 come from FED. BUREAU OF INVESTIGATION, CRIME IN THE UNITED STATES—2014 tbl. 4 (2015), *available at* https://www.fbi.gov/about-us/cjis/ucr/crime-in-the-u.s/2014/crime-in-the-u.s.-2014/tables/table-4.

126. MARC MAUER & NAZGOL GHANDNOOSH, THE SENTENCING PROJECT, POL-ICY BRIEF: FEWER PRISONERS, LESS CRIME (2015).

127. OLIVER ROEDER ET AL., NEW YORK UNIVERSITY SCHOOL OF LAW, WHAT CAUSED THE CRIME DECLINE? 22 (2015).

128. *Id.* at 23.

129. COMM. ON CAUSES AND CONSEQUENCES OF HIGH RATES OF INCARCERATION, *supra* note 122, at 155–56.

130. *Id.* at 155.

131. *Id.* at 150.

Chapter 7. Wisconsin's War on Drugs

1. MARC MAUER, RACE TO INCARCERATE 32 (2006).

2. Richard J. Bonnie & Charles H. Whitebread, II, *The Forbidden Fruit and the Tree of Knowledge: An Inquiry into the Legal History of American Marijuana Prohibition*, 56 VA. L. REV. 971, 1030, 1033–34 (1970).

3. 1935 Laws of Wisconsin Ch. 306, § 1.

4. *Id.* § 4.

5. 1967 Wis. Stat. § 161.28.

6. The Boggs Act, *reprinted in* DRUGS IN AMERICA: A DOCUMENTARY HISTORY 276, 276–77 (David F. Musto ed., 2002).

7. TASK FORCE ON NARCOTICS AND DRUG ABUSE, THE PRESIDENT'S COMMISSION ON LAW ENFORCEMENT AND ADMINISTRATION OF JUSTICE, TASK FORCE REPORT: NARCOTICS AND DRUG ABUSE 11 (1967).

8. DAVID F. MUSTO, THE AMERICAN DISEASE: ORIGINS OF NARCOTIC CONTROL 211–12 (1999).

9. 1967 Wis. Stat. § 161.02(3).

10. RUFUS KING, THE DRUG HANG-UP: AMERICA'S FIFTY-YEAR FOLLY ch. 28 (1972).

11. MUSTO, *supra* note 8, at 248.

12. 1971 Wis. Stat. ch. 161.

13. 1971 Wis. Stat. § 161.001.

14. DARYL HINZ, WIS. LEGISLATIVE FISCAL BUREAU, ADULT AND JUVENILE CORRECTIONS PROGRAMS 25 (1987).

15. DIV. LAW ENFORCEMENT SVCS., WIS. DEPT. OF JUSTICE, WISCONSIN CRIMINAL JUSTICE INFORMATION: CRIME AND ARRESTS 86 (1978).

16. ROBERT DEITCH, HEMP: AMERICAN HISTORY REVISITED 192 (2003).

17. *Id.* at 183.

18. MUSTO, *supra* note 8, at 260.

19. The bill was 1977 AB 325.

20. TED GEST, CRIME & POLITICS: BIG GOVERNMENT'S ERRATIC CAMPAIGN FOR LAW AND ORDER 112 (2001).

21. WIS. STATISTICAL ANALYSIS CTR., WIS. COUNCIL ON CRIM. J., CRIME AND ARRESTS: 1985, at 77 (1986).

22. MUSTO, *supra* note 8, at 264.

23. SANDRA SHANE-DUBOW ET AL., WISCONSIN FELONY SENTENCING GUIDE-LINES: PHASE I AND III OF RESEARCH AND DEVELOPMENT 261 (1982).

24. *Id.* at 321–22.

25. *Id.* at 324.

26. MUSTO, *supra* note 8, at 268.

27. *Id.*

28. GEST, *supra* note 20, at 117.

29. *Id.* at 118–19.

30. *Id.* at 120.

31. WIS. COCAINE TASK FORCE, FINAL REPORT (1986).

32. *Id.* at i.

33. *Id.* at 73.

34. *Id.* at 46.

35. 1987 Wis. Act 339.

36. Dennis McCann, *Hanaway Looks Ahead: Winner Plans Focus on Drugs, Organized Crime*, MILWAUKEE J., Nov. 5, 1986, at 10A, *available at* https://news.google.com/news

papers?nid=1499&dat=19861105&id=x2UaAAAAIBAJ&sjid=mSoEAAAAIBAJ&
pg=4434,4315805.

37. 1987 Wis. Act 332.

38. Musto, *supra* note 8, at 281–82.

39. 1989 Wis. Act 31.

40. Musto, *supra* note 8, at 281.

41. *Special Session Urged to Work on Drug Laws*, Milwaukee J., Aug. 21, 1989, at 2B,
available at https://news.google.com/newspapers?nid=1499&dat=19890821&id=WG8a
AAAAIBAJ&sjid=8isEAAAAIBAJ&pg=5089,5521900.

42. *Id.*

43. David E. Umhoefer, *Task Force Plots Anti-Drug Ad Effort*, Milwaukee J., Sept.
26, 1989, at 1B, *available at* https://news.google.com/newspapers?nid=1499&dat=1989
0926&id=s2kaAAAAIBAJ&sjid=YCwEAAAAIBAJ&pg=6569,3010614.

44. Wis. Cocaine Task Force, *supra* note 31, at i–ii, 30.

45. Johnnie L. Smith, *Local Law Enforcement View of the Cocaine Problem, in* Cocaine:
A Symposium 11, 12 (Carla J. Brink ed. 1985).

46. Interview with Janine Geske, Milwaukee County Circuit Court Judge, 1981–93,
Wisconsin Supreme Court Justice, 1993–98, in Milwaukee, Wis. (Aug. 26, 2013).

47. Charles E. Friedrich, *Tuning of Drug Bills Takes Longer Than Expected*, Milwaukee
J., Dec. 19, 1989, at 9B, *available at* https://news.google.com/newspapers?nid=1499&
dat=19891219&id=pW8fAAAAIBAJ&sjid=2X4EAAAAIBAJ&pg=3805,3530541.

48. 1989 Wis. Act 121.

49. Interview with Lynn Adelman, Wisconsin State Senator, 1977–97, U.S. District
Judge, 1997–present, in Milwaukee, Wis. (April 16, 2014).

50. 1989 Wis. Act 121, § 53m.

51. 1991 Wis. Act 39 §§ 2967r, 2703.

52. 1995 Wis. Act 448.

53. 1997 Wis. Act 283 § 371.

54. 1999 Wis. Act 48.

55. Jennifer Schwai, *Racial Bias Haunts Drug Sentencing but Commission Suggests Stiffer
Crack Penalties*, Wis. St. J., March 4, 1995, at 4A, *available at* 1995 WLNR 3920639.

56. 1993 Wis. Act 98 § 89g; 1993 Wis. Act 437.

57. 1999–2000 Wis. Stat. § 961.41; 21 U.S.C. § 841 (2002).

58. 1999–2000 Wis. Stat. §§ 961.41–961.50.

59. Nat'l Crim. J. Ass'n, A Guide to State Controlled Substances Acts
127–28 (1999).

60. Wis. Sent'ing Comm'n, Annual Report 5 (1993); Wis. Sent'ing Comm'n,
All Drug Offenses Committed on or After January 31, 1990 to June 30, 1992
and Sentenced After January 31, 1990 to June 30, 1992 (1992).

61. Michael Connelly, Wis. Sent'ing Comm'n, Judicial Response to Proposed Substance Abuse Treatment Legislation in Wisconsin: Results of
Three Focus Groups 7 (2005).

62. This number must be used with caution since the study's breakdown by drug

type excluded three-quarters of the probation cases. Still, even if *none* of the excluded cases involved heroin, the overall proportion of heroin cases would still have been much larger than in the later Sentencing Commission study.

63. I refer here to powder and crack cases subject to the five- and ten-year presumptive minimums, for which the mean sentence lengths in the early 1990s exceeded the five-year maximum for cocaine distribution that existed prior to 1986. It is true that the five-year maximum would have doubled to ten years for a second or subsequent offense. However, the commission data indicate that only 7 percent of the high-volume cocaine offenders were subject to this enhancer. Additionally, none were subject to the pre-1986 enhancers for distribution to a minor or a prisoner.

64. Data in this paragraph come from the biennial reports of the Wisconsin Legislative Fiscal Bureau on adult corrections. The drug imprisonment figures reflect those whose most serious offense was a drug offense.

65. Memorandum from Kevin Pranis, Justice Strategies, to Ron Kuehn 1 (Jan. 18, 2005) (on file with the author).

66. Although adopted in 1998, the TIS law only took effect with crimes occurring on or after December 31, 1999.

67. Paige M. Harrison & Allen J. Beck, U.S. Dep't of Justice, Prisoners in 2002, at 10 (2003).

68. The 2002 maximums indicated here reflect the adjustments made as a result of TIS II, which were adopted in 2002 but did not take effect until 2003. The various maximums are set forth in 2001–2 Wis. Stat. § 961.41 and its predecessor provisions, as summarized in tables 7.1–7.3.

69. Wis. Sent'ing Comm'n, Sentencing in Wisconsin: Drug Trafficking (2007).

70. Pew Research Center, America's New Drug Policy Landscape 8 (2014).

71. Governor's Task Force on Sentencing and Corrections, Final Report 2–3 (1996).

72. Pew Research Center, *supra* note 70.

73. Michael M. O'Hear, *Drug Treatment Courts as Communicative Punishment, in* Retributivism Has a Past, Has It a Future? 234, 234 (Michael Tonry ed., 2011).

74. Michael M. O'Hear, *Federalism and Drug Control,* 57 Vanderbilt L. Rev. 783, 825 (2004).

75. Memorandum from Jane R. Henkel, Senior Staff Attorney, Wisconsin Legislative Council, to Members of the Special Committee on Drug Law Enforcement 15 (Jan. 8, 1990) (on file with author).

76. *Id.* at 4.

77. Jesse J. Norris, *The Earned Release Revolution: Early Assessments and State-Level Strategies,* 95 Marq. L. Rev. 1551, 1571 (2012).

78. The 1986 Cocaine Task Force, for instance, found that "35% of the regular cocaine users began dealing cocaine to support their habit." Wis. Cocaine Task Force, *supra* note 31, at 13.

79. John M. Hagedorn, Wisconsin Policy Research Institute, The Business of Drug Dealing in Milwaukee 1 (1998).

80. Pranis, *supra* note 65, at 3.

81. Governor's Task Force to Enhance Probation, Final Report 27–28 (2000).

82. Wisconsin Sent'ing Comm'n, *supra* note 69, at 13, 15–27.

83. Pranis, *supra* note 65, at 2.

84. 2005 Wis. Act. 25 § 90m.

85. Felicia Thomas-Lynn, *400 Diverted into Treatment, Freeing Courts, Jail Space*, Milwaukee J. Sentinel, April 28, 2008, at B1.

86. Interview with David Liners, Executive Director, WISDOM, in Milwaukee, Wis. (May 20, 2015).

87. Leonard Sykes Jr., *Alternatives to Prison Offered*, Milw. J. Sentinel, March 13, 2004, at 2B.

88. Liners, *supra* note 86.

89. WISDOM, 11X15 Blueprint for Ending Mass Incarceration in Wisconsin 2, 4 (2014).

90. Liners, *supra* note 86.

91. Interview with Joe Ellwanger, Organizer, WISDOM, 2002–13, in Milwaukee, Wis. (June 2, 2015).

92. Liners, *supra* note 86.

93. Sykes, *supra* note 87.

94. Memorandum from Kevin Pranis and Judy Greene, Justice Strategies, to Michael Blaine, Drug Policy Alliance (Feb. 1, 2004) (on file with the author).

95. Liners, *supra* note 86.

96. 2005 Wis. Act 25 § 90m, Wis. Stat. 16.964(12)(c)(5).

97. 2005 Wis. Act 25 § 90m, Wis. Stat. 16.964(12)(c)(10).

98. Kit R. Van Stelle et al., Univ. of Wisc. Pop. Health Inst., Treatment Alternatives and Diversion (TAD) Program: Participant Outcome Evaluation and Cost-Benefit Report (2007–2013) 5 (2014).

99. *Id.* at 23.

100. Michael Fendrich & Thomas P. LeBel, University of Wisconsin–Milwaukee, Evaluation of the Milwaukee County Drug Treatment Court: Annual Report for 2013 (2014).

101. *Id.* at 9.

102. *Id.* at 16.

103. *Id.* at 54.

104. Michael M. O'Hear, *Rethinking Drug Courts: Restorative Justice as a Response to Racial Injustice*, 20 Stan. L. & Pol'y Rev. 463, 480 (2009).

105. *Id.* at 13.

106. Ashley Lutheran, *Heroin Deaths in Milwaukee County Jump by 72%*, Milwaukee J. Sentinel, Feb. 18, 2015, *available at* http://www.jsonline.com/news/health/heroin-deaths-in-milwaukee-county-jump-by-72-b99447450z1-292396321.html. By contrast, the

1986 Cocaine Task Force had trumpeted just *21* cocaine overdose deaths in the 1980s as a major public health concern and a justification for much tougher cocaine penalties. WIS. COCAINE TASK FORCE, *supra* note 31, at i–ii.

107. Prison data come from the biennial reports of the Wisconsin Legislative Fiscal Bureau on adult corrections. Prisoner totals are based on prisoners at about the midpoint of each even-numbered year. Prisoner admissions are two-year cumulative totals. Drug arrests come from the annual *Crime and Arrests in Wisconsin* (now *Arrests in Wisconsin*) series; data for 2013 and 2014 are not yet available. "Major drug arrests" refers to arrests for distribution of cocaine or heroin.

108. Arrest figures come from the annual reports on arrests in Wisconsin issued by the Office of Justice Assistance and its predecessor agencies. Imprisonment data come from the biennial reports of the Wisconsin Legislative Fiscal Bureau on adult corrections. Numbers are based on prisoners at about the midpoint of each indicated year.

109. Data come from the biennial reports of the Wisconsin Legislative Fiscal Bureau on adult corrections. Numbers are based on prisoners at about the midpoint of each indicated year.

110. E. ANN CARSON, U.S. DEP'T OF JUSTICE, PRISONERS IN 2014, at 16 (2015).

111. These figures are calculated based on numbers from the U.S. Bureau of Justice Statistics online Arrest Data Analysis Tool: http://www.bjs.gov/index.cfm?ty=datool &surl=/arrests/index.cfm.

Chapter 8. Lessons

1. Michael M. O'Hear & Darren Wheelock, *Imprisonment Inertia and Public Support for Truth in Sentencing*, 2015 BYU L. REV. 257.

2. For technical details, see *id.*

3. The first two results come from the 2013 poll, the full results of which are here: https://law.marquette.edu/poll/wp-content/uploads/2013/07/MLSP17Toplines.pdf. The third result comes from the 2014 poll, the full results of which are here: https://law .marquette.edu/poll/wp-content/uploads/2013/07/MLSP17Toplines.pdf. The final two results come from the 2012 poll, the full results of which are here: https://law.marquette .edu/poll/wp-content/uploads/2012/09/MLSP8_Toplines.pdf.

4. MICHAEL TONRY, THINKING ABOUT CRIME: SENSE AND SENSIBILITY IN AMERICAN PENAL CULTURE 36 (2004).

5. Interview with Tommy Thompson, Wisconsin Governor, 1987–2001, in Madison, Wis. (April 1, 2014).

6. The data come from the biennial Blue Book published by the Wisconsin Legislative Reference Bureau.

7. MATTHEW R. DUROSE ET AL., U.S. DEPT. OF JUSTICE, RECIDIVISM OF PRISONERS RELEASED IN 30 STATES IN 2005: PATTERNS FROM 2005 TO 2010, tbl. 9 (2014).

8. These results come from the 2012 poll. *See supra* notes 2–3.

9. Stephanos Bibas, *Plea Bargaining Outside the Shadow of Trial*, 117 HARV. L. REV. 2463, 2508 (2004).

10. Michael Tonry, *Making Peace, Not a Desert: Penal Reform Should Be About Values Not Justice Reinvestment*, 10 CRIMINOLOGY & PUB. POL'Y 637, 637–38 (2011).

11. Nour Kteily et al., *"Not One of Us": Predictors and Consequences of Denying Ingroup Characteristics to Ambiguous Targets*, 40 PERSONALITY & SOC. PSYCH. BULLETIN 1231, 1244 (2014).

12. Bernard E. Harcourt, *Reducing Mass Incarceration: Lessons from the Deinstitutionalization of Mental Hospitals in the 1960s*, 9 OHIO ST. J CRIM. L. 53, 64 (2011).

13. DAVID GARLAND, THE CULTURE OF CONTROL: CRIME AND SOCIAL ORDER IN CONTEMPORARY SOCIETY 133 (2001).

14. Harcourt, *supra* note 12, at 66 (quoting DAVID A. ROCHEFORT, FROM POORHOUSES TO HOMELESSNESS: POLICY ANALYSIS AND MENTAL HEALTH CARE 39 [1st ed. 1993]).

15. These results come from the 2014 poll.

16. These results come from the 2012 poll.

17. These results come from the 2013 poll.

18. O'Hear & Wheelock, *supra* note 1.

19. COMM. ON CAUSES AND CONSEQUENCES OF HIGH RATES OF INCARCERATION, NATIONAL RESEARCH COUNCIL OF THE NATIONAL ACADEMIES, THE GROWTH OF INCARCERATION IN THE UNITED STATES: EXPLORING CAUSES AND CONSEQUENCES 197 (2014).

20. 2005 Wis. Act 25, § 90m.

21. WIS. LEG. FISCAL BUREAU, INFORMATION PAPER 55: ADULT CORRECTIONS PROGRAM (2015).

22. E. ANN CARSON, U.S. DEP'T OF JUSTICE, PRISONERS IN 2014, at tbl. 11 (2015). Prisoners are classified based on their most serious offense of conviction.

23. DUROSE ET AL., *supra* note 7, tbl. 8.

24. *Id.*, tbl. 10.

25. WIS. LEG. FISCAL BUREAU, *supra* note 21, Ex. A-1.

26. Michael M. O'Hear, *Not Just kid Stuff? Extending Graham and Miller to Adults*, 78 MO. L. REV. 1087 (2013).

27. See, e.g., JOHN PAWASARAT & LOIS M. QUINN, WISCONSIN'S MASS INCARCERATION OF AFRICAN AMERICAN MALES: WORKFORCE CHALLENGES FOR 2013, at 1 (2013).

28. COMM. ON CAUSES AND CONSEQUENCES OF HIGH RATES OF INCARCERATION, *supra* note 19, at 75.

29. *Id.* at 76, 78.

30. AMERICAN LAW INSTITUTION, MODEL PENAL CODE: SENTENCING § 6B.02 (tent. draft no. 3, 2014).

31. PAMALA L. GRISET, DETERMINATE SENTENCING: THE PROMISE AND THE REALITY OF RETRIBUTIVE JUSTICE (1991).

32. COMM. ON CAUSES AND CONSEQUENCES OF HIGH RATES OF INCARCERATION, *supra* note 19, at 77.

33. KATE STITH & JOSÉ A. CABRANES, FEAR OF JUDGING: SENTENCING GUIDELINES IN THE FEDERAL COURTS (1996); United States v. Booker, 543 U.S. 220 (2005).

34. COMM. ON CAUSES AND CONSEQUENCES OF HIGH RATES OF INCARCERATION, *supra* note 19, at 76.

35. In the Matter of Judicial Administration Felony Sentencing Guidelines, 353 N.W.2d 793 (Wis. 1984).

36. These results come from the 2012 poll.

37. Ronald F. Wright, *Counting the Costs of Sentencing in North Carolina, 1980–2000*, 29 CRIME & JUST. 39, 40–41 (2002).

38. Michael M. O'Hear, *Beyond Rehabilitation: A New Theory of Indeterminate Sentencing*, 48 AM. CRIM. L. REV. 1247, 1248 (2011).

39. Kevin R. Reitz, *Don't Blame Determinacy: U.S. Incarceration Growth Has Been Driven by Other Forces*, 84 TEX. L. REV. 1787, 1795 (2006).

40. *Id.* at 1798–99.

41. Gina Barton, *Parole-Eligible Inmates Barred from Freedom*, MILW. J. SENTINEL, July 13, 2014, at 1A, 6A.

42. *Id.*

43. Michael M. O'Hear, *Good Conduct Time for Prisoners: Why (and How) Wisconsin Should Provide Credits Toward Early Release*, 98 MARQ. L. REV. 487, 542 (2014).

44. JAMES AUSTIN ET AL., ENDING MASS INCARCERATION: CHARTING A NEW JUSTICE REINVESTMENT 12 (2012).

45. COMM. ON CAUSES AND CONSEQUENCES OF HIGH RATES OF INCARCERATION, *supra* note 19, at 74–75.

46. Steven L. Chanenson, *The Next Era of Sentencing Reform*, 54 EMORY L.J. 377, 432–35 (2005).

47. MARC MAUER & NAZGOL GHANDNOOSH, THE SENTENCING PROJECT, POLICY BRIEF: FEWER PRISONERS, LESS CRIME 6–7 (2015).

48. WILLIAM J. STUNTZ, THE COLLAPSE OF AMERICAN CRIMINAL JUSTICE 254 (2011).

49. Wright, *supra* note 37, at 85–86.

50. MAUER & GHANDNOOSH, *supra* note 47, at 7.

51. JAMES AUSTIN, JFA INSTITUTE, THE IMPACT OF PLATA AND REALIGNMENT ON STATE AND LOCAL CORRECTIONS: THE USE OF ECONOMIC INCENTIVES TO REDUCE CORRECTIONAL POPULATIONS 10 (2015).

52. *Id.* at 12.

53. Karol Lucken, *Leaving Mass Incarceration: The Ways and Means of Penal Change*, 10 CRIMINOLOGY & PUB. POL'Y 707, 711–12 (2011); Heather Schoenfeld, *Putting Politics in Penal Reform*, 10 CRIMINOLOGY & PUB. POL'Y 715, 718 (2011).

54. Pew Center on the States, The Impact of Arizona's Probation Reforms (2011), *available at* https://www.acgov.org/probation/documents/PEWStudyonImpactof ArizonaProbationReform.pdf.

55. Lucken, *supra* note 53, at 712.

56. NANCY LaVIGNE ET AL., URBAN INSTITUTE, JUSTICE REINVESTMENT INITIATIVE STATE ASSESSMENT REPORT 24 (2014).

57. Harcourt, *supra* note 12, at 67–68.

58. AUSTIN, *supra* note 51, at 4–5.

59. MAUER & GHANDNOOSH, *supra* note 47, at 1.

60. Sociologist Alice Goffman more fully describes the alienation and social conflict that are engendered by "intensive policing" in poor neighborhoods. See ON THE RUN: FUGITIVE LIFE IN AN AMERICAN CITY (2014).

61. Brown v. Plata, 134 S. Ct. 1 (2011).

62. Michael Tonry, *Remodeling American Sentencing: A Ten-Step Blueprint for Moving Past Mass Incarceration*, 13 CRIMINOLOGY & PUB. POL'Y 503 (2014).

63. Wright, *supra* note 37, at 49–51.

64. PAUL BREST ET AL., PROCESSES OF CONSTITUTIONAL DECISIONMAKING 925–31 (5th ed. 2006).

Index

Page references in italics indicate an illustration, and those followed by a t *indicate a table.*

255